Southern Living®
1994
Garden
Annual

Yellow daylilies

Southern Living®
1994
Garden Annual

Book Division of
Southern Progress Corporation
P.O. Box 832463
Birmingham, Alabama 35201

ISBN: 0-8487-1141-6
Manufactured in the
United States of America
First Printing

Southern Living® Magazine
Garden Editor: Mark G. Stith
Senior Writer: Stephen P. Bender
Associate Garden Editor:
Linda C. Askey
Senior Garden Photographer:
Van Chaplin
Garden Photographer:
Sylvia Martin
Associate Projects Editor:
Julia Hamilton Thomason
Assistant Garden Design Editors:
Rebecca Dell Bull,
Joann Catherine Kellum
Production Manager: Kay Fuston
Assistant Production Manager:
Vicki Weathers
Editorial Assistant: Tena Z. Payne

Oxmoor House, Inc.
Editor-in-Chief: Nancy J. Fitzpatrick
Senior Homes Editor:
Mary Kay Culpepper
Senior Editor, Editorial Services:
Olivia Kindig Wells
Director of Manufacturing:
Jerry Higdon
Production Manager: Rick Litton
Art Director: James Boone

Southern Living 1994 Garden Annual

Editor: Rebecca Brennan
Designer: Eleanor Cameron
Editorial Assistant:
Rebecca C. Fitzgerald
Copy Editor:
Leslee Rester Johnson
Associate Production Manager:
Theresa L. Beste
Production Assistant: Marianne Jordan

Cover: *Peonies*

CONTENTS

Foxgloves

Daylily

Yellow
shrimp
plant

It seems to me that gardening is both an active and a passive process. Preparing soil, sowing seeds, burying bulbs, planting shrubs, and mowing the lawn are all labor-intensive acts we perform to realize the gardens of our hopes and dreams. Ah . . . but the hoping and dreaming, that's gardening, too.

   This book is a compilation of articles that have run in the past year's issues of *Southern Living* magazine. I hope that admiring the efforts of others will inspire you to take the time to plan, to dream, and to appreciate your own garden.

Japanese primrose

Mark G. Stith
Garden Editor

Homegrown Gardeners

Summer vegetables

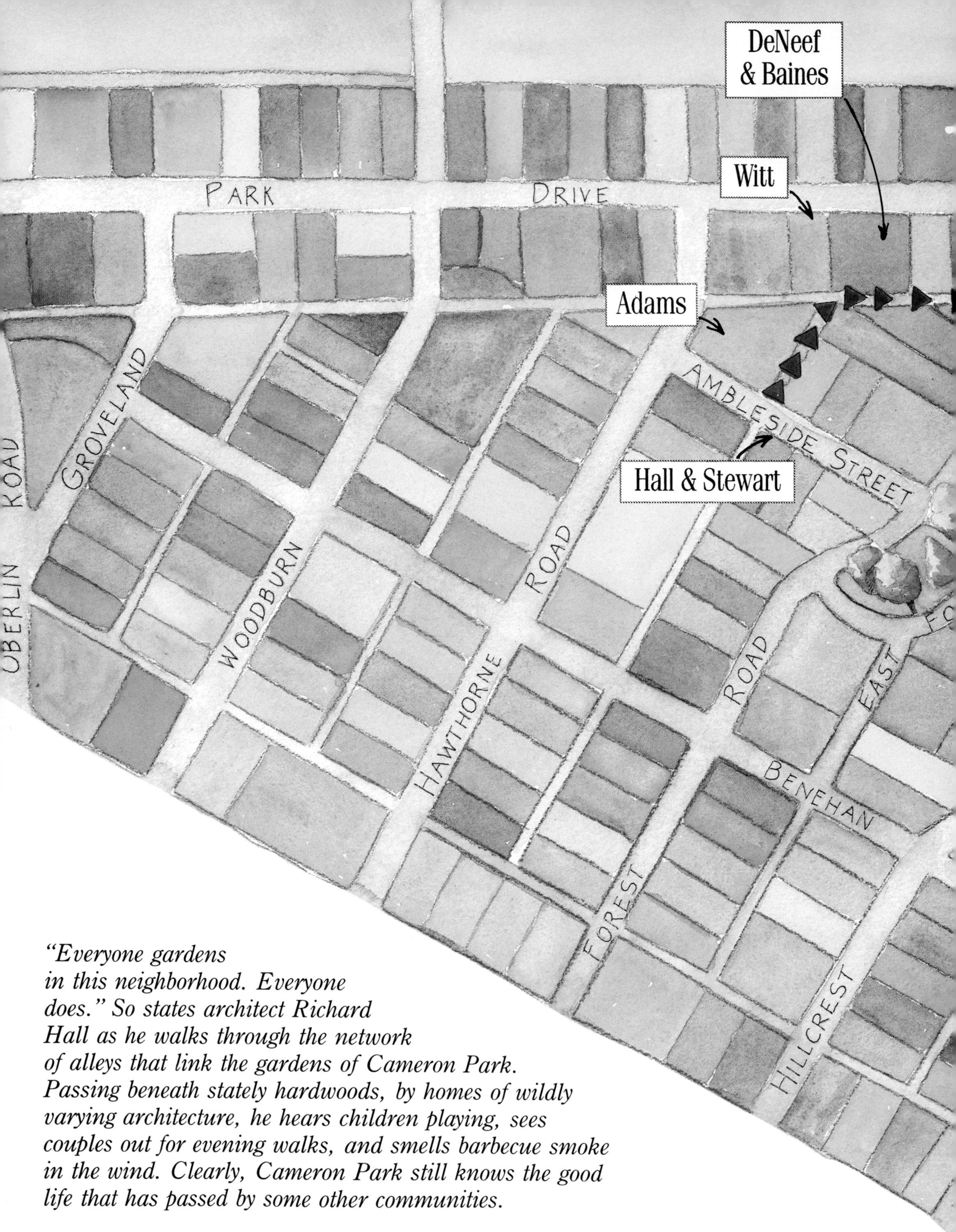

DeNeef & Baines

Witt

PARK   DRIVE

Adams

AMBLESIDE STREET

Hall & Stewart

OBERLIN ROAD

GROVELAND

WOODBURN

HAWTHORNE ROAD

FOREST

ROAD

BENEHAN

EAST

HILLCREST

*"Everyone gardens
in this neighborhood. Everyone
does." So states architect Richard
Hall as he walks through the network
of alleys that link the gardens of Cameron Park.
Passing beneath stately hardwoods, by homes of wildly
varying architecture, he hears children playing, sees
couples out for evening walks, and smells barbecue smoke
in the wind. Clearly, Cameron Park still knows the good
life that has passed by some other communities.*

Hopfenberg

A Neighborhood That Gardens

Looking for experts on growing vegetables, wildflowers, perennials, herbs, even bonsai? If you live in this Raleigh neighborhood, they're as close as next door.

One of Raleigh's oldest neighborhoods, Cameron Park owns a distinctive character largely defined by its academic heritage. Many families have at least one member working at nearby St. Mary's College, Meredith College, Peace College, or North Carolina State University. As you'd expect, all those classrooms foster a willingness to experiment, a willingness that extends to the garden. Gardeners here do the work themselves; they don't "hire it done." And as they share vegetables and flowers from their gardens, they also share expertise.

If you like English cottage-style gardens, you'll find no better example than at Richard Hall and Fred Stewart's place on Ambleside Drive. It's organized disorder at its finest. Instead of the usual grass between sidewalk and street, lamb's-ears and rosemary spill carelessly over the curb. Perennials poke between fenceposts, vines clamber upon an arbor, and hollyhocks soar skyward. No one minds if seedlings sprout in cracks between bricks. In this garden, freedom reigns.

Architect Fred Stewart designed the garden to complement the Sears-Roebuck catalog house that dates from 1914. He enclosed the front yard with a handsome fence in order to visually extend the house and give the garden

Herbs, perennials, and shrubs grow freely in a cottage garden designed to complement this 1914 bungalow.

structure. Behind the fence, a mélange of annuals, perennials, shrubs, and herbs run the show. No one takes hedge trimmers to floppy wildflowers; seedheads remain to drop their seed. Maintenance is low, because in the scheme of things, a brown leaf or errant branch isn't noticed.

Because this garden lacks a set pattern, it's full of surprises and continuous change. Some plants become invasive; others disappear, encouraging new combinations. Neighbors often donate "starts," each plant coming with a bit of gardening advice. One such neighbor, Ollie Adams, lives across the street.

A Jill of All Trades

On just about any pleasant morning, you'll likely run into Ollie Adams out in the yard tending plants. When it comes to gardening, this 30-year resident of Cameron Park is what you might call a "Jill of all trades." Her wildflower and shade garden is widely touted as the neighborhood's best. But she also grows vegetables and herbs, as well as unusual perennials and shrubs.

Ollie succeeds in her garden because, instead of

Ollie Adams shows off a giant chard, the product of her garden's rich, organic soil. (**Inset**) *In her own cottage garden, Ollie enjoys this mixture of larkspur (purple), rose campion (deep rose), and Jerusalem sage (yellow).*

fighting the situation, she matches plantings to the conditions she has. For example, vegetables and herbs need lots of sun, so a vegetable and herb garden occupies her yard's sunniest corner.

Several magnificent trees, for which Cameron Park is justly famous, shade most of Ollie's front yard. Thus, she devotes the lion's share of this space to shade-loving wildflowers, perennials, and shrubs, including hostas, bloodroot, trillium, gingers, lungwort, and azaleas. Where sun manages to peer through the branches fairly regularly, she maintains a cottage garden composed of rambling perennials and self-seeding annuals, such as larkspur, yarrow, and rose campion.

Curiosity may have killed the cat, but it usually rewards the gardener. Ollie delights in confounding neighborhood skeptics by trying out unfamiliar plants that authorities tell her won't grow in Raleigh. For example, Mexican orange (*Choisya ternata*) is a greenhouse plant for most Southerners. However, Ollie grows this rare, evergreen shrub in a sheltered corner of her backyard. "I must have the perfect place for it," she says," because it never gets hurt by the cold." "Each March, it bears wonderful

Peter and Inge Witt garden in raised planters that let them tend plants without bending over.

white, very fragrant flowers."

If there's one key to Ollie's garden, it's the way she cares for the soil. Time and again, she either mulches the beds with composted leaves or tills compost under to add organic matter. Fortunately, she has a ready source. "Gardening is special in Raleigh because the city furnishes us with free compost made from leaves they take off the streets," she explains. "They'll bring you as much as you need." The compost loosens the soil, keeps it cool, helps retain moisture, and adds nutrients. "Compost is all I use," declares Ollie. "I never use fertilizer. Never."

Garden clubs frequently tour Ollie's garden, but you needn't be a member to see it. "I garden next to a public alley, which makes it fun for everyone," she says. "You can just stroll about Cameron Park and take a look at what's going on. Sundays, in particular, are just great."

Gardening With Spiderman

You don't need to rob a bank or threaten the world to stand face-to-face with Spiderman. Just walk a short distance down the alley from Ollie's yard. "Spiderman," the nickname of retired scientist Peter Witt, was given to him by colleagues for his research into the behavior of spiders.

Today, Peter is involved in a different endeavor. He and his wife, Inge, grow plants inside special, raised beds.

Richard Hall and Fred Stewart designed the Witts' raised beds, based on a centuries-old idea. "In the Middle Ages, monks in Germany and France had herb and flower gardens in their courtyards," explains Peter. "But when the monks got older and couldn't bend down anymore, they used raised beds, called *pulvinus*."

Two such beds, actually wooden planters, stand side-by-side in the garden. Built from rot-resistant redwood, they stand 38 inches high, 36 inches wide, and 12 feet long. Lengths of 2 x 6 redwood form handy shelves atop each planter for resting elbows or laying down tools. Why two planters? "We weren't in agreement about what to plant, my wife and I," concedes Peter. "So Richard asked, 'Why don't we make one for each of you?' " Now Inge devotes her space to vegetables, while Peter prefers flowers.

The couple highly recommends raised beds to other gardeners getting along in years. "You don't have to bend down; the plants are orderly and away from weeds; and of course, it all looks lovely," Peter says.

A Short Course On Bonsai

Peek over the fence from the Witts' and you'll notice something a little strange next door — row after row of miniature trees and shrubs. The plants represent an Oriental art called bonsai. They belong to Educators Leigh DeNeef and his wife, Barbara Baines. He's the Associate Dean of Duke's graduate school, while she

teaches English at N.C. State.

Bonsai, for the uninitiated, involves dwarfing plants in a way that gives the impression of mature specimens in the landscape. Contrary to what you might think, this isn't done by starving the plants or denying them water. Rather, it's accomplished by pruning both the roots and top growth. The Chinese school of bonsai trains plants by pruning only. The Japanese employ pruning too, but also train plants by periodically wrapping the branches with copper or copper-coated aluminum wire.

In the eight years since Leigh fashioned his first bonsai, his collection has grown to more than 200 plants, including bald cypress, Japanese maple, trident maple, and dawn redwood. If you're thinking about getting into bonsai, Leigh suggests contacting local experts and reading books on the subject. (Many cities have bonsai societies.) But here are some general guidelines to get you started.

Subject matter—Look for plants capable of growing thick, gnarled trunks (simulating great age). The smaller the leaves, the better, because large leaves will be out of scale with the rest of the plant and ruin the desired effect. Juniper is an excellent plant for beginners because it's hardy, is easily shaped, has small needles,

Leigh DeNeef and his wife, Barbara Baines, display two of Leigh's prized bonsai—a trident maple (left) and Japanese beech.

and grows thick, twisted trunks.

Container—Bonsai containers are typically very shallow and hold only a small amount of soil. This restricts growth and keeps the container in scale with the plant. "The basic rule is that the depth of the container shouldn't be any more than the width of the trunk at its widest point," explains Leigh. To prevent overwatering, the container must also allow excess water to drain freely.

Light—Give bonsai the same amount of light as a normal-size plant of the same species would receive. For example, give a juniper bright sun and an azalea light shade.

Soil and fertilizer—The soil should be porous and well drained. Half gravel, half potting soil is a good mix. Feed every two weeks with water-soluble 20-20-20 fertilizer diluted to half-strength.

Watering—Bonsai dry out very quickly, especially in summer. One day without water can easily kill them. So be prepared to water once or twice every day without fail.

Most common mistake—"Most people think because bonsai are small and grow in pots, they're indoor plants," says Leigh. "Most of them are not. Outdoor plants, like junipers, need to stay outside."

If Leigh's advice has whetted your appetite for gardening, it's time to walk a few blocks southeast to a garden designed for big appetites.

They Garden To Eat

A person's garden tells the story of his or her life," declares Patsy Hopfenberg. "Come into our yard and you know immediately we're all about cooking."

But not just any kind of cooking. Patsy and her husband, Hal, residents of Cameron Park for 26 years, specialize in Italian cooking. It's a subject she covers frequently in food columns for the Raleigh *News & Observer*. Why the cuisine of Italy? "It's a glorification of ingredients," she explains, "a very healthy way of eating. The Italians make the most of fresh vegetables and herbs and try not to mask the flavors of what they're working with. If it's a tomato, they want it to taste as much like a wonderful, sun-ripened tomato as it possibly can."

Patsy grows such staples of Italian cooking as tomatoes, peppers, a special type of broccoli, basil, and parsley in a 25- x 40-foot plot in the backyard. She orders some of her seed from specialty catalogs, such as Shepherd's Garden Seeds in California; however, many varieties she likes aren't available in this country. Fortunately, Hal has research ties in Italy, allowing the two to travel there once or twice a year. Patsy seizes the opportunity to visit restaurants and gardens and have seed of coveted selections sent back home.

When asked about favorite garden dishes, she quickly replies, "My very favorite dish is simple, basic tomato sauce. A lot of Americans think that's a dish you cook for hours. But you want to cook it for only 10 to 15 minutes to retain the flavor of fresh tomatoes." For her sauce, Patsy uses Italian tomatoes. "They're very concentrated, very meaty and sweet," she says. "When you combine them with basil, garlic, and olive oil, you've got a tomato sauce in 10 minutes."

Of course, fresh basil is essential for many Italian dishes. For pesto, Patsy prefers the young, top sprouts of a narrow-leaved variety called Genova. For tomato sauce, she likes the large-leaved Italian basils.

Hal doesn't take a backseat to Patsy in the kitchen. Italian cooking is his hobby, too. All this cooking precipitates frequent dinner guests, who like to come early and participate. Arriving at the kitchen, they notice things at the Hopfenbergs' are a bit different. For one thing, Patsy and Hal don't own a microwave. They wouldn't hear of it. Instead, they cook on, in Patsy's words, "an ancient, cast-iron, six-burner restaurant stove that takes 30 minutes to preheat, is ready to cook on for the whole day, then takes another day to cool down." With Hal and Patsy frequently cooking at once, all six burners are gainfully employed.

More than a few of their guests from outside the South have changed their minds about Southern cooking. "People who come to the South are very surprised that there's sophisticated cooking going on," comments Patsy. "They think all we have are turnip greens, cornbread, and side meat." A single meal at her house, however, proves what Southerners have known all along—some of the world's best cooking happens right here below the Mason-Dixon. ◇

Food columnist Patsy Hopfenberg grows Italian vegetables and herbs for cooking. She also grows lots of flowers for decorating the dinner table.

The Common Sense Gardener

I haven't used one grain of fertilizer, one grain of lime, or one drop of pesticide in 10 years," David Bradshaw announced as we stood in the middle of his remarkably productive garden plot. And as if he could amaze us even further, he continued, "I don't consider myself an organic gardener; I am a common sense gardener." By using good cultural practices, choosing the appropriate plant selections, and carefully timing when he plants and harvests, he is able to pick something, usually several things, out of his garden all year long.

It is not simply David's insights into growing vegetables that set his Six Mile, South Carolina, garden apart; it is his philosophy of harvesting. "First, nobody comes to my garden without taking something away." (We helped him uphold this tradition.) "And secondly, the first of everything I harvest goes to someone else. I always take the first pink tomatoes to a widow who doesn't have a garden. And by giving away the first, I am always blessed by a whole lot more."

But David shares more than edibles. The garden is an educational tool as well. When he is not gardening, he teaches horticulture at Clemson. He opens the garden to students and Extension service tours; local television and radio garden shows are even taped in the garden.

Though his training and work have been in ornamental horticulture, his backyard gardens have provided years of experience in sustainable agriculture methods—that's what it's called in university circles. Practically speaking, it's just common sense gardening.

Soil Is the Secret

The secret to David's success in the garden is in the soil. It began as the slick red clay characteristic of the South Carolina foothills. But through the annual addition of organic matter, David has built some of the best soil you will ever see. We visited the day after 2 inches of rain fell on the garden. The soil was so well drained that it crumbled through our

David Bradshaw grew up on a peanut farm. Now he grows them in his backyard garden in rich, organic soil. But it did not start out that way. What we see now is the result of 10 years and lots of organic amendments.

fingers without leaving even a trace of clay on our hands.

David's wide beds are amended 12 to 15 inches deep. "I'll be doing research for the next 8 to 10 years to prove that we can do on a large scale what I've been doing in my backyard. Our health will be better, our earth will be better, and our ground water will not be contaminated. And you get better production if you follow the right techniques."

Some of his gardening recommendations include:
- Build healthy soil by adding massive amounts of organic matter to it. David started out applying a 4- to 5-inch layer of old, rotted sawdust to the surface of the soil each year for the first three to four years. Now he simply uses the compost produced in the garden.
- Arrange a mixed planting. David's garden is a patchwork quilt of two pepper plants, two celery plants, two tomato plants, two broccoli plants, etc. Then there are additional plantings of the same vegetables elsewhere in the garden. The diversity makes it difficult for insects and diseases to spread.
- Interplant crops by height, too. David optimizes space and light by growing cantaloupes in the same bed with tomatoes. The tomatoes grow up, and the cantaloupes spread around them to shade the soil and keep down weeds.
- Plant more than one variety of a vegetable, such as four kinds of lettuce, two kinds of carrots, and six kinds of tomatoes.
- Well-fed, vigorous plants are more resistant to insects and diseases. Even when pests are present in the garden, healthy plants will outgrow the problem without intervention with pesticides.
- Because no pesticides have been used, there is a good population of beneficial insects. David also collects egg cases of praying mantises and puts them in the garden during the winter. He encourages frogs and spiders as well. This past year he counted more than 30 species of birds in the garden, but had no problem with them eating his produce.

Vegetables, herbs, and flowers thrive inside raised beds filled with rich soil. These beds are pressure-treated 2 x 10s (see inset) faced with cedar siding to match the house. Their 4-foot width makes it easy to reach the middle from either side.

Gone Gourmet In Poplarville

"Arugula" isn't the name of a Caribbean island, a corrupt Roman emperor, or even that hangey-down thing in your throat between your tonsils. Rather, it's a gourmet green whose tangy, peppery taste jazzes up salads of gardeners-in-the-know.

Now, you probably wouldn't expect to stumble upon arugula among the bayous and backwoods of South Mississippi. But drive to Poplarville, about an hour north of New Orleans, and you'll find gardens lined in geometric precision with arugula, bok choy, Swiss chard, daikon radishes, and other such culinary treasures—all the handiwork of Allen and Julia Anderson of Wolf River Farms.

Julia began growing gourmet vegetables about 10 years ago while working in a New Orleans natural foods store. Soon, she and Allen were tending rows of lettuce and beans beside a 120-year-old log cabin in Poplarville, which has since become their home. As good gardeners invariably do, they grew much more than they could eat, but found nearby restaurants and grocery stores eager to buy the rest. They quit their city jobs, moved to the cabin, and started gardening full time.

Today, growing produce for market takes a backseat to another business. The Andersons design, build, plant, and maintain vegetable and flower gardens primarily for New Orleans residents who escape to weekend homes in the Mississippi countryside. Their clients want attractive, low-maintenance gardens that supply a steady stream of fresh vegetables and herbs not readily available at corner supermarkets. It's a tall order, to be sure. Here's how Allen and Julia do it.

(Right) *Mustard greens enjoy the cool weather of spring and fall. Julia's two favorite kinds are bronze-leaved Red Giant and green-leaved Savannah.* (Below) *Allen likes drip irrigation because it uses less water, puts water right at the roots, and doesn't wet the foliage.*

Start With Raised Beds

They begin with bottomless raised beds bordered with rough-cut pine 2 x 10s that are pressure-treated for ground contact. Iron reinforcing bars inserted several inches into the bottom timbers anchor the beds to the ground. Lengths of pressure-treated 2 x 6s cap the beds, providing seating and a finished look.

The beds vary in length, but are always about 18 to 20 inches high and 4 feet wide. "With a 4-foot bed, you can work from either side and easily reach the middle," says Allen. "It also gives you enough room to grow three rows of something." Aisles between the beds are 4 feet wide as well, to permit wheelbarrows and carts to pass through with plenty of room.

Soon after constructing a bed, Allen and Julia run an underground irrigation line up through its bottom, connect the line to a spigot in one corner, then hook up a drip irrigation system to water the bed individually. Allen extols this arrangement. "With drip irrigation, you use less water because you put water where you want it, right to the root zone of the plant," he declares. "And you don't cause a splash that washes soilborne diseases up on plants. Also, some of our vegetables, like the lettuces, are very delicate. I don't want a pulsating sprinkler blasting them because it tears them up."

Julia appreciates drip irrigation for another reason. "I used to drag soaker hoses around from one garden to another, which took incredible amounts of time," she recalls. Now automatic timers turn water on and off, whether Julia's there or not.

Perhaps the biggest advantage of raised beds is that they give gardeners almost complete control over the soil mixture inside them, ensuring good drainage even in areas plagued with heavy clay. Allen and Julia regularly amend the soil with copious amounts of composted horse manure, hay, oak leaves, grass clippings, and agricultural waste, such as spoiled grain and rice hulls. The goal—lots and lots of organic matter. "In these beds," explains Allen, "you're always going to have a lot of leaching. You want to create a soil that's very high in organic matter, so it will retain moisture and nutrients and will favor soil microbes."

Controlling Those Pests

Gardening near the Gulf means almost year-round problems with bugs and weeds. As confirmed organic gardeners, Allen and Julia reject synthetic chemicals in favor of natural controls. They use insecticidal soap for aphids, Bt (*Bacillus thuringiensis*) for caterpillars, and a mixture of 5% rotenone and 5% pyrethrin for beetles. Notes Allen, "Most often when I spray, I add fish emulsion and seaweed extract. In addition to having trace minerals, seaweed extract is also thought to have fungicidal properties."

Few weeds crop up in the beds because massed vegetables crowd them out. To discourage weeds between beds, Allen and Julia lay down black plastic, then cover it with several inches of pine straw. Pine straw, they observe, controls weeds much better than gravel. It's also cheaper, readily available, and easier to keep clean.

Although the Andersons grow a long list of vegetables, Julia's favorites are her gourmet greens, including chard, Chinese vegetables, and arugula. She's an excellent cook, so bounty from the garden makes it into almost every meal. They still grow much more than they can eat, but she doesn't mind. "To me, it's so exotic having more broccoli and cauliflower than I know what to do with." ◇

It Pays To Doctor the Soil

Full-time physician and part-time gardener Dr. Leon Hamrick is out here somewhere. His wife, Bunny, says so. But right now, he's hidden by the fruit and foliage of his labor. After she hollers "Leon!" a couple of times, he emerges from a narrow slit between tomato cages and trellised pole beans.

The woven peach basket he's carrying is full of red and green Better Boy and cherry tomatoes. From the looks of the plants, it took him a very short while to fill it. In other words, this garden yields and yields some more.

The Hamricks' cool, shady backyard opens out into a broad, hot, and sunny stretch of rich earth in north-central Alabama, a region known more for yielding iron ore and coal than beans and tomatoes. But the rows of over-your-head tomato vines and pole beans, monster-leaved squash, lush herbs, and more attest to the good soil—as well as the good gardener—that changed this place.

This success has a simple explanation. "There's some 30 years of leaves back here," Leon explains. Each autumn, he adds and tills under piles of leaves collected from his and the neighbors' yards (he often shreds

Leon Hamrick uses 6-foot-high wire cages to contain his healthy, productive tomato plants.

the leaves and adds a little fertilizer to help them break down more quickly). Over time, the hard and rocky red clay was transformed into rich, brown soil. He points to the very edge of the garden, which drops off steeply, to show what he started with.

Like most proud gardeners, he agrees to a walking tour of the quarter-acre spread. Every plant has a story. "The Cunninghams gave us

seeds for these yard-long beans about 10 or 12 years ago," he remembers as we walk by a row of them running up a trellis. "Ever seen them grow?" he asks, grabbing a fistful. "They look like a bunch of green snakes."

We move down the row a bit to some beautiful, purple-hulled beans. "See these Louisiana purple beans?" he says. "They turn green when you cook them."

The dark, rich soil is the result of 30 years of tilling fallen leaves into what used to be rocky, hard clay.

You can't help but think of the tender irony: Here is a physician, even in his spare time, taking pride in seeing life flourish.

As we amble along, picking this and poking at that, everything looks familiar, pretty much like you'd want a vegetable patch to be. Everything except a long, orange extension cord that leads out to a large, upside-down, white bucket with its rim propped up. What's that for? "Oh, I keep a radio in there," Leon says with satisfaction. "I tune it to a rock music station, and it keeps the woodchucks out of the garden. They probably don't like the high notes."

As the hot sun falls back over the treetops, other members of the Hamrick family arrive in the garden—daughters Catherine and Mary; Mary's husband, Mike; and their three young children, Emily, Keith, and Madeline, who scamper around like three young children ought to. They sit on the crossties that define the herb garden and share stories. One that gets the most laughter—and

moaning—is a common Southern tale, snapping green beans. "We'd have our friends over to visit, and we'd be so embarrassed that they'd think we were hicks or something because we'd be snapping beans," Catherine recalls. "But they thought it was lots of fun. So we'd all watch TV and snap bag after bag of green beans."

It seems like it would take a small army to consume the fresh produce from this garden, but the Hamricks don't have any problem handling the harvest. One wall of their basement is lined with assorted freezers and fridges—five, to be exact—and the Hamricks are experts at canning and pickling (Bunny makes superb pickled squash), making jellies, jams, and apple butter.

With true gardener's spirit, Leon and Bunny share the bounty—they donate generous portions of their jams, jellies, and other garden goodies to their church to sell at their fall fundraising event. It's just a gardener's way of saying thanks for the joy of growing. ◇

Tips For A Productive Garden

■ Start with good soil. If you don't have good soil, enrich it with generous amounts of organic matter. In most areas, leaves are some of the most abundant and easy-to-get organic amendments you can find.

■ A Rototiller is extremely handy for working in large amounts of organic matter. If you can't afford to buy one, most rental companies have them available.

■ For the most efficient use of your garden, plan beyond using fresh produce. Freeze, can, or otherwise preserve what you can't use right away.

■ Try growing herbs for one of the greatest delights a garden can give. Even small container gardens can host a variety of herbs appropriate for cooking, potpourri, and other uses.

Jerome Ridaught found these regal lilies growing in a ditch near his Alachua, Florida, home. He dug them up and transplanted them to his perennial border, where they thrive after their third year.

Lilies Flourish In Florida

We have trouble with perennials down here," Jerome Ridaught confesses. "All gardeners seem to want what won't grow in their area."

You wouldn't have ever guessed it from the looks of the place: Jerome and Reba Ridaught's garden, located about 12 miles north of Gainesville, Florida, isn't exactly hurting. There's a 100-foot-long and 10-foot-wide perennial border, filled with plants that look as happy to be here as a tourist from Toronto in winter. Regal lilies, five different types of salvias, old-fashioned roses, and garden phlox are all blooming their heads off in this north-central Florida garden.

"Now, we can't grow peonies or lilacs down here; we don't get enough cold weather," Jerome says. But the lilies do just fine; in fact, he found them growing in a ditch not far from the house. "I just dug 'em up and brought 'em home. This is their third year, and the first time they've had real good blooms."

Lilies aren't the only plants that thrive in this garden. Some 100 roses occupy a formal, octagonal display bed. Jerome is particularly pleased with the performance of his David Austin English roses, such as Graham Thomas, a beautiful yellow shrub rose. Other roses that have caught his eye include Alba Meidiland (a low-growing, white rose) and Seven Sisters (an old, pink rambler).

As for insects and diseases, "You name it, we've got it," he says with a laugh. They do have to spray to control insects and diseases (such as black spot) on roses, but try to avoid chemical sprays in the perennial border. Deer have been a major problem, too. "They love the roses," Jerome complains. "So we put an 8-foot-high fence around the backyard. The neighbors thought I was going to raise giraffes."

Jerome enriches the sandy soil typical of this area with generous amounts of compost and manure. "We add about a third (by volume) of manure or compost in the hole every time we plant something," he says.

The mild temperatures also allow the Ridaughts to try their hand at more cold-sensitive plants without too much risk. "We've tried some orange trees and tropical plants right along with the more Northern things," Jerome relates. "The good part about this area is that you get some of the best out of both worlds." ◇

Organic fertilizers, periodic aeration, and proper mowing produce a thick, green lawn for David and Carolyn Oldham, daughter Jennifer, and Roscoe the basset hound.

The Oldhams Go Organic

Nothing in the garden receives more chemicals than the lawn. Homeowners regularly douse their grass with chemical fertilizers, insecticides, fungicides, and weedkillers. But growing numbers of people today reject many chemicals in favor of organic products. Two such people, David and Carolyn Oldham of Dallas, claim their lawn is greener, thicker, healthier, and takes less time to maintain since they switched to organics three years ago.

The Oldhams' lawn care program contains three main components. The first is fertilization. Following the recommendations of Dallas gardening guru, Howard Garrett, they feed their St. Augustine lawn in spring and summer with bagged, composted manure. They like to use two brands widely available in Texas, Sustane and Greensense. These slow-release products condition the soil and add organic matter. From time to time, the family also applies a foliar spray of seaweed extract and fish emulsion, good sources of nitrogen and trace minerals. "With organics, you don't have to feed on any rigid time schedule," explains David. "You're not feeding plants; you're feeding the soil."

Regular aeration is the second step. Each spring and summer, David uses a sharp-spiked tool to aerate the lawn to a depth of 6 inches, particularly areas under stress. (You can also hire a lawn service to aerate.) Aerating loosens compacted soil, helping oxygen, water, and nutrients to penetrate, and increases the number of healthy soil microorganisms.

Proper mowing is the third step. "We used to mow the lawn really short and bag the clippings," recalls David. "Now we do just the opposite—we mow high (2½ inches) and leave the clippings." By mowing high, the Oldhams generate less clippings, which will disintegrate quickly and feed the lawn. "Our lawn looks better, doesn't turn brown after mowing, and uses less water than before," adds David.

Just getting started with organics was the hardest part. "When we first stopped using chemicals, we had more weeds for a while," he admits. "But they've gotten progressively fewer because our lawn is thicker and healthier and crowds out the weeds." Lawn diseases face a similar fate. During especially rainy periods, brown patch appears. But the vigorous grass soon outgrows it.

In David's opinion, organic lawn care isn't a passing fad. It's a coming trend. The best part is helping to save the environment. "Growing a lawn without strong chemicals gives me peace of mind," he states, "and a great sense of satisfaction."

J. Howard Garrett's Organic Manual is an excellent source of information on organic lawn and garden care. It's available from Lantana Publishing, P.O. Box 140650, Dallas, Texas 75214. The book is $15 including postage and handling.

Homegrown Gardeners was written by Steve Bender, Linda Weathers, and Mark Stith with photography by Van Chaplin and Sylvia Martin. ◇

January

Phalaenopsis orchid

CHECKLIST FOR JANUARY

ANNUAL PHLOX

In Florida, sow seeds of annual phlox (*Phlox drummondii*) for bloom in early spring. Sow it in open, sunny areas or under the light shade of trees with a high canopy. Be sure to water every day for at least a couple of weeks after sowing.

ANNUALS

In Florida, pinch or trim back petunias, lobelia, pansies, dianthus, and other cool-weather annuals that were planted in the fall and have grown leggy. Encourage new growth and more blooms by fertilizing with a slow-release 6-6-6 fertilizer.

BLACKBERRIES

In Texas, plant blackberries now. Among the best blackberry selections are Brison (South Texas), Womack (North Texas), and Rosborough (most of state).

CACTI

In Texas, this is the season cacti and other succulents grow very slowly, if at all. Reduce watering to avoid problems with root rot; wait until spring to resume fertilizing, if needed. Be prepared to move outdoor, container-grown specimens to a sheltered spot if hard freezes are forecast.

FIRE ANTS

In Florida, sprinkle a fire ant bait, such as Amdro, throughout your lawn and garden to kill existing mounds and help prevent new ones. It takes several weeks for the bait to destroy a mound, but it will be more effective than a chemical mound treatment that may not kill the queen. It helps if your neighbors treat their yards at the same time.

FREEZE DAMAGE

Marginally hardy plants may be hurt by sudden freezes, but don't be too hasty to remove injured branches. Wait until spring (when plants begin showing new leaves) to determine the extent of the damage. Then cut several inches below the dead tissue to ensure good recovery.

FRUIT TREES

Prune fruit trees now. For peach and plum trees, first remove any limbs that are broken or rub against other branches. Prune established trees to a flat V shape with an open center by leaving horizontal branches and removing vertical shoots. Trim newly planted trees back to between 24 and 28 inches. For apple and pear trees, keep the main trunk with side limbs spaced evenly around it. Remove inner branches to allow more sunlight to reach lower ones. In Florida, prune deciduous fruit trees now.

GARDEN STRUCTURES

During winter, the structures in your garden could use a checkup. Be sure that decks, gazebos, fences, and other features are structurally sound. Repaint, stain, or apply sealer to exposed wood (check the label for instructions on minimum temperatures for effective application). Inspect hinges, bolts, and brackets, and replace those that are rusted or badly worn.

GRAPES

Prune grapes this month while they are dormant, leaving about four leaders per vine. Use sharp shears or loppers (for heaviest stems) to make clean cuts.

HARDWOOD CUTTINGS

Now is the time to root hardwood cuttings. Take 6- to 8-inch cuttings from plants such as azaleas, camellias, and hollies. For faster rooting, dip the cut end in rooting powder, and place in a sterile potting soil mix or sand. Water the cuttings frequently.

HERBS

Fertilize windowsill herbs monthly with a water-soluble fertilizer that has a high middle number, such as 5-10-5. Also, check plants regularly for pale, discolored foliage and small webs, signs of spider mite infestation. To control, rinse the foliage thoroughly with water; then spray with insecticidal soap according to manufacturer's directions.

HOUSEPLANTS

Flowering plants, such as gloxinia, florist's cyclamen, and kalanchoe, are still in good supply and may be discounted following the holidays. Consider buying a few to brighten up your house.

MITES

In Florida, inspect the undersides of citrus and other evergreen fruit trees, leafy vegetables, and flowers and shrubs for the tiny spiderlike pests. To control mites, spray the undersides of the leaves and the tender new growth with insecticidal soap according to label directions.

MULCH

Winter winds and dry spells are harsh on plants. Replenish mulched areas that have become thin during the year. A 3- to 4-inch layer of mulch can protect roots and conserve moisture.

NASTURTIUMS

Sow nasturtium seeds indoors now; gardeners in the Coastal South can sow seed outdoors. Soak the seeds overnight; then plant ½ inch deep in moist potting soil. In colder areas, wait until after the last spring freeze to set out in the garden.

ORNAMENTAL GRASSES

Cut back old stalks of pampas grass and other ornamental grasses 6 to 8 inches above the ground. To speed their decomposition, shred the cut stalks in a chipper/shredder machine before adding to the compost pile.

PANSIES

For more profuse flowering, pinch back flowerbuds after hard freezes. The new growth that results will be fuller, with more blooms. Remove spent blossoms for continued flower production.

PEAS

Plant seed of Sugar Snaps and other edible-podded peas now; sow them about an inch deep and an inch apart. Harvest these peas just as the seeds begin to form.

PLANT MARKERS

Inspect or add plant markers to keep up with the location and identity of plants in your garden. A variety of materials are available; metal strips are the most weather resistant.

SHRUBS

Take advantage of warm spells to set out shrubs. Dig a hole twice as wide and 1½ times as deep as the root ball, and set the plant at the same depth it was in the container or to the top of the burlap. Backfill with soil; then water and mulch thoroughly.

TILLING

Get your flowerbed or vegetable garden in good shape for spring. Till in leaves, compost, lime, or other soil amendments to a depth of 6 to 8 inches. Don't till soil when it's wet.

TOMATOES

Gardeners in North Florida who want the earliest tomatoes can try selections such as Santiam and Oregon Spring whose blooms will set fruit without pollination. Sow seeds indoors now to plant in mid-February, and cover to protect from frost. These selections also need rich soil and plenty of fertilizer to produce an early crop.

TROPICAL FRUIT

In Florida, spray mango, citrus, avocado, lychee, and carambola with a nutritional spray to keep leaves green and healthy. You may need a trombone-type sprayer to reach the tops of full-sized trees. You can also apply micronutrients as a drench to the root zone of the trees. Mix with water according to label directions, and use a watering can or hose end sprayer to apply within the dripline of the trees.

VEGETABLES

In the Lower South, sow seeds of collards, turnips, radishes, and spinach now. Set out transplants of broccoli, brussels sprouts, and cabbage late in the month. Start seeds of tomatoes, eggplant, and peppers in a greenhouse or cold frame; then plant out in the garden after the danger of frost has passed. In North Texas, sow seeds of broccoli, cabbage, lettuce, and other cool-weather vegetables. Set out transplants of cabbage, carrots, onions, and spinach later in the month from Austin southward. Start seeds of tomatoes, eggplant, and peppers in a greenhouse or cold frame; then plant out in the garden after the danger of frost has passed.

WEEDS

In Texas, apply a pre-emergence weedkiller to dormant warm-season lawns now. Be sure to follow label directions; never apply a pre-emergence herbicide or weed-and-feed fertilizer to newly seeded lawns.

January Notes

To Do:
- Force spring bulbs for early blooms indoors
- Brush heavy snow from shrubs to prevent breakage
- Recycle cut Christmas trees
- Cut boughs from discarded Christmas trees to mulch perennial beds
- Scan garden catalogs to plan orders for spring
- Mist houseplants to maintain humidity

To Plant:
- In Middle, Lower, and Coastal South, trees and shrubs
- In Coastal South, cool-weather annuals and vegetables

To Purchase:
- Flowering houseplants for winter color

_____
_____
_____
_____
_____
_____

TIP OF THE MONTH

With so much emphasis on recycling, I have found an efficient way to reuse plastic soda bottles. Cut off the bottom of each bottle, leaving a rim 1½ to 2 inches high. Use this "dish" as a drainage saucer for potted plants. Place the pot and saucer inside a basket or other decorative container and no one will know what you have used. This is an economical and practical way to recycle old soda bottles.

Jane Dewane
San Antonio, Texas

Evergreen hollies and azaleas stand out against a tan Zoysia lawn. The lawn's change in color between winter and summer (see inset) gives this garden two different looks.

A *Lawn In Winter*

If your dormant grass leaves you longing for green this time of year, take another look.

BY STEVE BENDER
PHOTOGRAPHY VAN CHAPLIN, SYLVIA MARTIN

No matter how logical and calculated my argument, I can't convince my mother that brown grass in winter looks good. Mom lives in Maryland, a state awash in bluegrass and fescue, where most lawns maintain a semblance of green even in cold, cold January. But here in Alabama, I grow Zoysia, a superb grass for our warm climate; it forms a thick, soft, durable carpet. Of course, Zoysia, like other warm-season turf, turns brown in winter, and Mom hates that.

Others share my mother's aversion. The reason seems to be that brown grass looks dead to most people, and dead plants in the yard don't win you gardening awards. It may help to think of the winter lawn as a carpet and the garden as a living room. A carpet, aside from its practical function, serves to complement the room's other features and unite them into a coherent composition. That's exactly what a winter lawn does. It ties together shrubs, trees, ground covers, walks, and driveways. It emphasizes evergreen plantings. And by virtue of being a different color than surrounding plants, the lawn makes itself a dynamic design element.

But in order to do this, the lawn must be a solid sheet of tan, not pockmarked with winter weeds. Among the most common despoilers of warm-season lawns right now are wild onions, straw clumps of tall fescue, and violets. You can eliminate the first two with herbicides, although chemi-cals work more slowly in winter than in summer. To kill wild onions, spray them according to label directions with Weed-B-Gon. Spot treat clumps of tall fescue and other grassy perennials with Grass-B-Gon, being sure that your good grass is completely dormant first. Chemicals won't control established violets; you need to dig them out.

Brown winter lawns are most often sullied by deep-green annual bluegrass (*Poa annua*). It germinates in late summer and early fall. If you didn't put down a pre-emergence herbicide containing Balan three months ago, count on seeing this weed until it disappears in late spring. Mark your calendar now, so you'll remember to apply Balan by Labor Day.

Here are two other uniformity tips. First, rake the lawn every other week or so to remove fallen leaves, pine straw, small twigs, and pieces of bark. A power mower set at 2 inches will do the job faster and even better. You'll be surprised how much brighter a clean lawn appears.

Also, don't mix different warm-season grasses in your lawn, not even two selections of the same grass. They'll turn brown in fall and green up in spring at different times, resulting in a patchwork look. "Meyer Zoysia is notorious for going dormant early in fall," says M. C. Engelke, turfgrass specialist at Texas A&M University. "But Emerald Zoysia stays green a lot longer, usually through several frosts."

Despite every argument put forward, you, like my mother, may never believe that a brown lawn can be a plus. If so, there are several alternatives. Some folks like to spray paint brown grass green, although this strategy works a lot better on football fields. Or you can plant a hybrid bluegrass or tall fescue, provided these grasses thrive in your area. Or try overseeding your warm-season lawn next fall with annual or perennial ryegrass. The ryegrass stays green all winter, then dies in spring when warm-season grasses green up.

A final option—move to South Florida. Lawns grow year-round there, which is heaven to people who love to mow. ◇

KEYS TO A HANDSOME WINTER LAWN

■ Eliminate dark-green weeds, such as wild onions, tall fescue, and violets, by spraying or digging them up.

■ Apply a pre-emergence herbicide in late summer or early fall to prevent annual bluegrass.

■ Don't mix two warm-season grasses together, not even two selections of the same grass.

■ Consider overseeding warm-season grass in fall with annual or perennial ryegrass if you want it to stay green.

■ Rake or mow the lawn periodically to remove debris.

Camellias For Cold Climates

In the South, Japanese camellias are to winter what azaleas are to spring (actually, late-season camellias can bloom into azalea season). Their biscuit-size blooms are just expected, anticipated, and appreciated. So it is profoundly disappointing when the plants are hurt or even killed by a particularly harsh winter or a sudden cold snap.

But thanks to the work of some dedicated researchers and observant gardeners, there are many cold-hardy Japanese camellias (*Camellia japonica*) for gardeners in the Lower South. In addition, new crosses of related species of camellias promise to extend their range into the Upper South.

Betty Hotchkiss, horticulturist at the American Camellia Society headquarters in Fort Valley, Georgia, likes to refer to the "Camellia Belt" when describing the safe zone for Japanese camellias. For Southerners, it's an area extending south from Washington, D.C., along the Atlantic Coast, then across the Gulf Coast into Texas. It includes the bottom half of the Lower and all of the Coastal South.

"Generally, they can survive 10 degrees where the temperature doesn't regularly go that low," she adds. "Of course, if it's 70 degrees one day and 10 the next, you're going to have some damage."

You can refer to the box at right for recommended cold-hardy camellias, but the choices don't end there. Dr.

Pink Perfection

Empress or Lady Clare

William L. Ackerman at the U.S. National Arboretum has developed a number of even more cold-resistant plants. Produced by crossing a relatively obscure species, the tea-oil plant (*C. oleifera*), with the popular sasanqua camellia, these plants are said to be cold hardy down to minus 10 to 12 degrees, which means that gardeners in the Upper South and even into Northern states can grow them successfully.

Flower colors include pink, white, and lavender pink; the blooms—and plants—are similar in size to sasanqua camellias. Blooms appear from mid-October through mid-January, depending on selection. Look for these camellias soon at your local nursery or garden center.

Don't get the wrong impression: The flowers on most any camellia can't take below-freezing temperatures for long before they're reduced to soggy-cornflake brown goop. But if the plant is healthy, and the weather warms up a bit, there should be plenty of blooms coming to pick up where the others left off. In addition, early-season camellias, such as Alba Plena (which isn't particularly cold hardy), can strut their stuff and be done before real cold hits the Lower South.

Planting newly acquired camellias where they are sheltered from winter winds and direct sun can help ensure that you'll get lots of blooms at a time of year when color is a precious commodity. *Mark G. Stith*

Cold-Hardy Camellias

Red	Flower Form	Bloom Season
Blood of China	Peony	Late
Christmas Beauty	Semi-double	Early
Governor Mouton	Semi-double/peony	Middle
Pink		
Dr. Tinsley	Semi-double	Middle
Empress (Lady Clare)	Semi-double	Early-middle
Pink Perfection	Formal double	Early-late
White		
Finlandia	Semi-double	Middle
Purity	Rose-form double	Late
White Empress	Semi-double	Early-middle

For a more extensive list, contact the American Camellia Society, 1 Massee Lane, Fort Valley, Georgia 31030.

Simple Steps
To Pruning Crepe Myrtle

PHOTOGRAPHS: TINA EVANS

Select four or five of the strongest stalks to become the tree's main trunks. They should be evenly spaced and fan outward in a vase shape.

My friend, Rut, and I act like Southern neighbors should. A real handyman, he answers my questions about painting, plastering, wiring, plumbing, and other such weighty household matters. In return, I assist him with his garden. Last winter, I noticed his new crepe myrtle needed training to become tree-form—a shape that would promote both its health and beauty in the years to come. Like most beginning gardeners, Rut is unsure about pruning, so I volunteered to help him out.

The job took less than 30 minutes.

Here are the simple guidelines I followed, which you can use to train your crepe myrtle.

■ Prune when the tree is leafless and dormant. Mid- to late-winter is a good time. For most young plants, the only tool you'll need is a good pair of sharp pruning shears. Don't worry about painting the cut ends of branches—this isn't necessary.

■ Do your first pruning around the base of the plant. Most crepe myrtles send up numerous basal suckers, which, if not removed, will transform your tree into a twiggy mess. So cut to the ground any sucker that's less than the thickness of a pencil. Select four or five of the straighter, thicker stalks to become the tree's main trunks. They should be evenly spaced and fan outward in a vase shape. At 3 feet above ground, adjacent stalks should be a minimum of 6 to 8 inches apart.

■ Smooth, flaking bark is one of a crepe myrtle's prime assets. Show it off by removing all weak, spindly growth (again, defined as being thinner than a pencil) from the main stalks up to a height of 5 to 6 feet. This establishes a strong form. It also lets air circulate freely throughout the tree, reducing the chances of mildew on the leaves. If your plant is less than 5 feet tall, just remove spindly growth from bottom to top.

■ Some gardeners insist on removing any seedpods that formed after the plant flowered the previous summer. But this isn't mandatory. Leaving them on will not reduce flowering the next year. You should, however, shorten branches that bloomed last year if the weight of the flowers caused those limbs to curve downward. Cut to an outward-facing bud, so that the new branch will grow up and out of, not into, the center.

■ Keep at it. Like Rut's crepe myrtle, yours will require touchup pruning again next winter. But as the tree matures, the amount of annual pruning necessary will decrease.

Steve Bender

Clean out the center of the crepe myrtle by pruning weak, spindly growth. This promotes strong form and shows off the tree's handsome bark.

Phalaenopsis
The Easiest Orchid

BY LINDA ASKEY WEATHERS
PHOTOGRAPHY COLLEEN DUFFLEY

Orchids. Naturally these denizens of tropical forests must be grown by experts who have a greenhouse and lots of patience, right? Well, not always. One orchid, the phalaenopsis (pronounced fail-a-NOP-sis), is quickly becoming a favorite houseplant, one that will bloom year after year with no more care than an African violet. Sometimes called the moth or butterfly orchid, its sturdy blooms will each last up to three months. The parade of flowers opening up along the graceful arching stalk extends the season of bloom.

Another reason to cherish these orchids is that they typically bloom in winter. In fact, you will find them at their prime right now, selling for $20 to $35, depending on size and selection.

These houseplants hold their blooms longer than almost any other, yet they couldn't be easier to grow or more economical to buy.

Caring for Your Plant

"Phalaenopsis orchids like the same temperatures we do, ranging from 65 degrees at night up to 80 to 85 degrees during the day," says Owen Holmes, III, of Carter and Holmes Orchids in Newberry, South Carolina. They enjoy a couple of hours of direct sun in either the morning or late afternoon. However, if the leaves get hot, move the plant. Avoid drafts from windows or heat vents.

These orchids grow in fir bark, so water runs right through the pot. Water lightly, moistening the foliage and surface of the soil. The plant should be almost dry before watering again. Spray leaf surfaces lightly on sunny days. Always water in the morning so the cup formed by the foliage will dry before nightfall. Allowing water to sit overnight in this cup may lead to crown rot.

Feed by watering with a soluble fertilizer, such as 20-20-20, mixed one-half strength according to label directions. Do this every other time you water. About every two to three weeks, run water through the bark at the kitchen sink to rinse away excess fertilizer.

Phalaenopsis roots often grow out of their pot. Repot about every two years, or when you see that the roots are pushing the plant out of the pot. When you repot, trim the roots back to about 2 inches long; or, if you prefer, just trim the dead roots (those that are brown and wrinkled) and soften the live roots by misting them. Then coil these up in the new pot.

Intricately detailed blooms make phalaenopsis orchids one of the most desirable plants for the home.

(**Top**) *Intricately detailed blooms make phalaenopsis orchids one of the most desirable plants for the home.* (**Above**) *The long, arching stems give the plant graceful lines— light and airy, yet colorful.*

They'll Bloom Again

Assuming that you buy a plant already in bloom, you don't have to do anything besides water it for months. But if the stalk is still green after it has dropped all of its flowers, try cutting it back to just above the first (bottom) or second node (the lump on the stalk where a flower was attached). If the plant is strong enough, it will send out a branch and produce even more flowers, extending the blooming period into summer.

In the fall, when night temperatures drop into the 50s, phalaenopsis plants will form new flower stalks. If your plant has produced a couple of new leaves during the summer, it will probably be able to bloom again. Put it on a porch or in an unheated room until the new stalk appears. Then move it to a favorite spot, and enjoy the unfurling flowers. ◇

February

Mountain laurel

CHECKLIST FOR FEBRUARY

ANNUALS

Fertilize cool-weather annuals, such as calendulas, English marigolds, and pansies, with a slow-release or polymer-coated nitrogen fertilizer (such as Osmocote or Polyon) using the amount suggested on the label. You don't need to pull back the mulch when applying fertilizer; just water after application. In Florida, also fertilize dianthus and stock.

BARE-ROOT PLANTS

Set out dormant, bare-root roses, trees, and other plants as soon as possible. Set them at their original depth (grafted plants need the swollen part, or graft union, set an inch above the soil). If the roots appear dry or shriveled, soak them for several hours before planting. Keep the soil moist but not soggy.

BLOOMING BRANCHES

When buds of quince, forsythia, spirea, and dogwood swell, cut some branches for indoor blooms. Make long, angled cuts when collecting the branches, and place them in a large vase of warm water. Change the water every few days.

BLUEBERRIES

Plant blueberry bushes now (different selections pollinate each other; you need more than one selection for berry production). Choose early- to late-maturing types to prolong summer harvests. Rabbiteye blueberries do best in the Lower and Middle South. In Texas, blueberries do better in the acidic soils found in the east. Gardeners in other parts of the state need to add generous amounts of peat moss and shredded pine bark to the planting hole. Selections for Texas include Woodard (early) and Tifblue (late). In Central Florida, plant Misty and Sharpeblue. Climax, Woodard, Bluebell, Brightwell, and Powderblue are good for North Florida, including the coldest areas of the Panhandle.

BULBS

Check stored corms and tubers of caladiums and other summer bulbs for signs of rot. Dispose of any diseased bulbs before others become infected. The problem could be due to your storage area being too moist. If that's the case, move the bulbs to a cool and drier place. In Texas, set out caladiums, dahlias, and gladioli now. In Florida, begin planting summer bulbs. These include tiger lily (*Lilium tigrinum*), Aztec lily (*Sprekelia formosissima*), canna, caladium, gloriosa lily (*Gloriosa Rothschildiana*), dahlia, and gladiolus. These and other seasonal bulbs will be for sale now in garden centers. Fertilize the bulbs at planting time with a bulb fertilizer or a slow-release 6-6-6 applied at the rate recommended on the label.

FERNS

In Florida, for shady areas where you want to eliminate lawn, try evergreen ferns such as the popular, coarse-textured holly fern (*Cyrtomium falcatum*) or the rich-green teasel fern (*Polystichum setosum*). Both will tolerate sites ranging from moist to fairly dry and will do well under the shade of live oaks or pines.

FRUIT

In Florida, fertilize citrus and tropical fruit (lychee, guava, and avocado) with a citrus fertilizer that contains iron and other minor elements. For peaches, apples, pears, persimmons, loquat,

and pomegranate, use a fertilizer that contains zinc, magnesium, and manganese, such as a peach-and-pecan fertilizer. For blueberries, use an azalea-camellia fertilizer.

POTATOES

About a month before the last freeze in your area, potatoes are ready to plant. Cut seed potatoes into small, egg-sized sections containing at least two eyes. Leave the sections out on a newspaper for a few days until the cut areas have a thin callus. Add about ¼ cup of 8-8-8 fertilizer per 10 square feet of loosened soil; set the pieces about 3 inches deep and a foot apart. As the potatoes sprout, mound soil around the plant. Norland, Red La-Soda, and Kennebec are good selections for Texas gardeners.

PRUNING

Prune ornamental trees and shrubs that are overgrown or need shaping. Wait until spring-flowering shrubs (including azaleas) have finished blooming before cutting them back. In Florida, this is the last month to prune ornamental trees and shrubs and many roses before growth resumes. Even if the plants did not go completely dormant, don't wait. (For spring-flowering shrubs, such as azaleas and spirea, wait until after they bloom.)

ROSES

Prune hybrid tea and bush roses now. Remove all but four to six healthy canes if big blooms are your goal. Leaving more canes will result in a fuller, more attractive bush. Make your pruning cuts about ¼ inch above an outward-facing bud. Seal hollow canes with a bit of white glue to prevent wood-nesting bees from damaging the stem. Do not prune climbing roses now.

ST. AUGUSTINE

Brown patch is a fungus that causes large, irregular patches of yellowed-out grass. Spray these areas with a fungicide, such as Daconil, as soon as the symptoms appear.

SAVED SEEDS

Before you set out seeds that may not be viable, put 10 of them in a wet paper towel. Fold it up, put in a plastic bag to keep the towel moist, and set in a warm place (such as on top of your refrigerator). Check the old seed packet for germination times. Unwrap the towel after the appropriate time, and count the seeds that have sprouted. If it's less than half, it's probably not worth your while to plant the seed. Sow heavily if slightly more than half germinate.

SCALE INSECTS

Apply dormant oil early in the month to control scale insects on fruit trees and other ornamental shrubs. Spray on a day when the temperature is between 35 and 85 degrees Fahrenheit and no hard freezes are expected in the next couple of days.

SEED STARTING

Sow seeds of marigolds, zinnias, coleus, scarlet sage (salvia), and other warm-season annuals indoors. Use seed trays, large flats, or plastic foam egg cartons (poke a small hole in the bottom of each depression) filled with sterile soil media. Herbs that can be grown from seed include basil, parsley, and sweet marjoram. Gardeners in warmer areas of Texas and Florida can sow the seeds directly in the ground. In Florida, start seeds of tomatoes, peppers, and eggplants now.

February Notes

To Do:
- Prune summer-flowering trees and shrubs
- Cut back wisteria
- In Lower and Middle South, apply pre-emergence weed killer to lawn
- Trim old foliage of liriope
- Spray fruit trees with dormant oil
- Clean foliage of houseplants
- Force cut branches of forsythia, quince, spirea, redbud, and azalea into early bloom indoors
- Lime lawn and garden beds, if necessary

To Plant:
- In Lower and Coastal South, cool-weather vegetables, summer bulbs, and annual flowers
- In Middle, Lower, and Coastal South, trees, shrubs, and roses

To Purchase:
- Mail-order seeds and plants
- Pre-emergence weed killer
- Dormant oil spray
- Lime

_____

_____

_____

_____

_____

_____

_____

SULPHUR BUTTERFLIES

More of these pretty butterflies in shades of yellow or orange will come to your garden if you plant for them. The IFAS Cooperative Urban Wildlife Program suggests several cassias as food for the caterpillars; they include dwarf golden shower tree (*Cassia afrofistula*) and privet cassia (*C. ligustrina*). Pentas, papaya (male), and scarlet firebush (*Hamelia patens*) are three good sources of nectar to attract adult butterflies.

VEGETABLES

Start seeds of tomatoes, peppers, and eggplants now. Gardeners in the Lower South can sow spinach, carrots, collards, radishes, and English peas outside; onion, cabbage, broccoli, and cauliflower can be set out now. Wait until March to sow seeds outdoors in the Middle South and until April in the Upper South. In Texas, gardeners from Houston southward can set out onion, cabbage, broccoli, brussels sprouts, cauliflower, and other cool-season vegetables. Sow seeds of summer vegetables, such as tomato, eggplant, and peppers, in flats.

TIP OF THE MONTH

You can make permanent name tags for your plants using empty aluminum cans. Remove the ends of the cans; then cut the sides lengthwise into strips a half-inch to an inch wide and 2 to 3 inches long. Use a ballpoint pen to inscribe names or notes on the strips. To attach a tag to a plant, use a nail to punch a hole in one end; then thread a thin wire or fishing line through the hole. When you no longer need the tag, send it to your recycling center along with other aluminum products.

C. Fred Gerlach
Athens, Georgia

*B*looms
That Brighten
The Shade

BY STEVE BENDER
PHOTOGRAPHY
VAN CHAPLIN, TINA EVANS

"Tell us what we can plant to get some color in our gardens," the woman demanded. "What can we get to grow that will bloom in all this shade?"

She belonged to a local garden club that had invited me to speak at their monthly meeting. I had in mind to wax poetic about the joys of gardening, but these women wanted none of that. They were after brass tacks. Practically all first-time homeowners in their thirties and forties, they craved practical information on how to beautify the shadows with something other than the standard impatiens and English ivy. What kinds of shrubs, for example, would give them flowers under all of their big trees?

"Azaleas," I replied, hoping I wasn't insulting their intelligence by being *too* obvious. "You all know the evergreen kinds that everyone plants around their houses. But how many of you have tried the native azaleas, like Piedmont azalea, Florida flame azalea, and Alabama azalea? Some people call them 'wild honeysuckle' because of the long stamens in their flowers. Granted, native azaleas lose their leaves in winter. But they have an open, airy look that evergreen azaleas lack. And their flowers are often very fragrant."

Vulcan rhododendron is particularly well adapted to the South's heat and humidity.

A large, open shrub growing 8 to 10 feet tall and wide, Piedmont azalea offers sweetly fragrant, pink flowers in spring.

Their eyes brightened. Wow—two minutes into my spiel and already I'd said something useful. Got to keep the momentum going. "Of course, rhododendrons like shade," I continued. "Y'all know that. But you have to plant selections that do well in the South. Willis Harden, a rhododendron grower in Commerce, Georgia, recommends Anna Rose Whitney and Cynthia, which are pink, Vulcan and Damozel, which are red, and Dora Amateis and Anna H. Hall, which are white."

Pens and pencils scribbled hurriedly. I was cooking now. "What about hydrangeas?" I suggested.

"Oakleaf hydrangea is fantastic in the shade. You get huge flower spikes in spring and summer and burgundy leaves in fall. There's also French hydrangea, whose flowers turn blue or pink, depending on whether the soil is acid or alkaline. I also like a white, snowball-type called Annabelle, which grows 3 to 4 feet tall and blooms for months in summer."

Oakleaf hydrangea puts on a stunning show in late spring. The shrub also develops excellent fall color and is very easy to grow.

Writing hands started to cramp. Time to wrap this thing up. "Don't forget about Japanese andromeda," I urged. "It blooms white or pink in February and March. And for white summer flowers, you might want to try bottlebrush buckeye—*Aesculus parviflora*—or sweet pepperbush—*Clethra alnifolia.*"

The club members rose to thank me and invited me to stay for lunch. I therefore concluded that they liked my talk and headed straight over to find the desserts.

The Ins and Outs of Shade

Growing shrubs in shade involves more than simply plunking down plants at the foot of a big tree. You have to consider a number of factors. For example, how dense is the shade? Most shrubs bloom best in the high, filtered shade supplied by tall pines and hardwoods. In the dark shade of hemlocks, beeches, and Southern magnolias, however, they'll bear nice foliage, but few blossoms.

You might think shrubs in shade need less water than otherwise, but it ain't necessarily so. If your soil is dry and shallow and you're planting beneath large trees, those trees will suck up every molecule of available moisture during a drought and you'll end up watering more. If, however, the shade comes from either a nearby structure or trees growing some distance away, water requirements should lessen, especially if it's afternoon shade.

Shade cools the air, so don't be surprised if a hydrangea growing in shade blooms a week later than one in sun. The temperature told it to do that. Cooler air also helps flowers in shade last longer than those in full sun.

You may think that shade limits your selection of plants, but sometimes the opposite is true. For example, it lets gardeners in the Coastal South greatly expand their plant palette. "Shade helps us grow plants better suited farther north, such as weigela, Mock orange, and spirea (especially pink selections)," explains Alan Shapiro of The Plant Shoppe in Gainesville, Florida. "Without shade, these plants would burn up here." ◇

MORE FLOWERING SHRUBS FOR SHADE

Here are some lesser known candidates highly recommended by Carrington Brown, a landscape designer in Richmond.

- Japanese kerria (*Kerria japonica*)
- Mountain laurel (*Kalmia latifolia*)
- Leatherleaf mahonia (*Mahonia bealei*)
- Prague viburnum (*Viburnum* x *pragense*)
- Winter daphne (*Daphne odora*)

Mountain Laurel

Yellow Shrimp Plant

Turk's-cap

PHOTOGRAPH: VAN CHAPLIN

Nothing promotes vigorous plants more than loose, cultivated soil. For small areas, use a garden fork, after testing whether the soil is dry enough to work.

Get Your Soil To Loosen Up

Trying to grow plants in hard, compacted soil is like hopping into a car that's out of gas. You can fume and fret, but you won't get anywhere. Out of all the things that can make a great garden, none matters more than loose, cultivated soil.

Why?

Loose soil benefits plants in several ways. First, it allows root systems to freely expand. A vigorous root system strengthens the whole plant, therefore making it less prone to stress; this usually results in faster top growth.

Second, roots need oxygen to absorb water and nutrients. Loose soil contains plenty of air spaces. Third, water easily penetrates loose soil. Roots use what water they need, and the excess drains away.

When?

A good time to loosen compacted soil is in late winter or early spring prior to planting. But don't look to the calendar for guidance in picking out the exact day. Instead, do a simple soil test.

Grab a handful of soil from the garden and squeeze it in your hand. Then drop the soil from waist height to the ground. If the clod disintegrates, the soil is dry enough to work. If it holds together, the soil is too wet. Don't give in to the temptation to work wet soil. You'll squash out all of the air spaces and compact it even more. Then it'll dry as hard as a rock.

How?

To work up large areas of soil—more than 100 square feet or so—without killing yourself in the process, use a tiller. Rent one if you don't own one. A tiller will cultivate the soil about a foot deep.

For smaller areas, nothing works better than a trusty garden fork. Press the tines fully into the ground; then lift and turn the soil over. Use the head of the fork to break large clods. Work slowly backward from one end of the garden to the other, so you don't walk on soil you've just loosened.

What about soil amendments, such as sphagnum peat moss, sand, or gypsum? Can they help to loosen soil? The answer is "yes," but there's a catch. You can't simply spread a bale of peat over the soil or scratch in a bag of sand or gypsum and significantly improve the soil. You have to work amendments deeply into the soil by using a tiller or garden fork as previously described.

Organic matter, such as compost, chopped leaves, and pine straw, improves soil structure far better than sand or gypsum. It binds soil particles together, easing the passage of oxygen and water. It also increases the number of earthworms, which loosens the soil even more. If you can, work in large amounts of fresh organic matter every year.

Sometimes soil contains so much heavy clay and rocks that tilling or turning it doesn't seem feasible. In this case, consider building a raised bed of good soil atop the existing soil. Ten to twelve inches of loose soil provides ample leg room for most vegetables, flowers, bulbs, and shrubs.

Steve Bender

Nodding green blossoms resembling bell clappers appear atop the foliage in January and February.

Good and Green

Bearsfoot hellebores blend two shades of green as they bloom in this woodland garden on a mild winter day.

Imagine the result if I tried to convince you to eat bread that was all crust or an apple that was all peel. Yet here I am suggesting that you grow bearsfoot hellebore, a perennial that is all green. And you *should* grow it, really, because despite its lack of stunning color, it's one of the winter garden's premier plants.

Native to western Europe, bearsfoot hellebore (*Helleborus foetidus*) grows about a foot high. Leathery foliage, which apparently reminds some folks of a bear's clawed foot, gives this herbaceous evergreen its common name. Another nickname, "stinking hellebore," is downright slanderous because the plant bears only a slight scent.

How many perennials do you know that bloom in the dead of winter? This one does, although the flowers are probably like nothing you've seen before. In January and February, pendulous blossoms, resembling bell clappers, cluster atop the foliage. The flowers are green—ripe Granny Smith apple green—adorned with thin, rosy lips. The two-tone effect of flowers and foliage is both handsome and unusual. After seed matures, the flower stalks turn brown, at which point you just cut them off.

I like to use bearsfoot hellebore as a textural accent beside such stalwarts of the winter garden as Christmas fern, rhododendron, holly, mahonia, azalea, and boxwood. Its long, thin, black-green leaflets contrast dramatically with lighter greens and larger leaves around it. Come spring and summer, this plant proves a good companion to spring bulbs, hostas, caladiums, and deciduous ferns. Employ it in a mixed border, rock garden, woodland garden, or for edging a shady path.

Tolerant of drought and unpalatable to insects, bearsfoot hellebore isn't a difficult plant to grow. It does, however, require shade from tall pines or hardwoods. And the soil must be well drained. My plants thrive in rich, moisture-retentive soil that's supplemented annually with shredded leaves and other organic matter. They like a pH of between 6 and 7, so if your soil is strongly acid, be sure to sprinkle a handful of ground lime around each plant.

The best way to propagate this hellebore is to let it go to seed naturally. Seedlings will sprout at the foot of their parents in spring. Transplant this progeny as you will, or, even bettter, share with your neighbors. They may not know exactly what they're getting. But next year, they'll thank you.   *Steve Bender*

For sources of this hellebore, send a self-addressed, stamped, business-size envelope to Hellebore Editor, *Southern Living,* P.O. Box 830119, Birmingham, Alabama 35283.   ◇

BEARSFOOT HELLEBORE AT A GLANCE

Size: To 1 foot tall
Light: Shade
Soil: Fertile, moist, well drained, pH 6 to 7
Pests: None serious
Propagation: Seed, division
Range: Throughout the South, except Tropical South

A Neat Little Retreat

Sometimes, you just need to get away. Even if it's only to slip outside for a breath of fresh air. That was just the mission given to Landscape Architect Brian Zimmerman by the owners of this two-story brick home in the Eastover neighborhood of Charlotte.

"They wanted an outdoor room just off their family room on the side of the house," says Zimmerman. "There is a large terrace in the back, but it's open to the whole backyard. It just doesn't have the sense of intimacy and privacy that you have in this garden."

One slight problem arose: There was no easy way to get to the side yard, which, Zimmerman recalls, "was sort of nondescript—there were some leftover azaleas out there." So the two large windows on either side of the chimney were taken out and replaced with French doors. The side yard was then just a few steps away.

For privacy from the street and the neighbors, a 6-foot-high brick wall enclosed the matching brick terrace on the front and side. A 2-foot-high seating wall sets off the terrace from the rest of the yard.

The front wall, which would have looked a little cold and hard from the

street, was softened with plantings that blend with the existing shrubbery along the front of the house. Leyland cypresses on the neighbor's side of the wall give more separation. An iris sculpture fountain highlights a semicircular, raised pond on the wall opposite the house; a pair of spitting frogs flanks the iris. "The traffic noise from the street was louder than we realized, so the sound of the splashing water serves to combat it," Zimmerman says. In the middle of the terrace, a raised, rectangular planting bed contains a variety of perennials and other plants prized by the lady of

the house, who is an avid gardener. A built-in irrigation system helps keep plants looking their best.

Because both owners work, this terrace gets a lot of use as an after-hours retreat. A series of 12-volt uplights located throughout the garden adds a dramatic and practical effect for nighttime enjoyment.

"It's just a very simple place to enjoy the sound of the water and color from all the perennials," Zimmerman says. "There's enough seating for small parties, yet it's intimate enough for just the two of them."

Mark G. Stith

A 6-foot-high brick wall screens the terrace from the street and next-door neighbors. Seating is ample for small parties, yet the space is comfortable enough for two.

An iris sculpture fountain against the far wall serves as a focal point for the terrace. The gentle sound of water gurgling from the fountain has both pleasing and practical intents, helping drown out the sound of traffic from the busy street.

Two large windows on either side of the chimney were replaced with French doors. This gives easy access to the new brick terrace, located just off the family room on the side of this Charlotte home.

Bravoure

Saint Keverne

Ice Wings

Pink Charm

Rediscover
Daffodils

Good news: Some selections of these bright spring beauties last longer than you might think.

BY JULIA H. THOMASON
PHOTOGRAPHS VAN CHAPLIN

Plant several of these long-lasting daffodil selections to enjoy vibrant yellows, oranges, and pinks, as well as subtle pastels.

The first daffodils stirring in the garden are among the most welcome visitors of late winter and early spring. Once the daffodils arrive, we want them to linger.

Experienced gardeners have learned that certain selections produce flowers that are actually a bit thicker than most and have an almost waxy texture. These daffodils are more resistant to the elements, living in the garden for as much as a week longer than other selections. When picked shortly after blooming, the flowers will last an extra two to three days.

Brent Heath, of the Daffodil Mart in Gloucester, Virginia, has known the selection Ceylon to last six weeks in the garden and up to two weeks after being picked. But if the weather is too warm or dry, they do not last as long.

In addition to Ceylon, Brent recommends these selections for long-lasting blooms. **Bravoure**—Large yellow-and-white flowers, 18 to 24 inches tall. **Saint Keverne**—Golden flowers with a slightly frilled cup, 16 to 18 inches tall. **Ice Wings**—Two or three nodding ivory blossoms per stem, 12 to 14 inches tall. **Pink Charm**—White petals encircle a large cup banded in orange pink, 16 to 18 inches tall. **Gigantic Star**—Very large saffron-yellow blossoms with a vanilla fragrance, 18 to 20 inches tall. **Redhill**—Red-orange cup inside ivory petals, 16 to 18 inches tall. **Bella Vista**—White petals surround a small orange-red cup, 16 to 18 inches tall.

When these appear in the garden, pick a few to enjoy indoors. Cutting daffodils can damage the foliage; instead, just pick them with your fingers. The upper part of the stem is hollow and won't hold moisture. Reach down to the white portion of the stem, and snap it off. Be sure to leave the foliage intact.

Daffodils exude a liquid that is harmful to other flowers. Before arranging with other flowers, place the stems in 6 to 8 inches of lukewarm water for an hour or so; change the water, and let them stand another hour or more.

Daffodil stalks won't penetrate florist foam easily; instead, place glass marbles in a vase to hold the stems in place. In an opaque vase, use crumpled chicken wire or floral bases to anchor the stems.

Keep arranged flowers cool, out of direct sunlight, and away from dry heat. Cooler night temperatures also help keep them fresh. Place them near a window at night; they can tolerate temperatures to about 28 or 30 degrees. ◇

March

Peonies

CHECKLIST FOR MARCH

APHIDS

To prevent damage to tender new growth, control aphids now. Inspect plants on a regular basis, and spray with insecticidal soap; reapply as needed. Some plants, such as sweet peas, are sensitive to soap sprays. If you're not sure about a plant, spray just one or two leaves to see if it causes problems. Sometimes, a blast of water from the hose will do the trick.

BANANA SHRUB

One of North Florida's most fragrant shrubs is in bloom this month. Banana shrub (*Michelia figo*) is evergreen and grows to about 15 feet high. Each spring its small yellow blooms fill the air with a sweet fragrance likened to ripe bananas. Plant in a well-drained spot in sun or light shade.

CHRYSANTHEMUMS

If your garden mums are in full bud, don't be in a hurry to shear them back. There's plenty of time to cut them back so they can fill out and develop new flowerbuds for their fall display. In addition, some garden centers are starting to carry forced-bloom mums in spring that will bloom again in fall.

FIGS

Plant fig trees now. They survive winters well in the Lower and Coastal South but can also be grown in protected locations in the Middle and Upper South. Good selections include Celeste, Brown Turkey, and Texas Everbearing. In Texas, good selections include Celeste and Texas Everbearing; Alma is recommended for the southern half of the state.

FLOWERING SHRUBS

When shopping for azaleas, rhododendrons, or other flowering shrubs, buy plants in bloom. You'll be assured of getting the color and flower type you want. If you're starting a bed, plant large masses of the same bloom color.

FRUIT

In Florida, blueberries and pomegranates have ornamental qualities that make them great additions to the landscape. Blueberries do well from Central Florida northward; their foliage turns a brilliant red in fall. Pomegranates grow throughout the state and are covered in spring with red-orange blooms followed by red fruit.

GROUND COVERS

In Florida, divide aspidistra, clump-forming ferns, mondo grass, and liriope by separating parent plants into little plantlets and setting them out at the proper distance. Mow wedelia and Confederate jasmine early this month if you haven't already done so to remove old growth.

HEDGES

Trim overgrown or uneven hedges now. Prune them so the base is wider than the top, allowing sunlight to reach the lower branches. This will help avoid the sparse, "broccoli-top" look that plagues many hedges.

HOUSEPLANTS

Longer daylight hours means houseplants will be putting on new growth and increasing their uptake of nutrients. To keep new foliage healthy, apply a water-soluble fertilizer diluted according to the label directions every month. Remove dead or spindly foliage. It's also a good time to repot plants that have overgrown their containers.

LEAF SPOT

Photinias (red tips) are notorious for developing an unsightly disease called leaf spot that can even defoliate plants. To prevent leaf spot from worsening, spray with a fungicide, such as Daconil 2787, when new growth begins, and repeat the spraying at one- to two-week intervals until the foliage matures. Remove fallen, diseased leaves, and keep lawn sprinklers from wetting the foliage.

LIRIOPE

In Texas, cut back scraggly looking liriope before new growth begins; set your lawnmower at its highest setting or use a string trimmer. If new growth has already begun, take care not to cut it or the leaves will have clipped brown stubs on the ends.

MADAGASCAR PERIWINKLE

Consider using some of the outstanding, newer selections of this durable, sun-loving and drought-tolerant annual. Among the more recent types are Parasol (white with red center), Pretty in Rose, Pretty in Pink, or one of the new Cooler series, including Peppermint (white with red center) and Grape (purple).

PERENNIALS

Set out perennials now; be mindful of exposure (sun or shade), soil, and proper spacing for best performance. For shade, favorites include hostas, Southern shield ferns, Lenten rose (hellebores), astilbes, and coralbells (heuchera). For sun, daylilies, bearded iris, coneflowers, and butterfly weed are good. (See "Favorite, Foolproof Perennials,"*Southern Living*, May 1992, page 50.) In Texas, favorite perennials for shade include

hostas, holly and cinnamon fern (native to East Texas), astilbe, and coralbells. In Florida, plant stokesia, coreopsis, salvia, Shasta daisies, pentas, hostas, and other perennials now. Be sure the bed is well prepared with loads of compost or other organic matter. Avoid poorly drained spots in the yard. If your entire lot is low, raise the level of the bed by 6 inches using a brick edge, stone wall, landscape timbers, or railroad ties.

ROSES

If black spot was a problem last year, spray early in the season for control. For best results, spray weekly with Funginex, and reapply after rainy spells. In Florida, now is the time to choose roses, as garden centers are stocked with the biggest selection they will have all year. Old-fashioned landscape roses, such as The Fairy, Betty Prior, and Cherokee, do well in Florida's climate without much spraying or fuss. For a sturdy arbor or across the front of your house, try Lady Banks rose, a vigorous early-blooming climber with yellow blooms that has proven itself in Florida for decades. Be sure to plant roses in well-drained soil.

TEXAS MOUNTAIN LAUREL

In Texas, if you're looking for a striking plant for your garden, consider Texas mountain laurel (*Sophora secundiflora*). This native shrub produces clusters of purple, wisteria-like blooms in March. Typically reaching 10 to 12 feet in the landscape, Texas mountain laurel is ideally suited for the alkaline soils that are found in much of the state.

March Notes

To Do:
- Dig and divide crowded perennials
- Fertilize trees, shrubs, ground covers
- Feed the lawn
- Lime lawn, perennial beds, rose beds, and vegetable garden, if necessary
- Sow seed for cool-season grasses
- In Upper South, apply pre-emergence weed killer to prevent crabgrass

To Plant:
- Bare-root roses
- In the Lower and Middle South, broccoli, cabbage, lettuce, peas, carrots, potatoes, spinach, asparagus, collards, kale
- Trees, shrubs, perennials
- In the Upper South, pansies, Johnny jump-ups, ornamental cabbage and kale

To Purchase:
- Seeds
- Vegetable transplants
- Fertilizer
- Pots, stakes, tomato cages
- Pre-emergence weed killer

_____

_____

_____

_____

_____

_____

_____

_____

VEGETABLES

Sow seeds of spinach, edible-podded peas, turnips, Swiss chard, kohlrabi, and carrots now. Also set out transplants of broccoli, brussels sprouts, cabbage, collards, kale, and cauliflower. In the Middle and Upper South, there's still time to sow seeds of warm-weather vegetables, such as tomatoes, bell peppers, and eggplant, indoors for setting out after the last spring frost. In South Texas, beans, cucumbers, eggplants, squash, and tomatoes may be planted now from seed or transplants. Set out transplants of lettuce, early-maturing broccoli and cabbage, cauliflower, and spinach in North Texas; wait until late in the month to plant warm-season crops. In North Florida, start beans, corn, cucumbers, melons, squash, tomatoes, and other warm-season vegetables. Plant right away in South Florida or you'll be battling the scourges of summer—too much rain, insects, and disease. Eggplant, hot peppers, black-eyed peas, okra, and cherry tomatoes will be okay through summer, provided your garden has good drainage.

TIP OF THE MONTH

A plastic, openwork berry basket (like the ones you buy in grocery stores) is an ideal cover for tiny seedlings. It provides protection from small animals, heavy rains, or hail. In addition, it filters strong sunlight, so that the seedlings get the dappled light they seem to like best.

In the garden of Virginia's historic Stratford Hall, colonies of foxgloves stand tall.

Stately Spires

Foxgloves are a pleasure no gardener should miss—whether it's their impact at a distance or the charm of their freckled blossoms up close.

BY LINDA ASKEY WEATHERS
PHOTOGRAPHY VAN CHAPLIN

Foxgloves rocket skyward, lifting the eye from all the little beauties that bloom down low. In spring, they rise from the garden like long tapers atop a silver candelabra. "They're unobtrusive at first," observes Philip Page, superintendent of gardens and grounds at Dumbarton Oaks in Washington, D.C. "But when they bloom they make you sit up and take notice."

You might expect a flower this exciting to be difficult to grow, but it's as easy as setting out transplants in the fall. In the Middle and Lower South, the foliage is a handsome evergreen rosette measuring a foot or more across. During hard winters or in Upper South gardens, freezes may knock back the foliage but will not hurt the plant.

Foxgloves (*Digitalis purpurea*) are biennials, which means they grow leaves one year and bloom the next— that's why they are planted in fall. The flower stalk pushes upward until it stands 2 to 7 feet tall, depending upon the selection. By the time the tip of the stalk is blooming, the lower portions are ripening seeds. If you cut off the stalk at this point, the plant will usually sprout more spikes. Although they are never as big or showy as the first, there are usually several. Let these remain until the seeds are ripe, and they will provide plants for the coming year.

The freckled throats of foxgloves mark the trail that bees follow to the nectar.

Under ideal conditions foxgloves would live another year or two, but they usually become weak and bedraggled from the spider mites that attack the foliage in summer. It really isn't worth trying to spray because it is easier to pull them out each spring, replace them with summer annuals, and then plant strong, new plants in fall.

Self-sown seedlings may also suffer from spider mites. If so, don't bother to nurse them along unless you really enjoy a challenge. Your energies would be better spent on the summer garden. Then in fall, look for small foxgloves at your garden center. These will produce full-size plants the following spring.

But don't forsake the idea of having foxgloves this year. If your local nursery has mature plants for sale, you still have time to set them in your garden. They can be spectacular in an urn or other large container. Consider the impact they would have at your home's entrance or on the deck or terrace.

Foxgloves enjoy partial shade and moist, well-drained soil. If you have sand or hard clay, add plenty of organic matter before you plant. Space plants 12 to 18 inches apart to allow room for the foliage to expand. Sprinkle a tablespoon of slow-release fertilizer into the hole before planting.

Whether you buy plants locally or through the mail, you will find several selections. Excelsior Hybrids are probably the most popular, growing in a mixture of white, pink, and purple. Although the stalks are quite strong, they can grow 5 to 7 feet tall and can get heavy when the flowers are fully open. It is a good idea to stake them, or a spring storm could make a mess of a beautiful display.

For mail-order sources, send a self-addressed, stamped, business-size envelope to Foxglove Editor, *Southern Living*, P.O. Box 830119, Birmingham, Alabama 35283. ◇

Neat, lush plantings and the strong lines of fencing and curbs shape this handsome entry garden in New Orleans.

As Simple As Possible

According to an old Shaker hymn, " 'Tis a gift to be simple." The entry garden of New Orleans architect Barry Fox bears this aphorism out. Rather than hide his house behind a complex horticultural mishmash, Fox chose to complement its elegant, formal facade with lush, grouped plantings and clean, strong lines.

The scene wasn't always so tidy. When Fox and his wife, Maxine, bought the house, it had been boarded up for years. But the couple saw great potential in both the Garden District neighborhood and the 19th-century home. As part of the overall restoration, Fox designed a handsome entry garden to welcome guests to the front door. For assistance in selecting plants, he consulted Landscape Architect René Fransen.

A flagstone walk and steps take you to the front door. The home's large front windows needed a visual base, so Fox added an elevated planter made from reinforced concrete capped by the same flagstone. Needlepoint hollies anchoring each end of

Even a small lawn here would require constant maintenance. Instead, this panel of Japanese ardisia is practically care free and stays green all year.

the planter emphasize and frame the windows.

Using too many different kinds of plants in a garden this small would have reduced its impact and increased maintenance. So Fransen selected just a few types of broadleaf evergreens, such as cast-iron plant, holly fern, and dwarf sasanqua, to create interesting foliage combinations and keep the garden green year-round. An old, gnarled crepe myrtle, saved for its sculptural form, is the only plant remaining from pre-restoration days. In place of a small lawn, Fransen decided upon a panel of Japanese ardisia. "I like ardisia's lush texture," explains Fransen, "and the fact that you can grow other plants within it. Also, fallen leaves don't pile up on it, as they do with liriope. They seem to fall right through and be hidden."

Today the garden is easy to care for and always attractive. It's all because, as Fox puts it, "We tried to make everything as simple as possible."

Steve Bender

Little Wall, Big Effect

This 24-inch square column, 4 inches higher than the 16-inch-high wall, anchors the end of the curve.

My lot in an older neighborhood is 50 feet wide and backs up to an alley. Though the house was built in 1928, there was no privacy and no landscaping other than a cluster of dogwood trees. I had a two-space carport built and, at the same time, enclosed the rear and side yard with a paneled-and-capped fence. That left an undeveloped rear space of about 30 x 30 feet sloping down to the fence corner.

What to do? I looked and waited and welcomed advice. In the meantime, I moved flat, native stone from an old front walk to make a new walk bordering the area and placed three large stones as steps on a wide path down the slope. Someone suggested building a low retaining wall into the slope below the largest dogwood, but I didn't want to disturb its roots.

I eventually decided, instead, to wrap the *outside* of the nearly level area at the bottom of the slope with a low retaining wall and backfill with a fine gravel for a terrace. Gravel packs well and would let water and air get to the tree roots.

Using a hose to outline the proposed wall, I framed an area in and around a smaller dogwood near the fence. Fortunately, my landscape ar-chitect neighbor, Norman Johnson, pointed out I was about to stumble into that garden design embarrassment—a squiggle. Instead, Norman traced a strong, graceful curve *behind* the dogwood trunk and plunked down a large plastic container where I needed a low column to stop the wall.

My contractor, already building walks and steps at the front, included building the wall and adding the gravel at a good price (less than $500). Sam Bookout of Eastside Nursery suggested a substitute for gray gravel: a brick-colored slag known in Birmingham by the name "red dog." The color is friendly and relates well to the brick on the house.

The wall, which extends 20 feet, stands 16 inches high over the gravel, and can serve as seating. I am still surprised how much effect the little wall with its simple curve has. It distracts from the fence corner, creates a convivial arc of seating, and holds the loose-gravel terrace in place. The curve is a grand gesture in a constricted space. It makes a solid argument for seeking design advice on even modest garden projects, and proves the value of having a designer living on your alley.   *Philip Morris*

A low, 20-foot-long stone wall curves around a corner of this small garden, framing the gravel terrace.

PHOTOGRAPHS: VAN CHAPLIN

Peonies

Don't let them tell you peonies won't grow here. Generations of Southerners say it's not so.

According to ancient legend, peonies arose from moonbeams. While we modern and wiser folk may smile in amusement at this old belief, there's little argument that their blooms are among the most heavenly bodies on earth.

But peonies have gotten a bad rap in the South. For some reason, they're considered a Northern plant; something that you have to give up when you live or move here.

It's true that peonies need cold weather in winter to flower reliably in spring. And our trademark hot and humid summers can cause disease problems and poor flowering as well, especially with the selections that flower late in the season. However, enjoying the fat and fluffy blooms of peonies is far from a spectator sport: Gardeners as far south as Montgomery and Jackson, Mississippi, have been enjoying their plants, in some cases, for generations.

"The rootstock of these peonies dates back to at least 1879," says Mary Helen Irby, referring to the lush plants growing in her Jackson garden. "I've since divided them; now I've got four planted in a bed out beside the driveway." Several different types are planted throughout her garden.

Every fall, Sally Cooper would get a box full of peony divisions mailed to her Charlotte house from her mother-in-law, Mrs. William Hugh Cooper, in Orange, Virginia. "They were passed down through her family, and are well

(**Left**) *Back when she was a shy bride-to-be, Gertrude Miazza (soon to be Gertrude Irby) posed behind the peonies growing in her mother's yard in Jackson, Mississippi.*
(**Above**) *Phil and Mary Helen Irby tend the same peonies that Phil's mother, Gertrude, inherited from her mother; Mary Helen has since divided the plants in her garden. The rootstock of the original peonies dates to at least the late 1800s.*

BY MARK G. STITH
PHOTOGRAPHY VAN CHAPLIN, SYLVIA MARTIN

*For best performance in the South,
choose early-flowering selections.*

(**Above**) *Most of the crowd of peonies blooming in Sally Cooper's garden came from her mother-in-law, who would box up plants dug from her garden every fall.*

(**Right**) *Mary Ellen Bryan bought her peonies at a discount store some 20 years ago. "Even after they bloom, the beautiful foliage really looks good in the garden," she says.*

over 50 years old," Sally attests. "And there are three or four of them out in the garden that were my mother's."

If Mary Ellen Bryan had heard that peonies wouldn't perform in Montgomery, she would never have bought hers at a local discount store some 20 years ago. And they are doing just fine in her garden, thank you very much.

Although their cold-weather requirements pretty much disqualify them for gardeners in the Coastal and Tropical South, peonies are easy and enjoyable plants to grow. If you follow a few simple guidelines, you can be assured of fabulous flowers that will grace your garden for years and years.

■ Choose early-blooming selections. The later the flowering time, the more risk you run of getting disappointing blooms. Single- or Japanese-type flowers bloom reliably. If you simply must have one of the semidouble or double forms, go with early-flowering selections, such as Festiva Maxima, a beautiful white double that performs well in the South.

■ When planting the roots (best done in fall, although they can also be planted in spring), don't set them too deeply or they won't flower well. The red sprouts (called eyes) shouldn't be placed more than 1 inch below ground level.

■ Peonies need full sun or light shade, well-drained soil, and lots of water, especially in the spring. Apply a handful of low-nitrogen fertilizer (such as 5-10-10) around each plant in spring; overdoing it can cause too much foliage growth and fewer flowers. Also, stake the plants early in the season to support the weight of the foliage and flowers.

■ Cut back the foliage each fall after the first hard freeze to prevent the spread of disease. Thrips—thin, black insects smaller than a grain of rice—and beetles can ruin the blooms. Apply an insecticide such as Diazinon or Orthene Turf, Tree and Ornamental Insect Spray to control the thrips; carbaryl or rotenone will work on the beetles. Apply insecticide in the early morning or late evening; spray a small part of the foliage to check for damage. For non chemical control, keep beds weed-free and deadhead old blossoms.

■ Be patient—blooms will be disappointing the first year, but will improve in succeeding seasons.

■ Peonies *do* need cold weather to bloom well, so they don't do well for gardeners in the Gulf or Coastal South. But it's hard to generalize about this: At least one selection, Festiva Maxima, has been reported as blooming successfully as far south (and west) as Houston.

Depending on where you live and the selections chosen, peonies bloom from late-March to mid-April; late-flowering selections bloom up to a month and a half later. Don't limit your palette to only these selections at right; there are dozens of peonies to choose from. For a list of sources, send a self-addressed, stamped envelope to Peony Editor, *Southern Living,* P.O. Box 830119, Birmingham, Alabama 35283. ◇

The fat blooms of peonies make superb cut flowers; pick them early in the morning or late in the evening and immediately place in water. "They'll last longer if I cut them just when the bud is starting to show color," says Mary Helen Irby.

PEONIES RECOMMENDED FOR THE SOUTH

Selections	Flower Color	Flower Type
Dancing Nymph	White	Single
Edulis Superba	Pink	Double
Festiva Maxima	White/red flecks	Double
Krinkled White	White	Single
Lady Alexandra Duff	Pale pink	Semidouble
Largo	Pink	Single
Sarah Bernhardt	Pink	Double
Scarlett O'Hara	Red	Single
Charles White	White	Double

April

Louisiana iris

CHECKLIST FOR APRIL

BLACKBERRIES

In Texas, plant container-grown blackberries now. Set plants 3 to 4 feet apart (in rows of 6 to 8 feet wide, if you're planting several). Good selections include Brazos (all but West Texas), Brison (Central and South Texas), Rosborough (most of the state), and Womack (North and Central Texas). Navaho is a thornless selection well suited for most of the state.

BULBS

Don't cut off or braid the foliage of spring-flowering bulbs; it is needed to replenish the bulb for next year's flowers. As the leaves wither, they send nutrients to the bulbs, so let them fade naturally.

CALADIUMS

In Central and South Texas, plant caladium bulbs at the end of the month; wait until May in the Dallas-Fort Worth area northward. Plant masses of the same color for best effect; set them 4 inches deep and 18 inches apart.

CANNAS

In the Middle and Lower South and Central and South Texas, cannas can be left in the ground over winter, but this can lead to overcrowding and poor flowering. Dig up and divide overgrown plants now; space new divisions 12 to 18 inches apart and 3 to 4 inches deep. Water thoroughly after planting.

CITRUS

In North Florida, gardeners who want citrus with minimum risk of losing them to cold should choose satsuma. If you live on a lake or river, plant the tree as close to the water as possible where the ground still drains well; warmth from the water will help protect your tree. Or plant the tree in a container set on casters so it can be rolled into a garage or other protected area. A 25-gallon pot is usually large enough.

EASTER LILIES

In Florida, this classic lily dependably perennializes, so plant it in the garden after Easter. Give it a sunny spot in well-drained soil, and work Bulb Booster into the soil when planting.

FERTILIZING

Feed your Bermuda, Zoysia, St. Augustine, or other warm-season grass about two to three weeks after it starts to turn green. When using a drop spreader to distribute fertilizer, apply half the recommended rate in parallel lines. Then spread the rest at a 90-degree angle to the first application. A slow-release turf fertilizer can keep the lawn looking green longer without having to reapply as often. In Texas, feed your warm-season grass about two to three weeks after it turns green. In Florida, feed it now.

LAWNS

In Texas, it's an ideal time to set out plugs, sod, sprigs, or seed of warm-season grasses including Bermuda, centipede, St. Augustine, buffalo grass, and Zoysia. Water newly established lawns on a daily basis until the grass becomes established. Centipede is particularly slow to germinate and develop but becomes an attractive and relatively low-maintenance lawn once established.

MOSQUITOES

In Florida, cup-type bromeliads provide a breeding place for mosquitoes. Move these bromeliads under cover if possible. If planted in the ground, you may need to apply a mosquito killer that contains *Bacillus thuringiensis israelensis*, which kills the larvae.

OKRA

Warm soil is a must to germinate okra. Wait at least a month after the last frost to sow seeds. Soak seeds overnight, and then sow them ½ to 1 inch deep and 2 inches apart. When they are 2 inches tall, thin the seedlings to 6 inches apart. Good selections include Annie Oakley II Hybrid, Burgundy, Clemson Spineless, and Jade. In Florida, sow seeds now. Good selections of okra for Florida include Emerald Green and Perkins.

OLEANDER CATERPILLARS

In Florida, these hairy caterpillars will feed on full-sized and dwarf oleanders alike. They begin as tiny orange caterpillars and grow long tufts of black hair. They'll multiply rapidly and strip branches bare of leaves. Dust the plants with carbaryl as soon as the caterpillars appear.

PARSLEY

Parsley that survived winter in milder areas of the South will soon grow tall and bloom. Allow seeds to develop and fall into the garden where they will eventually sprout. You can ensure a continual supply of parsley by pulling out last year's plants and replacing them with new transplants.

PENTAS

If you're looking for a dependable flower that will bloom all season, try growing pentas (*Pentas lanceolata*), also known as Egyptian star-clusters. The purple, rose, or white flowers grow in 4-inch-wide clusters and sit atop shrubby, 18- to 24-inch-tall

plants. Buy transplants where available or sow seeds in a warm place (70 to 75 degrees). Pentas do best in full or partial sun and can even be grown as a houseplant in a sunny window. In extreme South Texas, they are perennials; otherwise, treat as annuals.

ROSES

To control black spot or powdery mildew on susceptible roses, spray as soon as new growth appears. Use Funginex or benomyl diluted according to directions. For best results, spray weekly and after heavy rains.

ST. AUGUSTINE

A new selection of St. Augustine, FX-10, has been developed by the University of Florida. It is shorter than Floratam but not as dwarf as Seville, Jade, or Delmar. It does show resistance to chinch bugs. Floratam, long planted for its resistance to the tenacious pests, is no longer resistant to some strains of chinch bugs.

SEEDS

Leftover seeds will keep for use later in the season if you keep them dry. Put opened and unopened packets into a glass jar, and seal tightly. Then store the seed jar in your refrigerator. Try a tablespoon of powdered milk wrapped in a tissue at the bottom of the jar to absorb extra moisture.

TOMATOES

Consider growing a few lesser known types of tomatoes along with your favorites. Yellow Pear produces large

---

April Notes

To Do:
- Leave bulb foliage alone until it turns yellow
- Prune dead wood out of winter-damaged trees and shrubs
- Be ready to protect newly planted flowers from unexpected frosts
- Visit the garden center early for the best selection of flower and vegetable transplants

To Plant:
- Caladiums, glads, cannas, and other summer-flowering bulbs
- Azaleas, rhododendrons, flowering shrubs
- In the Coastal, Lower, and Middle South, tomatoes, beans, squash, cucumbers, peppers, onions, okra, eggplant, corn

To Purchase:
- Flower and vegetable transplants
- Summer-flowering bulbs
- Any necessary insecticide, fungicide, or fertilizer
- Vegetable and flower seeds

_____

_____

_____

_____

_____

_____

_____

_____

---

quantities of small lemon-yellow fruit with a mild flavor; these are perfect in salads or summer vegetable dishes. Sweet 100 is a cherry tomato that bears lots of large clusters of sweet bright-red fruit.

VEGETABLES

In Texas, sow seeds of cucumbers, okra, Southern peas, and green beans now. Set out sweet and hot pepper plants and eggplants also; use organic mulch around the base to conserve moisture and reduce weeds. In Florida, sow seeds of Southern Peas now if you haven't already. Southern peas proven in the state include Mississippi Silver, Zipper Cream, and Pink Eye Purplehull.

TIP OF THE MONTH

When I'm preparing hanging baskets or containers for planting, I don't place gravel or broken pottery in the bottom for drainage. Instead, I use pine cones, either whole or broken up, depending on the size of the container. The cones provide good drainage and break down by the end of the season, enriching the soil. They also keep hanging baskets from getting too heavy.
Claudia S. Lynn
Keswick, Virginia

No Better *Iris* Than Louisiana's Own

BY STEVE BENDER
PHOTOGRAPHY VAN CHAPLIN

From their soggy home in bayous and swamps, these flowers won a home in Southerners' hearts. And to think we owe it all to a Yankee.

Louisiana iris bloom about two weeks later than bearded iris. Unlike bearded iris, these natives thrive in wet soil or even water.

*They also grow in well-drained soil, making fine companions to other perennials.
In warm climates, their swordlike foliage stays green all winter.*

Southerners like to blame Yankees for just about everything that's wrong with the world, from punk rock and bad manners to the fact that in the sequel to *Gone With the Wind,* Scarlett O'Hara moved to Ireland. Wouldn't it be nice to hear of a Yankee that actually did us a world of good?

John K. Small was such a person. Botanist, plant explorer, and curator of the New York Botanical Garden, he, more than anyone else, introduced Louisiana and the South to the beauty of Louisiana's own iris.

It was 1925 when Dr. Small, traveling by train from Florida to West Texas, glanced out of his window near New Orleans and observed vast swamps of wild iris in bloom. During the next six or seven years, Small spent weeks trudging through these wetlands collecting specimens. The extensive range of flower colors astonished him. In 1930, he collected over 8,000 plants representing "six various shades of violet-blue . . . sev-

enteen various shades of red-violet . . . fourteen various shades of lilac . . . nine various shades of cerise and magenta . . . fifteen various shades of pink and old rose . . . [and] twenty-six various shades of red, orange-red, and orange."

More than likely, Small had gathered just two native species—red flag (*Iris fulva*) and big blue iris (*I. giganticaerulea*)—along with a plethora of color variants and natural hybrids. By 1941, Small's enthusiasm for these plants resulted in the establishment of the Society for Louisiana Irises. Many members decided to breed their own hybrids, adding to the mix such parent plants as the leafy blue flag (*I. brevicaulis*), a cold-hardy species. Today, hundreds of selections exist.

They're Native— So What?

Perhaps you're not especially impressed with the fact that Louisiana iris are native. What concrete advantages do they offer your garden? There are several. For one thing, they represent "the widest color variation of any group of any iris known," according to Richard Johnson, curator of the Briarwood Nature Preserve in Saline, Louisiana.

Adds Josephine Shanks of Houston, "They're spectacular in bloom. Each stalk opens a flower at the top, then one at the bottom, then usually two to three buds in the middle open in sequence. There's usually another bud waiting behind each flower. So you get quite a lot of bloom." She notes that they make superb cut flowers without any special treatment.

Undoubtedly their biggest advantage is that they will grow almost anywhere. Unlike bearded iris, Louisiana iris like wet soil, thriving in mud and muck with their roots under water. But they'll also grow in the well-drained soil of a garden bed. Another advantage—in the Lower, Coastal, and Tropical South, their handsome foliage stays green all winter. Even better, pests seldom plague these irises.

Worried about winter hardiness? Don't be. Thanks to genes contributed by leafy blue flag, most Louisiana iris are surprisingly rugged. "I don't know anyone growing them in Alaska," comments Johnson, "but my sister grew them for years in Minnesota. So I'd say they're relatively hardy."

Louisiana iris are winter hardy throughout the South. Here, their colorful blossoms poke through a fence at the Antique Rose Emporium in Brenham, Texas.

Getting Started

If you'd like to try Louisiana iris, here are the basics to get you started. First, find a sunny spot. They need at least six hours of sun a day. (In hot, dry climates, however, afternoon shade is desirable.) Second, pay attention to the soil. Prior to planting, loosen the soil to a depth of at least a foot and work in lots of organic matter. Louisiana iris like acid soil with a pH between 5.5 to 6.5. If the pH of your soil exceeds 7.0, incorporate 2 to 3 pounds of garden sulfur per 100 square feet of flowerbed.

The best time to plant is late summer or early fall, when plants are dormant. If you plant in spring, keep your plants well watered. Promptly unwrap any roots that arrive in the mail, and store them in water until you plant them. Set these rhizomes at or slightly below the soil surface, spacing them at least a foot apart. Gardeners in the Lower, Coastal, and Tropical South should mulch with pine straw or shredded bark to prevent the rhizomes from getting sunburned. Feed in March and September with an organic fertilizer, such as cottonseed meal, blood meal, fish emulsion, or seaweed extract. You can also use Osmocote 14-14-14 or Bulb Booster.

For a waterside planting, don't plant the rhizomes directly into the water. Instead, place them on the water's edge, and let them creep into the water as they desire. Land-bound iris need no more moisture than your other perennials. But extra water in spring and fall results in better bloom.

Might as well admit it—for a Yankee, John K. Small was a pretty good guy. And thanks to all of his Southern followers, growing Louisiana iris today is no Small feat.

For mail-order sources, send a self-addressed, stamped, business-size envelope to Louisiana Iris Editor, *Southern Living*, P.O. Box 830119, Birmingham, Alabama 35283. ◇

Low Walls
Distinguish the Setting

BY PHILIP MORRIS / PHOTOGRAPHY VAN CHAPLIN

They may be called "decorative" or "accessory," but low, free-standing walls can be as exciting and useful as any design element. These masonry walls can help wed a house to its site, contain parking areas, or bring architectural weight to a landscape plan.

Robert Lewis is one of several landscape architects in Oklahoma City who treats low masonry walls as valuable tools in landscape design. "They are excellent ways to extend the lines of a house into its setting or to screen guest parking areas," he notes. "But care is needed in their use." A good caution: You can't just move them like you would a hedge.

For a handsome, older, stoneclad house in the Nichols Hills area of the city, Lewis developed a plan that employs a set of strategically placed walls made of the house's native stone. The house once sat high on the lot, with only lawn stretching from the street up to a newly installed curved driveway. About 100 linear feet of wall was used in three segments that vary in height and placement. One straight section, parallel to the housefront, screens the right side of the drive and also visually extends the house to balance it on the site. Stout columns anchor each end.

A larger L-shape section of wall begins just left of the front door and then turns toward the street. It features an inset bronze plaque with the house address on the segment closest to the street. The third wall brackets the left side of the drive and completes the composition.

"We suggested garden walls early on to screen cars, but the owner did not want a straight wall in front of the

Stout stone columns highlight the corners, adding definition to the new wall.

house," Lewis says. "That's when we came up with this plan."

Wall height varies with grade, but Lewis suggests a maximum height of 36 inches. The typical range is from 18 to 24 inches high. But these are all relative, depending on the site and how it's viewed. "We'd never go as high as 36 inches on a level site for this kind of wall," Lewis observes. And because the house setting is usually viewed from a passing car, the landscape architect asks clients to kneel down to examine proposed wall placements—the car-view level.

Although masonry walls are more expensive than shrubs, which can serve similar screening and containing purposes, they bring sharper definition and architectural substance to a setting that needs it. At the same time, they can be overdone. "We stay away from walls being really dominant in a plan," Lewis explains. "Sometimes you see a narrow driveway with a wall that's too tall, and it makes the drive seem narrower."

Care in placement of low walls near driveways is especially important. They should always be held back at least 24 inches clear of the driveway edge, because drivers cannot see over walls that are immediately adjacent to a drive.

Accessory walls almost always need softening as part of a larger landscape plan. In this case, Lewis introduced red oak trees both in front of and behind the walls in order to make them appear integral to the setting. Planting beds, edged with the same stone as the walls, fill the spaces between walls and driveway. Planting areas in front of some wall segments further tie them into the scheme. Evergreen materials create a year-round framework with seasonal planting

Landscape Architect Robert Lewis unified the design by successfully matching the native stone of the wall and the house.

spaces settled between.

"It's like weaving the walls and the plantings together to help make the plan work," Lewis notes. "We don't want to obscure the walls, so we use low materials for softening and heavier plantings on the ends to nestle them in."

The cost of walls will vary greatly depending on locale, materials, size, and other factors. But partial walls can be a reasonable component of a landscape plan. And they have both an immediate and a lasting effect, which is all the more reason to include them in a plan. ◇

TIPS FROM THE EXPERTS

The particularities of walls in landscape design are almost as varied as sites and designers care to make them. Oklahoma City area landscape architects share their experience.

■ "It is always best to use the same material found on the house exterior, or something very close. You can use combinations, like brick and stone, if the house is of either material, or you can introduce a precast stone cap. Pay attention to shadow lines and detailing to make the walls worthy of their prominence. Also, look at lighting in conjunction with them," says Scott Howard.

■ According to Brian Dougherty, "Walls are supposed to last, and it is important to have proper footings. This will vary both with the region of the country and the particular soil conditions. We think it is worth the extra cost to have a structural engineer check our plans, particularly if the walls are much over 2 feet high."

■ "You see cases where walls around a motor court at the front of a house simply take over the site. They must appear to fit in, to be part of the larger landscape. If there is a real question of necessity, I think plants are the best recourse," advises Warren Edwards.

DESIGN: SHEILA WERTIMER

This South Carolina city is famous for its gardens, yet many of the most delightful are hidden from view behind courtyard walls. Join us for a peek inside.

Charleston's Well-Kept Secrets

BY RITA STRICKLAND
PHOTOGRAPHY VAN CHAPLIN

(**Left**) *An open gate invites guests into Liz Young's courtyard garden. The grassy pathway leads visitors to the formal rose garden beyond.* (**Right**) *In Emily Whaley's garden, a fountain draws attention to the creeping strawberry geranium at its base.*

he story is often told of a venerable Charlestonian who was asked why she so seldom traveled. "Why should I travel?" she replied. "I'm here already." Those who have visited this South Carolina city can easily understand her complacence. Few places in the world can rival the blend of grace, beauty, history, and tradition. And the same might be said of Charleston's courtyards.

Although couched in the city's Historic District, these walled spaces are not museum pieces. Like gardens in your neighborhood, they are living places where real families play together, where friends congregate in the evening, and where caring hands till the soil. It is in these intimate courtyards that Charleston shows her true personality—friendly, warm, and unpretentious.

Originally, however, many of these areas were just about the furthest thing from pleasant gardens. Instead, they were places for carrying on the utilitarian business of life, where privies and other outbuildings were located and animals kept. But as times changed, these courtyards evolved into the wonderful gardens they are today.

Of course, not all of Charleston's courtyards came about in such organic fashion. Some are of later design, and others are formed completely by freestanding walls, rather than the old, surrounding buildings. But all share the seclusion that a courtyard garden fosters.

"People are very comfortable with the scale of these gardens," says Robert Chesnut, a Charleston landscape architect who has worked on numerous courtyard renovations. "There's a sense of enclosure—an intimacy—that makes a courtyard seem to be your own private world." Landscape Architect Mary Palmer Dargan agrees. "Our courtyards serve as outdoor rooms for such pleasures as reading, breakfasts, teas, cocktail parties, and receptions," she adds. "That's why they're very often located next to the dining or living room. When the weather is poor, the garden still serves the house by providing attractive views from the inside out."

A walk down almost any street in

A simple wooden balustrade bisects the courtyard of Marty Whaley Adams. Azaleas and camellias find shelter beneath an old, gnarled fig tree.

the city's Historic District will yield enticing glimpses past the gates of these wonderful courtyards. On one block, a rough-hewn arbor is draped by a Lady Banks rose bush in full bloom, its pendulous branches almost brushing the garden floor. Beneath it, a table set for a luncheon awaits the guests' arrival. On another street, a path of worn brick stretches from the sidewalk down a dark, covered corridor the length of the house. At its end, the sun shines on a small, emerald lawn surrounded by a bed of the purest white azaleas.

An Open Invitation

If you're strolling down the streets of the Historic District and pass a garden gate that's standing open, don't be bashful; step inside. By long-standing Charleston tradition, an open gate is an invitation. "That's really true," assures Liz Young, who has been one of the city's Registered Guides since 1952. "If the gate is open, you can go in. It means that the owners want to share the garden's beauty and ambience."

This time of year, more of the city's gates spring open, as if the vibrancy inside simply refuses to be contained. Camellias unfurl their season's last blossoms over ground blushed flame red or pink by the fallen petals of a winter's worth of blooms. Bright-yellow tangles of Carolina jessamine fill the air with fragrance, and wisteria's lilac-colored flowers hang heavy on the vines. Everywhere, azaleas burst forth in an exuberance of fuchsias, salmons, orchids, and scarlets, which their Charleston setting transforms from flashy to charming.

A more sure-fire approach to visiting Charleston's private gardens, however, is to seek the services of one of the city's Registered Guides, many of whom are available for private tours. "Most of the more experienced guides—the ones that have

Standing in a low pool, this statue is the focal point of Louie Koester's long, narrow courtyard. "In the morning, when the sun is up and reflecting on the statue, that's when I enjoy the garden most," declares Louie.

DESIGN: HUGH AND MARY PALMER DARGAN

been here the longest—have access to a lot of private gardens," says Young, who has been a guide longer than almost anyone. Not only can they show you to the very best in Charleston gardens, they can tell you something of the gardens' histories as well.

Once inside these gracious gardens, pay close attention. Charleston's courtyards brim with ideas you can take home with you. "The attention to detail is what attracts many people," says Chesnut. "They are charmed by the brickwork, statuary, and fountains."

Details do make the difference, especially when viewed close up. The carefully cut and fitted bricks in the cap of a wall, the skilled carpentry evident in an arched gateway, and the artful placement of garden ornaments all have added impact in these small areas. "It's attention to detail that impresses people with this city," adds Landscape Architect Sheila Wertimer. "We care about paving design and materials, how beds are bordered, even how catch basins are set."

You may notice that even the tiniest garden is actually a series of spaces. The first may be little more than an

entry or walkway bordered with plants of rich texture or color, but passing through it helps build your anticipation for what's to come. Inside, a simple wooden rail, a boxwood hedge, or a single step may be used to divide the garden into separate areas.

Fragrance is one element that sets gardens apart from other designed spaces, and nowhere does fragrance play a bigger part than in the gardens of Charleston. Plants such as daphne, jasmine, gardenias, roses, and tea olives are subtly placed by a gate, along a walk, or near a garden bench, so that each season has a fragrance all its own.

And rare is the Charleston courtyard where water plays no role. "Running water masks obtrusive sounds and is also serene and soothing," explains Mary Palmer Dargan. Most of the water features you'll see are really quite simple.

In one garden, a perennial border is reflected in a dark, still pool only an inch deep. A tiny statue of a maiden, tucked amid the boxwoods and azaleas, pours water from an urn into a shallow bowl where the birds can drink. And finally, a heard but unseen flow draws you inexorably to its source—a secret garden screened entirely from view by a mass of giant camellias.

Less than four years ago, many of Charleston's most delightful gardens were damaged by the wall of wind, mud, and salt water that was Hurricane Hugo. Undaunted, the city's residents began immediately to rebuild, repair, and replant. Today, few signs of that disaster remain, and Charleston's garden courtyards bloom more gloriously than ever.

Through April 17, the Historic Charleston Foundation is sponsoring its annual Festival of Houses & Gardens. Wednesday afternoons during the festival are devoted to tours of Charleston's "Glorious Gardens." For more information write HCF, P.O. Box 1120, Charleston, South Carolina 29402; or call (803) 723-1623.

For information on Registered Guides who specialize in Charleston garden tours, call the Charleston Convention & Visitors Bureau at (803) 853-8000. ◇

Draped in jasmine and antique roses, the gate to the garden of the historic Benjamin Phillips House, the home of John and Dianne Avlon, frames a view of the dining terrace and garden beyond. Clipped boxwoods and brick edging define the beds, while flowering crabapples form a canopy overhead.

May

*Spanish bluebells
and Bridesmaid azalea*

CHECKLIST FOR MAY

AGAPANTHUS

These blue-flowered perennials (*Agapanthus africanus*, also called lily-of-the-Nile) are terrific for partial shade, either in a flowerbed or a pot. Because of their blue color, they look best when combined with flowers having white or yellow blooms. Dependably hardy in the Lower South, they also will do well in the Middle South if mulched.

AZALEAS

Feed plants with azalea-and-camellia fertilizer now. If leaves are yellow with green veins, apply iron chelate or Greenol at the recommended rate (but the long-term solution is to treat the soil with aluminum sulfate).

BAGWORMS

Small, cone-shaped objects hanging from branches are actually homes of bagworms, which strip the foliage of junipers, cedars, and other evergreens. If there aren't a lot of them, simply pick off the bags; however, severe infestations may need to be sprayed with a systemic insecticide, such as Orthene.

BOUGAINVILLEA

For a profusion of blooms from spring to fall, it's hard to beat bougainvillea. Compact selections available in local garden centers include Helen Johnson (red) and Pink Pixie—both will do well in 6-inch pots. Other compact selections are Mardi Gras (gold), Rainbow Gold, Tropical Bouquet (orange fading to pink), and Royal Purple.

CANTALOUPES AND MELONS

If space is limited in your vegetable garden, try growing some space-saving selections. Musketeer cantaloupe can even be grown in containers; plants have a spread of only 2 to 3 feet. Bush Baby II Hybrid is a compact watermelon that yields round fruits of about 10 pounds that fit easily into the refrigerator.

CENTRATHERUM

This little-known annual provides a summer full of magenta flowers. It performs best in partial shade, and dead flowers never need removing. While the display is not as showy as a geranium, it is constant. Centratherum reseeds in most gardens, and butterflies love it.

CHINCH BUGS

Large, circular brown patches in St. Augustine lawns (popular in South Texas) are symptoms of a chinch bug infestation. To confirm, press a can with the bottom cut out into the edge of an affected area. Fill it with water, and wait a few minutes. If small, black insects with shiny wings float up, chinch bugs are the culprits. Spray the lawn with a recommended insecticide following label directions.

CHRYSANTHEMUMS

In Florida, cut the plants back by half now to prevent them from becoming too tall. Pinch back the stems again in June or July, and the flowers will bloom on much sturdier plants come October.

CLIMBING ROSES

Prune climbing roses back to 4 to 5 feet after they finish blooming. Train new growth to twist and turn around supports to double the number of flowers.

CUCUMBERS AND CANTALOUPES

Mildew is one of the worst pests of cucumbers and cantaloupes in Florida, so you need to plant resistant selections. Two popular mildew-resistant cantaloupes are Edisto 47 and Planters Jumbo. Two resistant cucumbers are Poinsett and Salad Bush hybrid. Leave at least 4 feet between plants in the garden; if plants are crowded, they are more susceptible to disease.

HEAT-TOLERANT FLOWERS

Tropical plants thrive all over Texas. Firebush, croton, mandevilla, hibiscus, pentas, allamanda, and cuphea all provide good hot-weather color.

HIBISCUS

Hibiscus like rich soil. Fertilize them with a slow-release 6-6-6 that contains extra iron. Spray the foliage or drench the ground with iron chelate. Be aware that the iron solution will stain concrete and painted surfaces.

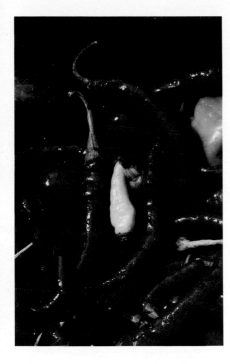

HOT PEPPERS

Spice up summer salsa with your own peppers. Jalapeños are probably the most familiar to fans of Tex-Mex cuisine. Thai Hot and Super Chili Hybrid are good selections for flavor as well as attractive bedding plants. Long, slender peppers such as cayenne are just right to harvest this fall for decorative pepper strings.

LAWNS

Repair small patches of lawn that have been damaged by diseases, insects, or wear and tear. First, remove the dead grass and work the soil; then cut a piece of sod to fit or sow seeds (try one of the new lawn-patching kits), and water thoroughly. Don't fertilize until you feed the entire lawn.

ROSES

If rosebuds fail to open or produce misshapen flowers, look for mites or aphids feeding on the buds. To control the pests, spray the plant with insecticidal soap, or use Orthene.

SCALE

Spray hollies, camellias, and euonymus for scale. Spraying now will help control the pests while they are still young. Scale insects are much harder to kill as they get older. Spray summer oil on stems and leaf undersides.

SWEET CORN

Make a second planting of sweet corn about mid-month in North Texas and early May in the rest of the state. Calumet, Sweet G-90, and Kandy Korn E.H. are all recommended types. Sow in double rows or blocks for good pollination, and don't plant different selections of sweet corn at the same time.

TRAINING

Guide new shoots of vines, such as clematis, to their supports. Stake tall lilies and provide supports for clumps of phlox, tall salvias, and asters.

VINES

Use vines to hide a chain link fence, provide shade on an arbor, or cover the ground where grass won't grow (or where you don't want to mow). Good evergreen vines for Florida include Algerian ivy, English ivy, and Confederate jasmine. Flowering vines, such as allamanda, mandevilla, bougainvillea, coral vine, morning glory, and wood rose, are outstanding ornamentals for a fence or arbor.

YOUNG PLANTS

Annual and vegetable transplants will experience a bit of shock when they are planted out in the hot sun. Give them a day or two of shelter by covering them with a floating row cover, handfuls of pine needles, or an old window screen propped up with a stake. Water the new additions to your garden. Their roots have not grown into the soil, so they will dry out more quickly than established plants.

May Notes

To Do:
- Replace cool-weather flowers with summer flowers
- Mark gaps in spring bulb displays so you can add bulbs this fall
- Mulch trees, shrubs, and flower beds
- Sow seeds of warm season grasses
- Spray roses for black spot

To Plant:
- Summer vegetables and flowers
- Container-grown trees, shrubs, and perennials

To Purchase:
- New garden hoses and sprinklers, if needed
- Flower and vegetable transplants
- Grass seed or sod

_____
_____
_____
_____
_____
_____
_____
_____

TIP OF THE MONTH

I have solved my slug problems with an environmentally safe treatment—eggshells. I rinse the shells and let them dry. Then I crush them into very small pieces. In spring, before the plants spread, I sprinkle the crushed shells on the beds. No more slugs. And the shells decompose naturally, adding calcium to the soil.

Maryann Brandon
Chicago, Illinois

GARDENING
PLANTS AND DESIGN

Views on Blues

*Sage advice
on how to use
a very cool color*

BY STEVE BENDER

It has long been a firm conviction of mine that the garden can never have too much blue. Oh, I suppose if I walked out one morning and found a bright-blue school bus parked in the yard, I might rethink my position. But engulf me with blue flowers, leaves, and berries, and I'm as happy as a toddler splashing in the mud.

Thus, it's disheartening to realize that not every gardener feels this way. Only a thorough and authoritative discussion of the ways blue enlivens the garden can remedy this sad situation. So I've called on several of the South's leading garden designers to help answer the following momentous questions about the color blue.

What's Special About Blue?

Blue gains value because of its relative scarcity. There are simply very few blues available for the garden. And the majority of these are adulterated blues. "If you look at most of the flowers we call blue, most of them are violet," observes Edith Eddleman of Durham, North Carolina.

Fred Thode of Clemson, South Carolina, agrees. "Occasionally, you see a clear, sky blue," he comments. "But most of the time, flowers have purple, red-violet, pink, or gray in them." This doesn't mean that purples, violets, and lavenders have no value. True, they're not purebred,

The strong contrast between purple ladybells (Adenophora confusa), *orange lilies, and miniature yellow daylilies makes each color look brighter.*

This mixture of (from top) white money plant, blue phlox, and white candytuft appears cool and serene, reflecting the feeling of early spring days.

but as members of the cooler end of the color spectrum, they serve the same function in the garden as blue.

What Does Blue Do?

"First, many blue flowers have a light-absorbing quality," states Eddleman. "They seem to recede from your eye and fade away." A subtle gradation of warm colors to blues, she says, can enhance a garden's feeling of depth and spaciousness. "On the other hand, blue foliage reflects light," Eddleman continues. "So plants with blue foliage brighten things around them." A blue-leaved hosta, for example, might help bring out the colors of dark-green ferns and hellebores in a shady corner.

In addition to the visual aspects, blue generates certain psychological effects. Unlike eye-catching, aggressive reds and yellows, blue minds its manners and waits for attention. Thus, it soothes rather than sizzles. Eddleman speculates that deep blues might even make you feel cooler on bright, torrid summer days.

Everyone Loves Blue—True?

Au contraire. Blue may be the color of choice when it comes to flower show ribbons and Elvis' shoes, but today's gardeners gravitate toward gaudier, hotter colors you can see from a distance. "The buying public usually doesn't buy blue," declares Thode. "They buy the brightest thing on a nursery's sales yard. You know, the pinks come out at you, the reds knock you down, yellow is sunny, and orange is hard to miss. Blue is the last thing people see."

Thode has a suggestion for gardeners who are comfortable with warm colors and nervous about trying blues. "Buy your blues last," he recommends. "Pick two or three kinds of blue flowers and get a half-dozen plants of each to get a good-size group. Then try it in combination with a stronger color."

What Are Good Colors To Use With Blues?

Blue's biggest asset is that it goes with just about every other color. So the color you mix it with depends on personal taste and the effect you're trying to create.

Many gardeners enjoy blending blue with white and silver. The latter colors "pop out" the blue, but the overall composition remains cool and serene. Likewise, blue and red-violet, Eddleman's favorite combination, joins colors in the spectrum that harmonize rather than compete.

If you're looking to excite rather than sedate, combine blue with orange, its color opposite. "The strong contrast between the two makes each look brighter," notes Eddleman. Mixing blue with yellow achieves a similar result. Bill Smith, an Atlanta landscape architect, sprinkles in another primary color when designing with blues. "I sometimes put a piece of red here and there to give the setting spice," he remarks. For a comparable, but more comforting effect, substitute pink for red.

Can You Help Me Choose Companions for Blues?

Our experts were happy to relate some of their most successful combinations involving blue. Thode favors pink azaleas with blue Spanish bluebells (*Hyacinthoides hispanicus*). Eddleman recommends combining deep-blue *Salvia guaranitica* with rose-violet ironweed (*Vernonia* sp.); blue-leaved rue (*Ruta graveolens*) with pale-pink roses; and blue phlox (*Phlox divaricata*) with White Nancy dead nettle (*Lamium maculatum* White Nancy). Smith enjoys mixing blue larkspur with silvery-leaved strawberry begonia (*Saxifraga stolonifera*) and Japanese painted fern.

Want a few more suggestions? Ed Givhan of Montgomery blends blue forget-me-nots with pink and red sweet Williams. Lena Caron of Ladew Topiary Gardens in Monkton, Maryland, praises two combinations: purple heliotrope and coral First Edition rose; and blue ageratum with a light-yellow yarrow called Great Expectations. And personally, I can't forget my father's combination of blue veronica shooting up through orange butterfly weed.

Any Last Thoughts About Blue?

Reflecting upon these experts' words, I've decided that as wonderful as blue is by itself, it's even better in the company of other colors. So I guess a garden *can* have too much blue. But that's better than having too little. ◇

DESIGN: ED GIVHAN, MONTGOMERY

The slender spikes of Spanish bluebells blend wonderfully with the salmon-pink blossoms of Bridesmaid azalea.

Red and pink sweet Williams add zing to this planting of light-blue forget-me-nots.

Inspired by a Swimming Hole

PHOTOGRAPHS: VAN CHAPLIN

If we asked you to describe this Dallas pool, the term "swimming hole" wouldn't likely pop to mind. Yet that's the look its owners envisioned when they asked landscape architect Rosa Finsley of Kings Creek Landscaping to design it. The owners were country people raised on ranches, and wanted the setting to look natural.

Despite the limitations of a small courtyard, the pool evokes images of a spring-fed pond nestled beneath a rocky hillside. To accomplish this, Finsley first gave the pool a natural-looking teardrop shape. To disguise the fact that the pool is relatively shallow (only 4 feet at its deepest point), she darkened the water by using dark-gray Gunite for the pool's sides and bottom.

A recirculating waterfall of Texas stone extends 18 inches into the water, lending the pool's edge a natural, irregular shape. A small hollow beneath and behind the spillway stone magnifies the sound of tumbling water, while supplying a great spot for the kids to gather for a rollicking shower. It also mimics the effects of a real waterfall, in which rushing water gradually undercuts the stone beneath the spillway.

A manmade waterfall, no matter how well constructed, can look pretty unnatural in the middle of a flat yard. To overcome this, Finsley enveloped the rock face within a lush planting of yaupon, wax myrtle, and Texas mountain laurel. The planting helps soften the hard look of the stones and visually extends the small garden while also blocking the view from neighboring houses.

The end product is a welcoming, wonderfully private place that's fun for kids and restful for adults. You might say it's like an old-fashioned swimming hole—minus the mud and critters, of course.   *Steve Bender*

Thanks to its teardrop shape, rock waterfall, and lush planting, this pool resembles a spring-fed pond. Given the chance, you'd duck under the waterfall too. The hollow beneath the spillway stone amplifies the sound of falling water.

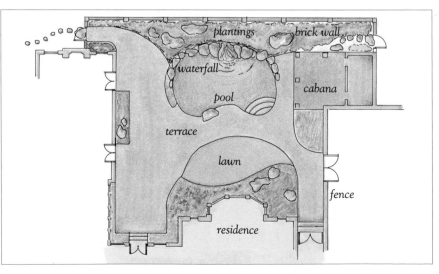

Pergola
At the Edge

The open roof has 2 x 8s crisscrossed for an interesting pattern.

Usually, putting up a fence, hedge, or wall at the property line can look a little confining, especially on the typical subdivision lot. But this doesn't always have to be true.

In the case shown here, a screening fence and pergola (PER-ga-la) built at the edge of a modest-size lot in Waynesboro, Virginia, actually created a more spacious feeling as well as an outdoor entertaining area.

When the owners decided to make improvements to their 1960s-era house, they devoted much of their attention to the setting. Landscape architects Douglas Associates of Charlottesville decided to enclose three sides of the corner lot with a 6-foot-tall, white-stained fence. There is just enough spacing between the 2 x 4 verticals to keep the fence airy and open—both actually and visually.

Built right against the fence toward one corner of the lot is a pergola of rough-sawn timber, also stained white. With a brick terrace beneath and roses trained overhead, the structure serves as a landscape focal point and a place to entertain. The pergola is placed at an angle to the fence to produce a more dynamic effect. Brick walks leading from two sides of the house pick up the angle in their alignment. *Philip Morris*

PHOTOGRAPHS: MARY-GRAY HUNTER

This new garden structure, placed at an angle against the 6-foot fence, functions as a garden focal point and a place to entertain.

PERGOLA OR GAZEBO?

Though often built of similar materials, these two garden structures fulfill different roles. A gazebo is usually roofed, with rounded lines, and functions as a strong, free-standing focal point. A pergola tends to be more linear, like an arbor, and links elements of a garden together. The structure in this garden is something of a hybrid. While it serves as a focal point, the open roof and linear shape help link the fence, terrace, and garden.

If you're interested in the use of a gazebo in the garden, see our September 1992 cover story, "This Gazebo Is a Classic."

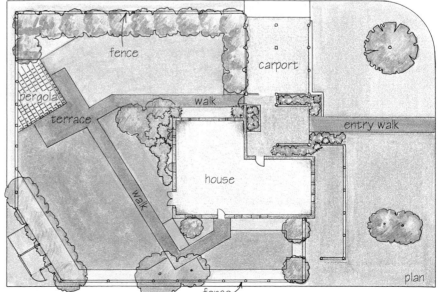

(Left) *One bed of peanuts in the garden will give your family a homegrown treat.*
(Bottom, left) *After they are dug and washed, peanuts can be boiled or dried and roasted.*

Snacks From the Garden

Peanuts are hardly new to the South. We traditionally think of them as a field crop. But give them a place in your garden and they will delight the entire family— even before you dig them. Perhaps the children will be a little more enthusiastic about the vegetable plot if they know it's producing their own peanut butter.

Peanuts grow on vines and develop from a pollinated flower. So how do they get underground? At the point where each leaf attaches to the stem, a bright, golden flower blooms on a thin stalk. Once pollinated, the stalk bends down and grows into the soil until the developing peanut is underground. Farmers call this process "pegging

down." This continues along the growing vine, so that the youngest peanuts are the farthest from the central taproot and the most mature peanuts are the closest.

One reason that peanuts are so closely associated with the South is that they require a long growing season—about four months of warm weather. Don't plant them until the soil is warm; that's late May or early June in the Middle South, and earlier or later depending on your specific location.

David Bradshaw of Six Mile, South Carolina, grows the big peanuts he remembers from his family farm in eastern Virginia. "When I moved down here, the farmers said to grow the little red Spanish-type peanuts," he remembers. "But I went back to Virginia and brought back a pint of seeds. They have produced beautifully."

Like most plants, peanuts prefer loose, fertile, well-drained soil, and full sun is an absolute necessity.

Seeds are individual nuts without the shell. Order them from mail-order seed companies, or buy them from a local farm supply store. To be sure of exactly what you are getting, don't plant the raw peanuts from the grocery store.

Set seeds 1 to 2 inches deep and 8 to 12 inches apart for large selections, 3 to 5 inches apart for small selections. You can plan on the vines spreading 2½ to 3 feet wide. Peanuts like a fairly rich soil, so add manure or compost at planting time and lime (about ½ cup per 3 feet of row) during the summer when the plants are about 6 inches wide.

You'll know your peanuts are mature by digging a few. When the shells are entirely filled and beginning to fall off the roots, they are ready. Dig up whole plants and spray soil from the nuts with your garden hose.

One good way to dry them is to stretch a cord between fenceposts or under a shed, drape plants across it, and let the nuts air dry. Once there is no evidence of moisture in the shells, pull off the nuts and toss the vines in the compost bin. If your weather is extremely wet, pick the nuts and spread them on a screen in an attic or other dry, well-ventilated place for several weeks.

Bradshaw recommends hanging the dried nuts in a mesh bag in a pantry or garage until ready to use. They will keep for about a year. He also shells raw, dry peanuts and freezes them. This keeps them fresh up to three years.

He roasts them with or without the shell by spreading them on a cookie sheet in a warm oven (375°). Stir frequently until golden brown. He says that if you scorch them your peanut butter will taste a little like coffee.

But no matter how careful you are to dig when the nuts are fully mature, some peanuts will be more mature than others because they develop sequentially along the vines. Bradshaw has found that the little half-mature "saps" growing near the ends of the vines can be boiled in salted water and eaten—shell and all. That leaves the rest for regular boiled peanuts or drying.
Linda C. Askey

Japanese Primrose: Simply Spectacular

All you can say is, it's ironic. The stated purpose of the Mount Cuba Center in Greenville, Delaware, is to preserve, promote, and propagate native piedmont plants. Yet one of the signature plants of this garden isn't native at all. It's the Japanese primrose, a water-hungry perennial whose glorious blossoms garnish the banks of Mount Cuba's pond each spring.

Which isn't so terrible. Japanese primrose (*Primula japonica*), after all, is a very fine garden plant. From a tuft of bright-green, spinachlike leaves, it produces a flower stalk as tall as 2 feet. Whorled tiers of blooms, like floral candelabras, occur up and down the stem. Colors range from white to pink to red to purple.

Just as important as how Japanese primrose looks is where it grows. It's one of the few perennials that blooms well in wet soil. The banks of a stream or pond usually provide a good site. According to Dick Lighty, Mount Cuba's director, the soil should contain plenty of organic matter and be evenly moist, but not inundated. If the soil is too wet, the plant may be heaved out of the ground in winter, particularly in the Upper South. If it's too dry, the plant often dies shortly after blooming and setting seed. The soil is right, he says, "when the soil surface glistens a little bit, but you don't see any free water."

Japanese primroses also demand shade. "You never see a good planting of them where they get direct sun for more than an hour," states Lighty. He recommends high shade from tall hardwoods or pines.

While individual plants generally live but a few years, they reseed readily. "On a wet site," observes Lighty, "the planting renews itself." To establish a new planting, set out transplants or start plants from seed. If you prefer the latter, the time to sow outside is when the seeds ripen (late summer to early fall). Either scatter seed over bare soil where you want seedlings to sprout, or refrigerate dry seed until early spring and then thinly sow in flats and transplant the seedlings after danger of frost has passed. Lighty believes that direct sowing gives better results than transplanting. "The plants that do the best and last the longest are the ones that germinate *in situ*," he notes.

For a list of mail-order sources, send a self-addressed, stamped, business-size envelope to Japanese Primrose Editor, *Southern Living,* P.O. Box 830119, Birmingham, Alabama 35283.   *Steve Bender*

(**Top**) *Japanese primroses thrive in moist, acid soil and light shade. Here they lend sensational color to the banks of a pond at Mount Cuba Center.*
(**Above**) *Whorled tiers of blooms appear up and down tall flower stalks in spring.*

JAPANESE PRIMROSE AT A GLANCE

Size: 1 to 2 feet (with blooms)
Light: Light shade
Soil: Consistently moist, acid, lots of organic matter
Pests: None serious
Method of Propagation: Seed
Range: Upper, Middle, Lower South

The White Garden at the North Carolina State University Arboretum offers great ideas, as well as a quiet spot to linger.

Gardening in White

To garden on a theme requires extraordinary restraint but can produce remarkable results. This Raleigh garden is a good example. In this sheltered grove of green only white flowers grow, but the scene is striking in its simplicity.

The White Garden is a prime gathering spot at the North Carolina State University Arboretum. Just inside the entry, it welcomes visitors into a refreshing glade. Students gather in lawn chairs around their teacher, learning horticultural Latin. In the last hours of the day, the white flowers softly shimmer when other colors would have surrendered to the darkness, making it a favorite setting for weddings and twilight receptions.

J. C. Raulston directs the development and use of the arboretum. "In the summertime, we do an annual potluck picnic for the Friends of the Arboretum," he explains. "When it gets dark, we do a slide show in the garden. People sit on their blankets and enjoy the evening show. At the end, we turn on the lights, and they go back to their cars."

Yes, the garden is lighted, but not in the sense of an auditorium. It's more in the romantic fashion of a stage set for theater. Flowerbeds glow in pools of light, and spotlights gleam on the satin trunks of Natchez crepe myrtles.

The lighting, like so many aspects of the garden, was a student design

project. The garden was designed about 10 years ago by landscape architect Curtis Brooks, who is landscape superintendent and urban forester in Chapel Hill, North Carolina.

He explains, "The theme of white provides a real opportunity to emphasize other aspects of plant materials. So we paid a lot of attention to the forms of the plants, their structure, and the enclosure they provide. For example, a cluster of three Natchez crepe myrtles frames a walkway. Then we repeat the upright, vase-shaped trees with a group of three Merrill magnolias in another area."

Although the garden is about a half

Easter lilies planted outdoors perfume the garden in May and June.

PHOTOGRAPHS: VAN CHAPLIN, SYLVIA MARTIN

A SAMPLE OF PLANTS FROM THE WHITE GARDEN

Annuals
Cleome
Cosmos
Dianthus
Impatiens
Madagascar periwinkle
Pansies
Snapdragons

Perennials
Candytuft
Siberian iris
Miss Lingard phlox

Bulbs
Easter lilies
Daffodils
Hyacinths
Amaryllis
Agapanthus

Vines
Moon vine
Clematis

Shrubs
Camellia
Gardenia
Quince
Slender deutzia
Snowmound Nippon spirea

Trees
Dogwood
Merrill magnolia
Natchez crepe myrtle
Star magnolia

Variegated Leaves
Box elder
Glacier English ivy
Japanese aralia
Mock orange (*Philadelphus coronarius*)
Silver Dragon liriope
Fatshedera
Yucca

Silver Leaves
Dusty miller
Lamb's-ears
Willowleaf pear

acre in size, little nooks and personal places in the garden create a feeling of intimacy. Visitors enjoy the gazebo, the focal point of the garden. But no path leads directly to it—guests must meander through the plantings before reaching the gingerbread-trimmed structure.

Brooks notes, "We use a lot of annuals because they give us the flowers we need to make the theme work." Deborah Harvey, curator of The White Garden, says that last year she grew 25 different annuals. Winter highlights include white pansies, while in summer impatiens are the mainstay. "Dr. Raulston wanted to show people that impatiens will grow in sun as well as shade," she points out. And

they do, lush beds of them carpeting the garden.

Deborah regularly pulls out reseeding annuals that are not white. "We call it de-pinking," she says with a grin. "You can tell which ones will be pink or red before they get large enough to bloom. The stems of those flowers are red; white-flowered seedlings have green stems."

But visitors find much more than just white forms of common annuals. A horticulturally challenging assortment of vines, shrubs, and trees fills the garden. By planting different selections, Deborah manages to have a succession of daffodils in bloom for four months each spring. But the garden is not limited to white flowers;

plants with variegated and silver foliage bring their own charm as well.

Deborah advises, "Enjoy your garden, especially if it's a white one. Go out and look at it in the moonlight; you won't be able to see the weeds! No wonder it's so soothing."

Linda C. Askey

Narrow
But Nice

BY CAROLE ENGLE-AVRIETT
PHOTOGRAPHY ART MERIPOL

Making the most of a leftover side lot, this house and garden work as one attractive unit. Lots of windows and doors connect inside and outside spaces.

Leftovers. If you are talking about something in the kitchen, this term may be greeted with little enthusiasm. The same is true of homesites, unless, of course, you bring a great deal of talent and imagination to the lot. Such was the case when architect John Brooks Walton and landscape architect Clare Ashby worked together to transform a narrow side-lot into a retreat for Tulsa homeowners Marion and Dick Teubner.

"I designed the house with one side of the lot at the minimum setback required, so that the other side could receive maximum space," explains Walton. "Placing the garage at the front helps buffer the house from the street and also works to create a feeling of seclusion. The rooms

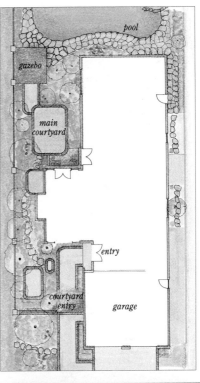

(**Left**) *A series of gardens extends down the side of the house. Here a narrow path leads to the main courtyard just off the living room.* (**Above**) *The main courtyard gives access to the living room and gallery passageway.*

are arranged one behind another, with a gallery passageway for easy circulation."

Ashby's garden plan complements the interior design. "We created a series of outdoor rooms also in a linear pattern," she says. "In some places along the side of the house, the garden narrows to a very small space but it always continues to draw you down the path."

The outdoor rooms form four distinct areas. At the front, a small entry court just past a romantic, roofed gate welcomes visitors. The entry court also includes a seating area surrounded by a variety of plantings chosen for year-round color and texture.

Down a small path is the main courtyard off the living room. The Teubners often have breakfast or entertain guests here.

Adjacent to the main courtyard, a gazebo creates the third outdoor room, a spot for relaxing or dining. The pavement changes from old brick in a basket-weave pattern to a simple pattern of concrete squares edged with brick. Beside the gazebo, a gently curving pool fills the space between house and fence across the entire rear of the lot. A small waterfall offers the delightful sights and sounds of moving water.

Both the interiors and exteriors of the house comprise wonderful spaces, so Walton wanted to ensure a strong connection between the two. Large French doors with high transoms bridge between inside and out. The transoms extend to the ceilings, an airy 10 feet in the main rooms and 9 in the rear bedroom. With an open floor plan across the front—the living, dining, and kitchen area form one large space—almost all rooms benefit from the light and vistas to the gardens.

Though square footage is only about 1,100 on the lower floor, the house lives big, especially when the French doors are thrown open and guests can move back and forth from one area to another. ◇

Across the rear of the house, a gently curving pool and waterfall bring the sound of running water to the garden.

Trumpet honeysuckle needs the support of a garden wall, fence, trellis, or arbor.

The heaviest flowering occurs in spring, then on and off throughout summer and into fall. Blossoms may be red or yellow.

Trumpet Honeysuckle Minds Its Manners

If you would rather be sentenced to an accordion festival than plant honeysuckle in the yard, take note. Here is a honeysuckle that won't strangle your dogwood, throttle your hydrangea, or yank the gutters off your house.

It's trumpet honeysuckle (*Lonicera sempervirens*), a Southern native that's among the best of all ornamental vines. Climbing by means of twining stems, it features elliptical, blue-green leaves that are evergreen in all but the Upper South. Showy clusters of tubular, 2-inch-long flowers appear on the ends of shoots in mid-spring. Spring sees the heaviest bloom, but flowering occurs off and on throughout summer and into fall. The blos-soms give rise to small, red berries eagerly gobbled by birds.

Red is the customary flower color (and the one to pick if you like hummingbirds), but many folks enjoy yellow-flowering selections as well. Recommended selections include Magnifica (red), Sulphurea (yellow), and a cold-hardy hybrid called Dropmore Scarlet.

You might also keep an eye out for woodbine honeysuckle (*L. periclymenum*), a vine that differs from trumpet honeysuckle in ways only a botanist could detect. Among the better selections—Graham Thomas (creamy white) and Serotina Florida (creamy white, yellow, and red).

These honeysuckles need the sup-port of a trellis, garden wall, fence, or arbor. But don't worry—unlike Japanese honeysuckle (*L. japonica*), neither is rampant enough to be destructive. The vines' lower stems become bare eventually, so plant low shrubs or perennials around the base. If flowering becomes sparse, look to one of three causes—too much shade, too much fertilizer, or pruning in fall instead of early summer.

Steve Bender

For a list of mail-order sources, send a self-addressed, stamped, business-size envelope to Trumpet Honeysuckle Editor, *Southern Living,* P.O. Box 830119, Birmingham, Alabama 35283. ◇

TRUMPET HONEYSUCKLE AT A GLANCE

Size: 15 to 20 feet depending on size of support
Light: Sun or light shade
Soil: Moist, fertile, well drained
Growth rate: Moderate
Pests: None serious
Prune: Early summer
Range: Throughout the South

June

*Stargazer lilies, daisies,
carnations, dried yarrow,
peony blossom, and assorted
summer flowers*

CHECKLIST FOR JUNE

ANNUALS

There is still time to set out the most heat-tolerant annuals, such as gomphrena, melampodium, and vinca, for hot, sunny spots. Set out transplants, and water them regularly until well established. Fertilize bedding plants when you set them out. In Texas, set out some heat-tolerant, sun-loving annuals now, including celosia, copper plant, Joseph's coat, marigolds, and zinnias. For partial shade, plant coleus, begonias, caladiums, impatiens, nicotiana, and salvias now.

BASIL

You can still sow seeds of lettuce-leaf basil (for pasta), or flavored types, such as cinnamon basil, now. Purple Ruffles basil is popular as an ornamental. Start the seeds directly in the garden or in a small pot placed in the shade. Transplant when the seedlings are 2 or 3 inches tall.

BLACKBERRIES

In Texas, remove fruit-bearing canes on blackberries after harvest. Prune new canes to encourage side branching. If purchasing container plants, Brazos and Rosborough are good selections.

BUTTERFLIES

Two woody summer shrubs that attract butterflies to the garden are butterfly bush (*Buddleia* sp.) and lantana (*Lantana camara*). Both are deciduous in North Florida and well suited for growing in pots. Set the pots on a terrace to enjoy butterflies up close.

CALADIUMS

Set out tubers in well-drained areas of the garden, as well as in containers and window boxes. Most selections perform best in shade. The colorful leaves often have more impact than flowers and are most effective when planted thickly in masses of a single color.

CONTAINER PLANTS

Hot and sunny weather can quickly dry out plants in containers. To reduce the need for frequent watering, move the container to a less exposed location, and keep a saucer under the pot. Add water-retaining gels to newly potted plants.

COREOPSIS

Perennial selections of this bright plant bloom like an annual—all summer long. Plant in a sunny, well-drained location, and regularly remove faded flowers so seeds don't develop. In Texas, good selections include Early Sunrise and Sunray.

CREPE MYRTLES

To get the color you want, buy crepe myrtles when they are in bloom. Consider planting one of the fast-growing, mildew-resistant selections, such as Biloxi (light pink), Tuskegee (dark pink), Natchez (white), or Basham's Party Pink.

DAFFODILS

It's still not too late to dig and divide overcrowded clumps of daffodils as the foliage fades. Rather than replanting the bulbs right away, store them in mesh potato or onion bags in a cool, dry basement or garage. Then replant in fall just as you would new bulbs purchased from the garden center.

FAMILY GARDENING

You can build children's enthusiasm for gardening by preparing a small garden plot with rich soil in an area with lots of sun. Plant large-seeded flowers, such as four-o'clocks, zinnias, or sunflowers. They're easy and fun to grow.

FRUIT DROP

Don't be too alarmed if citrus, avocado, and mango trees shed some fruit this time of year. The plants are "self pruning" down to the amount of fruit they can bear. However, watering during dry spells can help maximize production.

HARVEST TIPS

In the Upper South, be sure not to wait too long to cut broccoli and cauliflower heads. They won't get bigger, but will get mealy if the florets begin to open and expose the yellow petals. In warmer areas, be sure to pick cucumbers and summer squash while they are small. Not only will they taste better, but if left on the vine, they will prevent the plant from producing more.

HYDRANGEAS

French and oakleaf hydrangeas bloom this month. Most plants should be left alone to grow to full size, but if pruning is necessary to control height or form, do so right after the blooms fade.

IMPATIENS

If you grew these annuals in your garden last year, watch for familiar seedlings. Although they may not be exactly the color you had in mind, sometimes volunteers have a spontaneity of placement that a determined gardener cannot match. Thin them to 8 to 10 inches, and let them bloom.

IRON

In sandy soil where there is little iron, the leaves of many plants will yellow, especially between the veins. Green them up again by applying liquid iron (iron chelate) to the soil or the foliage. Mix according to label directions; don't apply in the heat of midday. Also remember that the iron solution will stain driveways and painted surfaces.

LAWNS

Replace sparse turf under trees with a shade-loving ground cover, such as ajuga or liriope, or have an arborist thin limbs to let light through. Or plant shade-tolerant grasses, such as St. Augustine or fescue blends. Water and fertilize regularly to satisfy the needs of both trees and grass. In Florida, replace sparse turf growing under trees with a shade-loving ground cover, such as ajuga or liriope, or plant shade-tolerant grasses, such as Seville, one of the most shade-tolerant St. Augustine selections. In Texas, replace sparse turf under trees with a shade-loving ground cover, such as ajuga or liriope, or have an arborist thin limbs to let light through. Or plant shade-tolerant grasses, such as St. Augustine (south of Waco) or fescue blends (north of Dallas). Water and fertilize regularly to satisfy the needs of both trees and grass.

MALABAR SPINACH

A climbing vine, this heat-tolerant summer green needs stakes or a trellis. Soak seeds overnight to speed germination. Thin plants to 8 to 10 inches. Begin picking leaves when the vines are 6 inches tall.

PERENNIALS

Set out summer- and fall-blooming perennials now for a late-season display. Good choices include perennial salvia, purple coneflower, asters, helianthus, and Japanese anemones. Water thoroughly after planting. In Texas, good choices include Mexican bush sage, purple coneflower, asters, and Mexican mint marigold.

ROSES

Spread about ½ cup of 12-6-8 or similar fertilizer beneath each plant. Scratch the fertilizer lightly into the soil with a hand cultivator, and water gently to wash the nutrients down to the roots.

SHRUBS

If you have spring-flowering shrubs that need pruning, do it now before they set flowerbuds for next season. Examples include spirea, weigela, beautybush, quince, forsythia, and azaleas.

STRAWBERRIES

After harvesting, fertilize strawberry rows with ¼ pound of 15-5-10 per 10 feet of row. Wash fertilizer off the foliage, and apply mulch to conserve soil moisture.

SUMMER ROSES

In Florida, landscape roses can continue blooming through summer with little fuss if you remove the old blooms when they fade. The Fairy, Nearly Wild, and Bonica will bloom in cycles from spring to Thanksgiving or later in North Florida. Plant in well-drained soil, and fertilize with a slow-release rose food every couple of months.

June Notes

To Do:
- Fertilize warm-season grasses
- Prune spring-flowering trees and shrubs
- Remove faded blooms from annuals
- Divide bearded iris
- Apply post-emergence weed killer to lawn

To Plant:
- Container-grown trees and shrubs
- Glads for summer flowers
- Summer annuals
- Tomatoes for fall harvest

To Purchase:
- Lawn fertilizer
- Post-emergence weed killer
- Transplants and seeds of summer annuals

_____
_____
_____
_____
_____
_____
_____
_____
_____
_____
_____

TIP OF THE MONTH

Sometimes, my cabbages mature faster than I can use them and they split open. To prevent this, I take a knife and cut halfway through the root. The cabbage stops growing, and the head stays firm.

Lucy Sauer
Jasper, Tennessee

Daylilies

The Lazy Man's Plants

No need to dote on these tenacious perennials, notes Julian Hardy. With even a little care, they'll bloom their heads off.

BY STEVE BENDER
PHOTOGRAPHY SYLVIA MARTIN

Disco Rose

Tom Wise

Carol Colossal

The summer show features blossoms of widely varied colors, forms, and sizes.

Some folks derive inordinate pleasure from catering to plants that revel in disease, kick off without warning, and only bloom during a solar eclipse. Chances are, you're not one of them. Neither is Julian Hardy.

He grows daylilies—and not just three or four like you or I might grow. At his home in Demopolis in south-central Alabama, over 1,400 named selections fill his backyard. Why daylilies and why so many? Two reasons. First, few other plants offer flowers in such an extraordinary range of color combinations. Second, few perennials are as easy to grow.

"I call them 'the lazy man's plants,'" declares Julian. "Give them half a chance and just a little attention, and they perform really well."

For proof, grab a handful of what passes for soil in Demopolis. It's thin, heavy, and low in organic matter. It's also alkaline, thanks to subterranean limestone laid down by an ancient sea. In hot, dry weather, the soil parches; during wet stretches, it bloats like a sponge. Still, Julian's daylilies persist, blooming even in the fullest summer sun.

El Camino

Don't get the idea that he abuses his plants. On the contrary, to get sumptuous blooms and plenty of them, Julian has learned to pamper his daylilies a bit. He constantly improves the soil, working in good topsoil along with every bit of compost and leaf mold he can lay his hands on. When droughts set in during blooming time, he douses his plants with plenty of water.

Fertilize for Better Blooms and Color

Vigorous daylilies work up healthy appetites, so Julian attends to their nutrition. In spring, around March 1 and again several weeks later, he broadcasts a generous amount of cottonseed meal and alfalfa meal throughout the garden and scratches it in. These natural fertilizers improve the soil and release nutrients slowly, feeding for months.

Then, just as his plants begin budding, he sprinkles pellets of ammonium nitrate around each plant, 1 quart per 100 square feet. "The extra nitrogen results in bigger flowers and more vivid colors," he asserts. Don't overdo the nitrogen or leave pellets on the foliage, he cautions, or you'll burn your plants.

Transplant Almost Any Time

Nothing demonstrates the resilience of daylilies better than their acceptance of transplanting and dividing. "You can take plants up and divide them at almost any time of year the ground isn't cold or frozen," says Julian. "But it's best not to dig them in July or August because those months are just so hot." Ideal times for planting and transplanting, he says, are April 1 through May 30 and September 1 through November 15.

In this garden, cleanliness is next to comeliness, so Julian and his wife, Ellen, doggedly strip away old daylily foliage and police the area for weeds. In addition, each morning during bloom season, he removes the spent blooms from the day before, not because this forces more bloom, but because he likes things tidy.

The best part of his hobby, says Julian, is the many friends he and Ellen make when folks visit their garden. "Our yard is open to the public seven days a week," he proclaims. "During peak bloom in June and July, there's always somebody milling about." So if you find yourself in Demopolis some day, pay Julian and Ellen a call. Don't worry that you don't know the way. In Demopolis, everyone knows everyone else. Somebody will point you in the right direction. ◇

(**Top**) *Disco Rose,*
(**Center**) *Carol Colossal,*
(**Bottom**) *Tom Wise*

PHOTOGRAPHS: VAN CHAPLIN

A Perfect Spot for a Chimney Pot

(**Top**) *The Scotts' spacious courtyard features rectangular planting areas filled with mondo grass and other low-growing plants. The panels of greenery serve to break up a large expanse of hard paving, and lavender verbena encircles the base of the pot.* (**Above, left**) *Another chimney pot, filled with yellow lantana, adds to the classic character of the wall-mounted fountain.* (**Above, right**) *On summer evenings, moonflower's huge, fragrant white blossoms open up to adorn the brick wall framing the terrace.*

Like most folks, Tom and Jane Scott like to sit out back when the weather's nice. But they didn't particularly like the setting for their sitting.

"When we moved into the house about four years ago, there was just grass with a narrow brick walkway in the back," recalls Jane. A brick wall enclosed the space nicely, but the scenery wasn't so great. "There was a flowerbed between the wall and walkway, but there was no order to it," explains Jane, who is an avid gardener.

The Scotts turned to Atlanta landscape architect Diane Dunaway, who worked with Tom on some general ideas he had. Dunaway insists that the Scotts' involvement was as much hands on as it was conversation. "A lot of their front yard was installed according to my plans. But the design of the backyard was much more spontaneous," Dunaway says.

The major improvements to the patio consisted of expanding the brick walkway, enlarging the sitting area, and getting rid of the grass. Bluestone pavers, which the Scotts installed themselves, replaced the middle third of the lawn. The remaining turf on either side was removed and replaced with mondo grass. A healthy rosemary bush and a Chinese fringe tree (*Chionanthus retusus*) were planted in the panel of mondo grass nearest the kitchen door. The flower border against the wall was filled with a pleasing mixture of annuals, perennials, vines, and other plants. Sounds perfect, doesn't it? Well . . . almost.

Tom and Jane felt that there was something missing—a focal point. "We had a talk about using different features but hadn't come up with any-thing," Dunaway remembers. "One day, they called me from a place that sells architectural relics and said, 'Hey, what about a chimney pot?' " (For those who might confuse a chimney pot with a chamber pot, a chimney pot is essentially an ornamental smokestack that is set atop chimneys in older style homes.)

It worked. Not only did the gray-concrete chimney pot become the crowning touch to the center of the terrace, many others (eight at last count) found new homes as containers throughout their garden. To perform the conversion from chimney pot to flowerpot, Tom added bricks or pieces of wood as crosspieces inside the chimney. Then the Scotts slipped in a container full of plants, and where there was once smoke, there are now flowers.

Mark G. Stith

PHOTOGRAPHS: VAN CHAPLIN

Kirilow indigo is a common sight in the Lower and Coastal South. Here it forms a handsome skirt beneath an old live oak in Baton Rouge.

Kirilow Indigo Quietly Marches On

No one names parades after kirilow indigo. No one writes poetry about it. It isn't a plant that catches the eye. But that doesn't mean this shrub is without merit for the garden. On the contrary, in the right spot it forms a handsome ground cover.

Native to China, Korea, and Japan, kirilow indigo (*Indigofera kirilowii*) is a cousin to the famous indigo plant (*I. tinctoria*) that provided blue dye to early Southerners. It's a low, spreading shrub, growing 2 to 3 feet tall and wide, featuring graceful, arching branches. Lacy, compound leaves lend the plant a soft texture.

Throughout the summer months, pendulous, 5-inch spikes of lavender-pink blossoms hang beneath the branches. When viewed from a distance, the blooms are hardly noticeable; close up, they definitely make an impression.

This plant spreads steadily by underground stolons to form small colonies. Therefore, it's a good choice for covering banks or carpeting the ground beneath large trees with protruding surface roots. It also combines splendidly with plants having coarser foliage, such as cast-iron plant (*Aspidistra elatior*), holly fern (*Cyrtomium falcatum*), hidden lily (*Curcuma petiolata*), and English ivy (*Hedera helix*).

Kirilow indigo performs best in light shade. It prefers loose, moist, well-drained soil that contains plenty of organic matter. Few pests bother it. Prune, when necessary, in late winter, removing older, woody canes. The easiest way to propagate this shrub is to divide it in late winter or early spring.

Spikes of lavender-pink blossoms appear all summer amid the lacy foliage.

Many nurseries in the Lower and Coastal South carry kirilow indigo. Elsewhere, it can be much more difficult to come by. For a good mail-order source send $3 for a catalog to Flowerplace Plant Farm, P.O. Box 4865, Meridian, Mississippi 39304; or telephone (601) 482-5686.

Steve Bender

KIRILOW INDIGO
AT A GLANCE

Size: Up to 2 to 3 feet tall and wide
Light: Light shade
Soil: Loose, moist, fertile, well drained
Pests: None serious
Propagation: By division or by cuttings

A new driveway threatened to damage the roots of these beech trees. Plastic drainpipes
under the pavement provide air for the roots.

Piping Saves Precious Roots

Remember the "scissors, paper, and rock" game you played as a child? You know, rock breaks scissors, paper covers rock, and all that. Well, there are some real-world versions of that game in the landscaping business, and one of them goes like this: Concrete smothers roots.

Protecting a beautiful grouping of large beech trees was very much on the mind of Louisville, Kentucky, landscape architect Bill Ray. In order to build a new approach to the Phillip Allen residence, he needed to install a concrete driveway right over a significant portion of the beech trees' roots. "And American beech trees don't like any of their roots disturbed," Ray says.

To avoid this predicament, Ray laid a series of 4-inch-diameter polyethyl-

ene drainpipes over the original soil level and at right angles to the proposed driveway. The perforated pipes, each about 30 feet long and spaced 3 feet apart, are open at both

Plastic grates conceal the drainpipes
and keep out debris.

ends, allowing air and water to reach the roots. A 4- to 6-inch layer of washed river gravel was added between the pipes. The pipe-and-gravel aeration system was covered with black plastic. Finally, a gravel roadbase and concrete aggregate driveway were poured on top of the pipe-and-gravel aeration system.

"The concrete supports itself and doesn't mash down on the plastic pipes," Ray adds. Plastic grates keep out debris.

And so, thanks to Ray, the Allens can enjoy their new, *tree-lined* semicircular drive. "That neighborhood is relatively new, and hundreds of trees were lost during construction," Ray recalls. "People were amazed that we were able to save those trees."

Mark G. Stith

Quick Summer Flowers

Becky Baxter of Atlanta reflects the beauty and diversity of her own garden in the flower arrangements she creates. This particular one is delightfully simple. She just arranges various cut flowers as though they are growing from green moss.

To create an arrangement similar to this, use a straight-sided, waterproof container. If you want to use a basket, place a liner inside. You will need enough florist foam to fill the container or liner and a piece of green moss to cover the foam. Select a variety of fresh flowers in different colors, and include a few dried ones if you like. Cut some foliage, such as lamb's ears, ivy, hosta leaves, and boxwood, from your garden.

Condition the flowers and greenery by soaking them in lukewarm water for a few hours. Let the florist foam stand in water until it's completely saturated. Add the foam to the container; then trim the moss to fit, and place it over the foam.

Select some of the darker flowers with the longest stems, and place them in the center of the arrangement. Insert stems through the moss down into the foam. Use a knife or ice pick to make an opening in the moss if it resists. Then fill out the arrangement, adding flowers that are progressively shorter and lighter in color. Add leaves and flowerbuds around the edge.

Julia H. Thomason

(**Top**) *Fit a plastic liner into a basket, and fill it with florist foam that's been soaked in water.*
(**Center**) *Cover the foam with a circle of green moss, and insert taller flowers in the center. Fill in with flowers that become progressively shorter as you near the edge of the container.*
(**Right**) *When complete, this arrangement includes stargazer lilies, daisies, carnations, dried yarrow, a dried peony blossom, and other flowers of different heights.*

As part of the "Don't Bag It" program, I used a mulching mower to return grass clippings to the lawn. How did it work? Great.

Let the Clippings Out of the Bag

A few years ago, the Texas Agricultural Extension Service initiated a lawn care program called "Don't Bag It," designed to reduce the mountains of grass clippings deposited in landfills each year. By carefully following instructions, participants found they could leave clippings on the lawn and enjoy beautiful grass that demanded less work and fertilizer. But one question still remained: Would this program work for the thicker Bermuda and Zoysia lawns common in the Southeast, where annual rainfall is much higher?

To find out, last summer I took part in the first "Don't Bag It" program sponsored by the Jefferson County Office of the Alabama Cooperative Extension Service. Along with dozens of other participants, I received a set of instructions, a bag of slow-release fertilizer, and a fertilizing schedule. I also received a new mulching mower to use for the summer.

The basic idea behind the "Don't Bag It" program is simple. Instead of bagging your grass clippings or raking them into the curb, you leave them on the lawn. They quickly decompose, returning nitrogen, phosphorus, and potassium to the soil and feeding the remaining grass. Despite what you've probably heard, clippings do not cause a buildup of thatch.

The key to the program is mowing correctly. You must mow often enough so that you don't remove more than one-third of the grass blades in a single cutting. In other words, if you typically mow your lawn to 1½ inches, don't let it get more than 2 inches tall before you cut it again. And never mow when the grass is wet.

You can use either a special mulching mower or a regular rear- or side-discharge type. Under normal circumstances, the first type grinds clippings into tiny particles that practically disappear into the lawn. The latter types leave trails of clippings, but a soft rake quickly spreads them evenly over the grass, where they then decay.

How did the "Don't Bag It" program work for me? Just great. Following the fertilization schedule provided, I fed my Emerald Zoysia front lawn and my St. Augustine back lawn with slow-release 24-6-12 fertilizer on the first weekend in May and again on Fourth of July weekend. Because the summer of '92 was very rainy in Birmingham, I seldom had to water. On the average, I mowed the lawn every seven days. Only once did my lawn grow so lush between mowings that the mower choked slightly while cutting. I just backed the mower off for a second, and then continued.

The best part of the program was this—95% of the time after I finished mowing the lawn, there were no visible clippings. While my buddy two houses down the street was busily hauling clippings to the curb, I was already indoors quaffing a cool drink.

Most of the program's other participants experienced similar success. They spent an average of 23% less time working on the lawn versus the year before. Only 10% complained of unsightly clippings on the lawn, while over 80% rated their lawn's color and quality as better than in previous years. And 91% said they hoped that the Extension service offered the program again next year.

A few folks reported disappointing outcomes, but this almost always resulted from not following directions. They either allowed the lawn to grow too tall between cuttings or cut it when it was wet.

Committing yourself to "Don't Bag It" does mean mowing more often. But in return, you'll spend less time raking and bagging and less money for fertilizer. And think about this—sooner or later your city landfill will stop accepting grass clippings, which now comprise about 20% of the material deposited there. Unless you compost the clippings, you'll have no place to dump them. So why not leave them right on the lawn?

Steve Bender

To find out if your town or county offers a "Don't Bag It" program, ask your Agricultural or Cooperative Extension service.

The garden combines care free perennials that bloom for a long time. Among them are purple coneflower, black-eyed Susans, loosestrife, Victoria mealy-cup sage, and Shasta daisy.

Dazzling in Dallas

BY STEVE BENDER / PHOTOGRAPHY VAN CHAPLIN

Stepping from the car in front of Dean and Linda Linderman's home, I suddenly had the sinking feeling that I boarded the wrong airplane earlier that day.

"This can't be Dallas," I muttered to myself, gazing in stupefaction at the perennials before me. "It looks like a garden in the Blue Ridge Mountains or maybe even New England. You can't grow perennials like this in Dallas."

With good soil and the right plants, you can grow beautiful perennials in tough climates. Just ask the Lindermans.

I was completely wrong, of course. Dean and Linda's perennial garden has astounded their Dallas neighbors for the last five years.

The Lindermans began with a front yard containing a semicircular drive bordered on the street side by a high privacy wall. To achieve a friendlier, more natural look, they called on landscape architect Walter Dahlberg of Lambert's Landscape Company. Dahlberg lowered the original wall

It's hard to imagine a more inviting front walk. Notice how the plants appeal to passersby while also screening the house.

This is one garden with no bad side. Viewed from the house, it's just as lovely.

and faced it with native stone. He then used the same stone to add a graceful front walk and broad steps. Perennial beds flanking the walk provided the final touch.

Before the first perennial could be set out, however, the original soil—alkaline and infertile—had to go. Off came the top 8 inches of dirt, supplanted by good soil rich in organic matter. Then Dean selected perennials that need no coddling. You'll find his choices in the box at right. To keep flowers coming from April to September, sturdy, ever-blooming annuals supplement the perennials. They include globe amaranth, wax-leaf begonia, verbena, and narrow-leaf zinnia.

If you suspect this spectacular display requires a mass infusion of chemical fertilizers and pesticides, think again. Maintenance includes only organic products. For example,

twice a year they fertilize the beds with 10 pounds of both bat guano and earthworm castings per 1,000 square feet. This may sound bizarre, but you can't question the results. The perennials grow so vigorously that pests rarely bother them. For added insurance against disease, Dean waters only in early morning so that the foliage dries quickly.

Every successful garden boasts at least one secret. This one happens to boast four:

■ Start with loose, fertile soil.
■ Ensure good drainage.
■ Group plants together that enjoy similar growing conditions.
■ Choose care free plants adapted to your climate that bloom for a long time.

Gardens differ from place to place, cautions Dean, so don't depend too much on secondhand knowledge gleaned from books. "You can read

about gardening until you're blue in the face," he declares. "But the reality is, you have to experiment."

Well, from what I've seen, I'd say the Lindermans have hit upon the magic formula. ◇

DEAN'S LIST OF TOUGH PERENNIALS
■ Purple coneflower (*Echinacea purpurea*)
■ White Swan coneflower (*E. purpurea* White Swan)
■ Goldsturm black-eyed Susan (*Rudbeckia fulgida* Goldsturm)
■ Loosestrife (*Lythrum* sp.)
■ Victoria mealy-cup sage (*Salvia farinacea* Victoria)
■ Shasta daisy (*Chrysanthemum* x *superbum*)
■ Perennial phlox (*Phlox paniculata*)

Splendid
Garden

BY STEVE BENDER / PHOTOGRAPHY VAN CHAPLIN

The past steps

into the future at the

Missouri Botanical Garden,

St. Louis' showcase

for plants and sculpture

and a center of great

learning.

Gerhard Marcks,
The Three Graces

In the spring of 1819, an 18-year-old Englishman named Henry Shaw sat upon his horse, looked out on the prairie just west of St. Louis, and pronounced it good. This year, nearly two centuries later, more than 800,000 visitors will gaze upon the garden he left on that prairie and pronounce it great.

Welcome to the Missouri Botanical Garden, arguably the finest botanical garden in the United States. Within its 79 acres, roses bloom, banana trees fruit, fountains gush, and sculptures inspire. Ph.D.s in lab coats endeavor to unlock the secrets of the rain forest. Retirees and preschoolers alike learn that amazing things grow from fertile soil.

To the locals, this place will always be simply "Shaw's Garden," an affectionate tribute to the generous man who made it possible. A shrewd trader and speculator, Henry Shaw amassed a fortune in the first half of the 19th century, as St. Louis swelled from frontier trading post to mercantile metropolis. In 1851, while attending the London World's Fair, he visited the gardens at Chatsworth in nearby Devonshire. Their

Viewed from the Carl Milles Sculpture Garden, the Climatron, the world's first geodesic-dome greenhouse, rises to 70 feet with no internal supports.

Seiwa-En, covering 14 acres, is the largest Japanese garden in North America. Each of its features has both symbolic meaning and aesthetic purpose.

beauty inspired him to create a garden of his own. With the help of America's premier botanists, he collected exotic plants from around the world. Word spread—by Shaw's own account, more than 40,000 people visited his garden in 1868.

After Shaw died in 1889, his will established the Missouri Botanical Garden, stipulating that it always be open to the public. In the century since, a series of visionary directors, together with the St. Louis community, have led the garden to the forefront of world horticulture. Yes, at its base, it's a haven for plants. But it's also a gallery for stunning art and a center for great learning.

A Haven For Plants

The Missouri Botanical Garden isn't a single garden, states Ann Case, a volunteer guide for the last 16 years. Rather, it's a series of distinct gardens. Indeed, as you walk the grounds throughout the year, you'll see matchless displays of azaleas, roses, iris, daylilies, bulbs, succulents, and scented plants. At the newly opened Center for Home Gardening, you'll eventually encounter a butterfly garden, a family vegetable garden, a children's garden, and a garden designed to attract birds.

> ...as you walk around the garden, it unrolls for you.

But first, visit the extraordinary Climatron. Based on American architect and inventor R. Buckminster Fuller's geodesic dome, this wondrous greenhouse stands 70 feet tall with no interior supports. Light penetrating its 2,425 panes of glass illuminates more than 1,200 species of tropical plants, including banana, cacao, coffee, and coconut trees.

Inside, you'll encounter a tropical rain forest, replete with dripping foliage, rocky cliffs, a native hut, and waterfalls. Children find it every bit as fascinating as adults. Norita Robey of nearby St. Charles, Missouri, brings 5-year-old Amanda and 3-year-old Wade with her during visits to the Climatron. "Both of them like the orchid exhibit," she remarks. "They like finding which flowers have aromas and which ones don't."

Your second must-see is 14-acre Seiwa-En, which means "garden of pure, clear harmony and peace." It emphasizes forms, lines, and textures. Each element, from lake to bridges to boulders, serves both aesthetic and symbolic roles. Because of its size, Seiwa-En is a strolling rather than contemplative garden. "It reminds you of a Japanese scroll painting where you never see the whole," observes Case. "But as you walk around the garden, it unrolls for you."

A Gallery For Stunning Art

Approximately 40 pieces of original sculpture, including famous works by Henry Moore and Carl Milles, grace the grounds. Some belong to the garden, while others are on loan. Selected by a review committee, the pieces echo and evoke natural forms embodied in the plants that surround them.

According to committee member George McCue, the sculpture elicits feelings of peace, repose, contemplation, and harmony with nature. "The landscape and sculpture work beautifully together," he comments. "You can let your gaze wander from roses to a piece of sculpture and back without feeling you've been distracted."

A Center For Great Learning

For a botanical garden to be truly great, it must do more than showcase pretty flowers. It must also instill in visitors a fundamental respect for plants and teach them a bit about how plants function. The Missouri Botanical Garden does this on a grand scale. In 1992, more than 110,000 people took part in its educational programs.

Many of the garden's students are schoolchildren. Grades 3 to 8 learn the basics of botany, geology, ecology, and natural history. Moreover, an extensive program of adult education targets those pursuing personal interests as well as professional enrichment.

"Most of the classes are quite good because the people who teach them are very dedicated," comments Tom

(**Clockwise, from top**) *Majestic trees testify to the age of the garden, which opened to the public in 1859. On a hot summer day, you can't keep kids out of the Shapleigh Fountain's curtain of water. So better bring a towel. Beneath stately oaks and sassafras, a green-roofed mausoleum houses the remains of the garden's founder, Henry Shaw. Tower Grove House, Shaw's country home, stands at the end of the path. Spectacular daylilies and other perennials adorn the Dry Stream Garden.*

Kuehling, a St. Louis architect. Kuehling has taken more than 20 courses on such subjects as lawns, vines, perennials, soils, garden lighting, and insects. "I took a course on tree pruning," he says, "and now I prune all the street trees in my neighborhood."

The garden's educational efforts stretch far beyond St. Louis. Its botanical research program, initiated long ago by Shaw, now employs over 40 Ph.D.s. Stationed primarily in Central and South America, these scientists race against time to search out and document the world's endangered tropical plants. Collecting plants that are screened for chemical agents found useful in fighting cancer and other diseases is a top priority.

If Henry Shaw returned to the Earth tomorrow, he might not recognize St. Louis. But he'd recognize his garden. Though its enterprise surpasses even his dreams, its purpose remains to serve and enlighten. Shaw would be proud.

> Most of the classes are quite good because the people who teach them are very dedicated.

When You Go

The Missouri Botanical Garden is located at 4344 Shaw Avenue, just off I-44. Open 9 a.m. to 8 p.m. Memorial Day through Labor Day, 9 a.m. to 5 p.m. all other days. Closed Christmas day. Admission is $2 for adults, $1 for seniors over 65, and free for children under 12. For more information call (314) 577-9400 or (314) 577-5141. ◇

July

Snowhill hydrangea

CHECKLIST FOR JULY

CHRYSANTHEMUMS

Cut chrysanthemums back by about one-third so they won't fall over when in bloom this fall. New growth can be pinched when a few inches long to encourage fullness. Don't pinch after mid-August when the flowerbuds appear.

CREPE MYRTLES

Encourage a second flush of blooms in six weeks by snipping off the tips of the flowering stems as soon as the trees finish blooming.

FOLIAGE PLANTS

Coleus and caladiums set out in the garden now will look good longer into the fall than those set out earlier. Be sure to water these and other newly planted specimens often. Pinch back coleus as they grow for fuller, more attractive plants.

GLADIOLA

In Texas, there's still time to set out gladiolus corms. Plant 3 to 4 inches deep in well-drained soil so the tall flower stalks won't flop over, or stake them before covering with soil. Full sun or some afternoon shade is best.

HERBS

Cut these plants often to keep growing. Basil actually needs to be cut back to encourage tender new growth. Pinch off flowers as they appear. Perennial herbs, such as rosemary, thyme, oregano, sage, and marjoram, can be pinched as needed.

HOSTAS

Traditionally considered a cool, shade-loving plant, there are a few that can take the scorching summer heat and a good dose of morning sun just fine. Among the top performers in recent tests for tolerance to sun and heat were Hosta Gold Standard and *Hosta plantaginea*. *H. plantaginea* showed almost no leaf scorch,

and Gold Standard held its variegated color well.

LAWNS

There is still plenty of warm weather left to start a new lawn or repair an existing one. Water the plugs or sod every day that there isn't a good afternoon thundershower. This is especially important with plugs as they dry out faster than sod. Use a root stimulator or starter fertilizer to ensure the roots grow as fast as possible. Never apply more than the recommended rate of fertilizer.

MAGIC LILIES

To grow these remarkable flowers, choose a spot with fertile, well-drained soil in sun or part shade. Plant the bulbs 5 inches deep and 6 to 8 inches apart now. Don't trim the straplike leaves that sprout in spring; let them die down. And avoid disturbing established bulbs or they'll skip a year or two of flowering. Spider lily (*Lycoris radiata*) would be a better choice for gardeners in Central and South Florida. It will grow in North Florida, too. Gardeners in East Texas (north of College Station) should get reliable flowering; magic lilies probably won't bloom dependably in other parts of the state. Along the coast, spider lily (*Lycoris radiata*) would be a better alternative.

MEXICAN FIREBUSH

In Texas this annual bedding plant (*Hamelia patens*) offers masses of tubular coral-red blossoms that attract hummingbirds and butterflies. It's not particular about soil and thrives in the sun but will tolerate partial shade. In addition, the foliage turns bright red in fall. Plants reach about 2 feet high and will resprout most springs in South Texas.

PEAT PELLETS

To get pansies, fall annuals and perennials, and (in the Lower and Coastal South) a fall crop of warm-

season vegetables off to a good start, sow the seeds in peat pellets. Just soak pellets overnight in a deep saucer. Use a pencil to poke a hole in the center depression; then add a couple of seeds. Thin to a single seedling, and plant in the garden when about 4 to 6 inches tall.

PERENNIALS

Groom fading flowers from daylilies to keep plants neat. Doing the same to purple coneflowers and black-eyed Susans may encourage a second bloom.

PESTICIDES

Avoid using fertilizer or pesticides if your plants are stressed or you will risk injuring them. Wait until you have watered or it has rained. Do not spray plants while they are still wet. The water on the leaves will dilute the chemicals and then give inconsistent results.

SQUASH VINES

If your squash, cucumber, and melon vines have suddenly wilted, look for damage to the stem. Slice it open lengthwise with a knife and you'll probably find a fat, white larva tunneling through it. Evict this little squash vine borer, and bury the damaged portion of the stem to encourage rooting. Just pull up vines that are severely infested—there's still time to replant.

TOMATOES

Keep plants watered during drought to prevent the onset of blossom-end rot. If brown patches are already a problem on tomatoes, apply calcium chloride (Stop-Rot) and continue regular watering. For autumn tomatoes in Texas, Surefire is a new, fast-maturing tomato developed by Texas A&M that's ideal for planting this time of year. Typically, only 65 days are required from transplanting to the first ripe fruit.

VEGETABLES

In Florida, only the most heat-tolerant vegetables can be planted now. Sweet potatoes, okra, Southern peas, chayote, and tropical vegetables, such as malanga and cassava, are good examples. Sow seeds of tomatoes indoors or outdoors in the shade to start transplants for a fall crop; set them in the garden next month. In Texas, set out eggplant and pepper plants now for the fall garden. Plant snap and lima beans by mid-month in the Panhandle area. Greencrop Bush and Topcrop are good snap beans; try Fordhook 242 or Henderson Bush lima beans. Keep fruit picked on established plants for continued production.

July Notes

To Do:
- Mow lawns higher in hot weather
- Watch out for spider mites on flowers and shrubs
- Give lawns an inch of water a week
- Water shrubs and young trees deeply
- Cut back leggy annuals to encourage more blooms

To Plant:
- Replant empty areas in the vegetable garden
- Seeds of biennial and perennial flowers

To Purchase:
- A rain gauge to measure how much water the lawn and garden receives each week
- Insecticidal soap for spraying spider mites and aphids

ZINNIAS

It's not too late to sow seeds of these sun-loving annuals directly in the garden. They'll sprout after about six days and bloom in a few weeks. If attacked by powdery mildew, just pull out affected plants and sow more seeds.

TIPS OF THE MONTH

Are voles eating your bulbs and the roots of your plants? Here's what to do. Place a mousetrap baited with peanut butter at the exit hole of a tunnel. Then place a bucket over the trap to make it dark.
R.S. Pierce
Suffolk, Virginia

To spray individual weeds in a flowerbed with weedkiller, cut the bottom out of a gallon plastic milk jug. Place the jug over the top of each weed, and spray it through the mouth of the jug. The jug will keep spray off nearby flowers.
Laura E. Franklin
Columbus, Georgia

White Clouds
In the Summer Garden

BY MARK G. STITH

PHOTOGRAPHY VAN CHAPLIN, SYLVIA MARTIN

DESIGN: BEN PAGE AND ASSOCIATES

The dramatic blooms of hydrangeas add the crisp, refreshing look of linen and lace. And they couldn't show up at a better time.

*F*inally. One of those choreless afternoons when you can sit out and watch the world go by from your lawn chair. Overhead, the hazy blue sky is filled with puffballs of drifting, white clouds. And you are lost in a summer daydream.

Not all of summer's cool, white clouds are way up in the wild blue yonder. Billowy masses of white-blooming hydrangeas can inspire much the same feeling as their airborne cousins. Refreshing, inviting, and long-lasting, the flowers of these deciduous shrubs are as welcome as a cool breeze on a sultry day.

"I adore hydrangeas," says Nashville gardener Margaret Ann Robinson. You could say she's grown up with them. "In the old garden here with them. "In the old garden here back in the 1930s, my mother had about two dozen old-fashioned pee-gee hydrangeas up against a fence."

When landscape architect Ben Page suggested planting a row of Annabelle hydrangeas (*Hydrangea arborescens* Annabelle) against a stucco wall facing north in her garden, Margaret knew she was in for a treat. "They get about a half-day's sun there and have done beautifully," she adds. "These have three different bloom colors. First they come out an apple green, then turn white, then in September become a pinky beige."

Peegee hydrangea (*H. paniculata* Grandiflora) is perhaps the best known of the white-blooming hydrangeas. Large (up to a foot or more), long-lasting flowers literally weigh the branches down, creating a pleasant, informal look. Mature plants can reach 20 feet or more, although about half that size is more typical. Peegee will grow in full sun to partial shade but needs a good, rich soil. To get the largest flowers, thin the plant to 5 to 10 good-sized shoots in late winter or early spring.

Once you've been introduced, there's no confusing oakleaf hydrangea (*H. quercifolia*) with any other plant. Or losing it in a crowd, either—it can easily grow 12 feet in height and spread. Sure, the large, deeply serrated foliage looks like red oak leaves on multivitamins. But this plant, native to hillsides and streams in the Deep South, boldly asserts its identity with four seasons of interest.

Tightly packed tufts of greenery spurt out of buds in spring and quickly clothe the once-barren stems in dense foliage. In summer, double scoops of vanilla blossoms covering the plant attract more attention than an ice-cream truck (well, almost). Such selections as Snowflake have

Huge masses of cloudlike flowers sit atop these Annabelle hydrangeas. Their long stalks make them perfect for cutting and displaying indoors. The blooms may also be clipped and dried for long-lasting winter arrangements.

(**Above**) *Smooth or wild hydrangea displays delicate, white saucers perched among the loosely formed shrub.*
(**Right**) *Heavy flower heads of peegee hydrangea nod gracefully in this garden at Fearrington Village, North Carolina.*
(**Below**) *Cone-shaped flower clusters and dramatic, coarse foliage of oakleaf hydrangea combine for a fabulous display. This selection, Snowflake, has blooms that can measure 15 inches or more in length.*

DESIGN: RYAN GAINEY

even larger and showier flowers (up to 2 feet long) than the native form (4 to 12 inches). The dramatic, wine-red fall color of the foliage is a special bonus. And when the leaves finally drop in late winter, the peeling "skin" of older stems reveals the attractive brown inner bark.

Another handsome native hydrangea is smooth or wild hydrangea (*H. arborescens*), from which Annabelle hydrangea was derived. Comparing smooth hydrangea to its cousin, oakleaf, is like comparing American cheese to extra sharp Cheddar. Smooth hydrangea is mild and unassuming—almost invisible until its graceful, 4- to 6-inch-wide, soft-white blooms appear. Snowhill is a selection that features 6- to 8-inch-wide flower clusters.

Both oakleaf and wild hydrangeas like the same growing conditions. "In the warmer South, they'll do well in partial to deep shade," says Dick Bir, a horticulturist with the Extension service in Fletcher, North Carolina. "But in the cooler South, like in the hills of Virginia, West Virginia, and up here in the North Carolina mountains, both will thrive in full sun. Neither is finicky about soil, but oakleaf has to have adequate moisture to look good," Bir adds.

As a general rule, most hydrangeas will do well throughout the South, but the limit appears to be as far west as East Texas, all but the extreme Coastal South, and as far south as Orlando. "The heat and humidity can really cause a lot of disease problems for them south of here," explains Camille Reynolds Humphrey of Leu Botanical Gardens in Orlando. "In addition, it doesn't get cold enough for them to set flowerbuds properly."

Don't restrict your list of hydrangeas to the few singled out here. There are many fine selections out there, and it was difficult to prune the field down to the ones we featured. In a sense, it was like trying to choose the best vanilla ice-cream cone I've ever eaten—they all were.

For a list of sources for these and other hydrangeas, send a self-addressed, stamped, business-size envelope to Hydrangea Editor, *Southern Living,* P.O. Box 830119, Birmingham, Alabama 35283. ◇

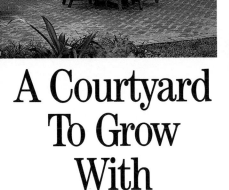

A Courtyard To Grow With

(**Above**) *The brick terrace is a favorite spot for adults while an arching trellis invites children to run through to the lawn beyond.*
(**Far left**) *The McCalebs' courtyard provides a pleasant view for the kitchen's bay window.*
(**Left**) *An Italian oil urn seems to float on the water. Copper piping was used to convert the urn into a fountain.*

"This is our forever home," says Teresa McCaleb of San Antonio. "Ten years from now we still want to be able to use our backyard for entertaining." As the parents of four young children, Teresa and her husband, Ben, needed an area suitable for today's tricycle derby yet able to meet the family's changing needs as well. With those criteria in mind, landscape architect Terry Lewis designed an outdoor living area that can host a wide range of activities—from children's birthday parties to grown-up get-togethers.

"The McCalebs wanted a place for the kids to play ball but also needed an outdoor space for the adults," Lewis says. His first step was to design a new terrace just outside the family room. D'Hanis brick, named after the nearby Texas town where it is made, was laid in a herringbone pattern to create a richly textured surface. This cozy spot hosts lazy summer suppers and doubles as a children's play area (within sight of adult supervision). A 6½-foot-high stucco wall extends from the side of the garage and creates a courtyard effect without totally screening the backyard. An arching cedar trellis frames the view of the lawn beyond, which beckons children to

kick off their shoes and run.

The courtyard's crown jewel is also its focal point: water bubbling over the lip of an Italian oil urn. Perched on an underwater pedestal, the urn fountain gives the illusion of floating in its small pool. The hollow pedestal houses a submersible pump which keeps the water recirculating. Terracotta containers of caladiums and umbrella plants add a splash of color.

The wall serves as a backdrop for the fountain, which would otherwise have to compete for attention with the rest of the yard. Capped with D'Hanis tile to match the paving, the wall also hides the barbecue grill.

Although the completed courtyard looks great now, during the planning stages Lewis had to convince the McCalebs that building a wall in the middle of their backyard was the way to go. "In most backyards, you see all the way to the fence, and I was used to that," says Teresa, "but this works nicely. I guess the best thing about this courtyard is that we won't ever outgrow it." *Jo Kellum*

Fairyland
OF
Flowers

*Spirits inhabit this garden.
The ones you see are magic lilies.
The one you feel is that of
the gardener who planted them.*

BY STEVE BENDER /
PHOTOGRAPHY VAN CHAPLIN

N o, Eleanor Bridges couldn't escape death. Quietly, it called upon this feisty octogenarian six years ago as she lay in her hospital bed. But today, throughout the grounds of her former garden in Homewood, Alabama, you feel her presence like a warming ray of sunshine. In the plants she nurtured and then passed on to friends, Eleanor lives.

Born into a well-to-do family near the turn of the century, Eleanor led a colorful life that her contemporaries couldn't help but envy. She wintered in Florida, traveled regularly to exotic places, and studied art at the Sorbonne. In her early twenties, she married Georges Bridges, an accomplished sculptor. In honor of the event, her father built them a house. But at Eleanor's insistence, it wouldn't be just *any* house.

Amid the weekend cottages and sleepy bungalows of the surrounding neighborhood rose an imposing, pink-

(**Left**) *Each August, hundreds of magic lilies sprout without warning throughout Eleanor Bridges's former garden.* (**Above**) *Eleanor loved animals as much as plants.
She was one of those who led the fight for the Laboratory Animal Welfare Act in the 1960s.*

Eleanor's spirit is there in the garden, and it always will be. Diana Hansen

(**Above**) *Today, Eric and Diana Hansen maintain Eleanor's garden as she would have liked, conserving her plants as well as her husband Georges' sculpture.*

stuccoed, Mediterranean-style house, replete with fountains, fishponds, ornate stone urns, and Georges' sculpture. Every feature had to make a statement, the more audacious the better. During its construction, she reportedly told her father, "I want a fireplace big enough to roast a missionary."

Flamboyant to a fault, Eleanor laid bare her eccentricity for all to see. A tiny woman, she often dashed about atop platform shoes, her face nearly hidden by a huge, floppy hat. She appeared comical to some—until she spoke. Then her eloquence and astounding breadth of knowledge captivated listeners. Jane Raybon, who attended one of Eleanor's garden club lectures, recalls, "The first time I saw her, I couldn't believe it. She wore Carmen Miranda shoes, a big hat, and epaulets on her shoulders. She looked like a little general.

But when she opened her mouth, I knew I was in the presence of someone brilliant."

If a green thumb signifies gardening skill, then Eleanor's thumbs were solid jade. She grew fussy plants that confounded others and decorated her garden terraces with botanical rarities collected while traveling. Many of her plants were old Southern treasures, such as clerodendrum, ricepaper plant, crinum, spider lily, alstroemeria, starflower, and cardinal climber.

Active in numerous civic causes and local charities, Eleanor was generous with her plants as well. She often bestowed them on ailing friends or those who needed some cheering up. Observes Evelyn Stough, a longtime friend, "She loved the fact the flowers did something to raise the human spirit."

Her favorite plant to pass along was magic lily (*Lycoris squamigera*), also called naked lady. In spring, this remarkable, long-lived bulb produces straplike leaves, which soon die down. Then, without warning, in

late July and August, whorls of light-pink trumpets appear atop 3-foot stalks. (For tips on growing magic lilies, see this month's Garden Checklist.) Spectacular drifts of magic lilies adorned Eleanor's grounds each summer.

Some of Eleanor's lilies thrive today in Sue Oztekin's garden in Hoover, Alabama. Sue received them one Sunday afternoon when she and her children passed by Eleanor's garden on their way back from church. "The children were enchanted," Sue remembers. "Her garden was a fairyland of flowers." Eleanor invited the family into her garden and asked if anything struck their fancy. "I would never have asked for any plants," notes Sue, "but my children did." They requested "fairy flowers"— their name for the lilies that had appeared from nowhere.

During Eleanor's half-century in Homewood, her garden hosted a slew of civic functions, including art shows (she was a talented artist), garden club meetings, and campaigns to reduce the suffering of laboratory animals. Eventually, she herself knew suffering, as five family members died in a single year. In her garden, Eleanor found a refuge from the pain. "She told me the garden saved her sanity," explains Evelyn, "because you see the cycle of life repeating itself in the plants, and when you sit on the ground, you draw strength from the soil."

Just before Eleanor died, her daughter, London, sold the home to a young couple, Eric and Diana Hansen, on the condition that they preserve the house and garden as is. The Hansens, who knew Eleanor, eagerly agreed. Today, using Eleanor's notes and old photos of the garden, they scrupulously maintain her botanical legacy, caring for her plants as if she were watching.

And maybe she is. Last winter, Eric and Diana planted a young dogwood into what they thought was empty ground. When spring warmth coaxed the garden's dormant bulbs to sprout foliage, the Hansens discovered they had planted the tree exactly in the center of a ring of old magic lilies without damaging a single one. A coincidence? Diana isn't so sure. "Eleanor's spirit is there in the garden," she declares, "and it always will be." ◇

PHOTOGRAPHS: VAN CHAPLIN

Unique flower spikes, like the heads of geese, appear atop deep-green foliage in summer.

Caution Is Key With Gooseneck Loosestrife

In my favorite childhood book, *The Thirteen Clocks* by James Thurber, an evil duke dispatches his niece's suitors by running them through with his sword and feeding them to the geese. (This sounds a whole lot less gruesome to an 8-year-old than it does to an adult.) Well, here's a flower that not only looks like a goose, but will gobble your garden up, if you let it. Fortunately, it has a good side as well. Its name—gooseneck loosestrife.

Native to Japan, this herbaceous perennial also goes by the botanical name of *Lysimachia clethroides*. If you know anything about the genus *Lysimachia*, you know its members are

born with their track shoes on. Gooseneck loosestrife invades entire garden beds, spreading by means of underground runners. Planting timid columbines and pinks next to this rapacious ruffian is like tossing lambs to the lion.

Given gooseneck loosestrife's predatory nature, why in the world would anyone plant it? There are a couple of good reasons. First, summer flowers combined with tidy, deep-green foliage makes for a very handsome plant. Second, it easily fends off diseases and insects. Third, sun or light shade, rich or poor soil make no difference to this tough customer. Finally, when prop-

erly confined it forms a dense, attractive border.

"Properly confined" is the operative term, according to Sam Jones of Piccadilly Farm in Bishop, Georgia. You need to plant this perennial in a raised bed bordered by brick, stone, or wood, so its roots can't escape and

(Above) *The plant spreads rapidly, forming a dense border. Keep it confined in a raised bed.*

wreak havoc in your garden.

Sam grows it in front of his nursery's office inside a raised bed edged in railroad ties and filled with gravel. The bed's original purpose was to catch rainwater from the roof. But now, brimming with loosestrife, it serves as a showy display bed for customers.

In the final pages of *The Thirteen Clocks*, a hideous monster destroys the evil duke, while a handsome prince rescues his niece. A happy ending, indeed. By exercising caution when planting gooseneck loosestrife, this gardening tale will end on a positive note as well.   *Steve Bender*

For a list of mail-order sources, send a self-addressed, stamped, business-size envelope to Gooseneck Loosestrife, P.O. Box 830119, Birmingham, Alabama 35283.

> ## GOOSENECK LOOSESTRIFE AT A GLANCE
> **Size:** 2 to 3 feet tall
> **Blooms:** June and July
> **Light:** Sun or light shade
> **Soil:** Almost any
> **Pests:** None serious
> **Range:** Upper, Middle, and Lower South

Southern Living®
JULY 1993

High Country
GARDENING

BY LINDA C. ASKEY
PHOTOGRAPHY SYLVIA MARTIN

It's summer in the Blue Ridge, and flowers abound. Here, souls and bodies are refreshed and gardens flourish in the agreeable climate.

When the sun peeks over the ridge crest, its rays pierce the cool, clean air of the High Country. That's what they call this area atop North Carolina's Blue Ridge around Grandfather Mountain. Because the nights are cool, mists invariably rise from the streams that trickle down every fold in the land. So when the sun streaks through the trees, you see not only ferns and moss in nature's spotlight, but also the light itself, primal and pure at the birth of a new day.

No one puts away their sweaters here. Even though the midday air is warm enough for shorts, morning's chill returns by three o'clock.

The High Country is probably as close as Southerners can get to gardening in England. Spring comes late—mid-May to early June—and doesn't get into full swing until July. That's when the delphiniums, astilbes, and roses are at their peak. And if a gardener is fastidious and cuts away the spent flowers, many will bloom again.

By virtue of this distinctive climate, these mountain communities have a style all their own. The old homes are rustic, with elements of natural surroundings built right in. Most noticeable are the houses clothed with chestnut bark. Stripped from trees felled by the chestnut

blight, this durable bark has lasted a hundred years on some of the older structures.

Picking up on the rustic theme, Charles Holden of Appalachian Highlands Nursery (located on U.S. 221 about a mile north of Crossnore) makes many of the twig benches, locust arbors, moss planters, and birdhouses that ornament the gardens of this area. In fact, his handiwork is popping up in other parts of the South as the souvenirs of refreshing summer vacations.

Like Europeans, the residents seem to have an innate appreciation for gardens. For one thing, flowers naturally thrive. More than one homeowner has exclaimed, "You just stick something in the ground and it grows!" There seem to be fewer

(Left) A unique opportunity for Southern gardeners exists among these rolling hills, and the lush plantings show it off.
(Above) As this garden gate proves, sometimes simple is best.

insect pests, and with plentiful rainfall, watering is seldom necessary.

Tuberous begonias do not have a reputation for thriving in the South, but they are at home in the High Country. Roses bloom endlessly with big blossoms that other parts of the South get only in spring and fall. And delphiniums grow 6 feet tall—year after year. Gardeners also blend native plants with their cultivated favorites. Queen Anne's lace, Carolina thermopsis, cranesbill, phlox, aster, ironweed, and ferns grow among astilbe, delphinium, lupine, and such.

In planning a garden in the mountains, remember that the early-spring garden is natural. Bloodroot, trillium, spring beauties, hepaticas, and a host of other wildflowers pop up with the first warmth of spring. By adding late spring and summer flowers to nature's garden, the charm of the mountains is amplified, not overwhelmed, and the color is extended through the season.

Although color is a personal choice, some colors naturally look better. Red, orange, and gold are warm tones that seem foreign to this area. The light is naturally blue, colored by mist and mountain shadows. Pink, mauve, blue, and white abound in these gardens, and harmony between these colors is easy to achieve. Even the yellows are a greenish hue, drawing on the background of foliage.

The dark soil that fills the valleys between the ridges is the product of minerals washed down from rocky crests and is enriched by the compost of thick forests. In beds bounded by walls of native stone, this fertile ground provides a beneficial foothold for gardens.

But that is not to say that the beauty of these gardens lies only at your feet. Above the flowers are the gracefully tiered hemlocks, as well as vistas to ridges that are layered one on another. In this contrast of near and far, small and grand, managed and natural, lies the magic of this region, the paradox of this highland paradise.

(**Right**) *Tended by its third generation, this garden features a crimson rose, whose name has been lost to time.*
(**Below**) *In these mountain gardens, native plants mingle with exotic favorites. Here, Carolina thermopsis blooms beside hybrid lilies.*

(**Right**) *Ornaments made by craftsman Charles Holden of Newland, North Carolina, are a good match for the rugged natural landscape.*

Summer cottages clothed with chestnut bark give the gardens of the High Country their characteristic charm.

The ruggedly natural quality of stone and bark provides counterpoint to the abundant flowers and foliage of the highland garden.

TIPS FOR THE HIGH COUNTRY GARDENER

Those who are just beginning to garden in the mountains may notice that some techniques that are generally recommended for the South may not always apply.

■ Mulch should be removed in the spring so that the sun can warm the soil.

■ Plants that may not perform as well in other regions of the South will thrive here. Such plants include delphiniums, tree peonies, and lupines.

■ Because the season is relatively brief, annuals such as cosmos, zinnias, and cleome are set out as transplants, even though they can be easily grown from seeds sown directly in the garden.

■ The season is shortened, and so is the se-

quence of bloom among perennials. Take this into account when planning your borders.

■ Invigorated by cool nights and rich soil, annuals and perennials need to be cut back regularly.

August

Flowering tobacco and cleome

CHECKLIST FOR AUGUST

BANANAS

Apply about 2 pounds of slow-release 6-6-6 per full-grown plant every six to eight weeks until the fruit ripens. Broadcast the fertilizer under the leaf canopy, and water it in. Also remove suckers (small sprouts arising from the base) from plants that are bearing fruit or the suckers will take up energy needed to ripen the bananas. Plant suckers elsewhere for a bigger harvest next year.

BEES

When cutting flowers, don't be caught unaware by sleeping bees. In early morning or late evening you may find the little stingers taking a nap. As soon as the sun warms the air, they'll wake up and fly away. Just don't get stung in the meantime.

BIENNIALS

Sow seeds now of hollyhocks, wallflowers, foxgloves, sweet William, honesty, myosotis, and Iceland poppies. Sow directly into a well-prepared bed or into a flat for transplanting.

BOUGAINVILLEA

To keep bougainvillea in bounds in Florida, prune it now. Its blossoms set in the shorter days of fall, so later pruning will remove flowerbuds. Cut plants as far back as needed. They'll sprout again just below the cut. After pruning, fertilize with a cup of 6-6-6 or other slow-release fertilizer.

BULBS

Mail order your spring-flowering bulbs now. When they arrive, store them in a cool basement, garage, or vegetable drawer of your refrigerator until you are ready to plant (October in the Upper South, November in the Middle, Lower, and Coastal South). Check your garden center for colchicums and spider lilies. Plant these bulbs right away, and they should bloom in only a few weeks.

CHINCH BUGS

Be on the lookout for chinch bugs in St. Augustine grass. Visible damage usually shows up as a spot of yellowing, drying grass near the street or driveway. The spot gets larger as the chinch bugs spread, and the grass inside the spot gets browner and drier as the insects feed. Apply Dursban around the infested area to control the insects.

CONTAINER PLANTS

The hot sun can quickly dry out pots, hanging baskets, and other containers. Check them daily, and water as needed. If you'll be away on vacation for more than a day or two, ask a neighbor to water them for you, or consider an automatic irrigation system. When re-potting, add a water-retaining polymer to the soil.

CONTAINERS

If your potted plants get so dry that the soil has shrunk or hardened, just watering the surface won't be effective. To thoroughly wet the soil, put several inches of water in the bottom of a bucket; then set the entire pot in the water, and let the dry soil soak up the moisture. After an hour or two, remove the pot, and drain excess water.

FALL ARMYWORMS

In Florida, these pests appear in hordes, devouring blades of grass and the foliage of tomatoes and many other vegetables. They have a white, Y-shaped mark on their foreheads and three thin yellow stripes and a heavier yellow and red stripe down their backs. To control, apply carbaryl insecticide. If you're treating the lawn, water it well the day before spraying.

GRAPES

In Texas, bunch grapes and muscadines should be ready for harvest this month. Wait until the whole bunch is completely ripened before picking. If birds getting at your fruit is a problem, use netting, aluminum foil strips, or predator decoys to help keep them away from your vines.

HERBS

Dry herbs from your garden now. Gather sprigs of oregano, marjoram, thyme, basil, rosemary, sage, bay, and chives. Spread them individually on cheesecloth in a warm, dark, well-ventilated place, or bundle them with rubberbands and hang to dry.

HOSE HELPERS

A water stop lets you cut off the water without going back to the faucet, making it easier to change from a watering wand to a power nozzle. A short section of hose with a coiled spring helps prevent kinks near the faucet but will also do a good job next to the nozzle.

LAWNS

Most lawns will let you know they are thirsty by turning slightly gray and being slow to spring back from footprints. Water for several hours in the early morning. When the sun hits the lawn, excess moisture will dry off. If you have a built-in sprinkler system, make sure that it is functioning properly. Thoroughly check all parts of the system, including the heads, valves, and timers.

MARI-MUMS

This group of marigolds was developed especially for long-lasting fall displays. Good selections for Texas include Discovery Yellow and Discovery Orange. Both reach about 8 to 10 inches in height and have bright, non-fading blooms. Plant them about 8 inches apart in well-prepared soil; they need full sun to flower well.

PETUNIAS

Perk up leggy petunias by cutting them back about one-third to encourage new branches and flowers. Then use liquid fertilizer, mixed according to label directions.

ROSES

Minimize disease problems by watering the soil beneath the bush and not the foliage. Use mulch to insulate rose roots. Remember, fungus problems, such as blackspot and powdery mildew, can only be prevented, not cured. Roses that are susceptible to these diseases should receive preventive sprays of Funginex mixed according to label directions.

SHRUBS

In Texas, fertilize shrubs now with 1 tablespoon of 12-6-6 or similar granular fertilizer per foot of height. Water thoroughly the day before fertilizing, and then again after application. Spread the fertilizer evenly around the root zone. There's no need to pull back mulch when applying fertilizer, but wash off any granules that might get on the foliage.

SUMMER SQUASH

In Texas, it's not too late to sow seeds of summer squash for a late harvest. Gardeners in most of the state have until late September to plant seeds. In the Panhandle, you should get them in the ground by mid-August.

TREE BORERS

Peach, plum, and apricot trees are vulnerable to damage from these destructive insects. Dead or dying limbs and sap oozing out of the trunk are signs of damage. Spray the base of the tree up to the first set of branches with Dursban insecticide. Use a pump-up or hose-end sprayer to cover the trunk thoroughly.

TREES

Avoid nicking the bark of trees when mowing or using a nylon-string trimmer around their trunks. The wounds could girdle the tree and cut off the flow of sap up the tree, killing it. Keep mulch around the base of the tree, or plant ground cover.

VEGETABLES

It won't be long until it is time to plant fall vegetables, particularly in the Upper South. Check the seeds left over from the spring garden to be certain you have all you need for a fall crop of lettuce, radishes, carrots, turnips, mustard, and peas. If not, place your order now, or look for an end-of-the-season sale at your local garden center. In Texas, seeds of cool-season crops, such as lettuce, English peas, spinach, mustard, radishes, and turnips, can be set out in gardens from San Antonio northward. It's also time to set out transplants of broccoli, cabbage, cauliflower, and kale. Gardeners in South Texas as well as those along the coast should wait until next month before they plant their fall gardens. In Florida, gardeners north of Orlando should choose tomato and snap bean selections that mature early to ensure harvest before frost. Some tomatoes that mature in eight weeks or less include Early Girl, Champion, Burpee's Early Pick, and Burpeeana Early. Bush-type snap beans for the state include Blue Lake, Burpee's Tenderpod, Contender, Provider, Topcrop, and Roma. They begin bearing in seven to eight weeks.

WREATHS

Now is the time to prepare dried wreaths to enjoy year-round. Green material is much easier to work with than dry. Use artemisia, rosemary, thyme, boxwood, or wild grasses to cover the form. Then fasten bundles of pods (such as poppy, milkweed, or iris) and fresh material that dries easily (such as strawflowers, rose hips, or lamb's-ears) to the covered form.

August Notes

To Do:
- Continue to give extra water to shrubs, trees, flowers, and lawn to make up for summer drought
- Control fleas in the lawn
- Continue to remove faded blooms from annuals
- Layer branches of hydrangea
- Replace vegetables already harvested with vegetables for fall—cabbage, broccoli, cauliflower, Brussels sprouts, collards, and kale
- Watch out for bagworms on evergreens; handpick and discard
- Put out a hummingbird feeder

To Plant:
- Colchicums, autumn crocus, and other fall-blooming bulbs
- Cool-weather vegetables for fall

To Purchase:
- Pesticide to control fleas in the lawn
- Transplants of cool-weather vegetables
- Fall-blooming bulbs
- Hummingbird feeder

_____

_____

_____

_____

TIP OF THE MONTH

A child's plastic swimming pool is an ideal tool for keeping outdoor potted plants watered when you're away. Put the pots in the pool; then fill the pool with several inches of water. The pool should be in partial shade to help reduce evaporation. This method kept my plants watered for more than two weeks.   _Miriam P. Kitchen_
Augusta, Georgia

GARDENING
PLANTS AND DESIGN

Winged Wizards

Hummingbirds fascinate us with their astounding aerobatics and pugnacious personalities. If you'd like them to visit your garden this year, here's how.

BY STEVE BENDER

PHOTOGRAPHY VAN CHAPLIN, SYLVIA MARTIN

Whrrrrrzzzzzip!

What the heck was that? Something just buzzed past my ear, rocketed straight up, hovered like a UFO, then zoomed away faster than I could wink. Maybe it was a bumblebee on its ninth cup of coffee. No, there it is again, over in the salvias, dashing maniacally from flower to flower. It's the size of a peanut, has the iridescent sheen of a dragonfly, and its wings move faster than a used car salesman's lips. Only one thing fits that description—a hummingbird.

Few creatures curry more favor with Southerners than do hummingbirds. But before we discuss strategies for attracting these winged wizards to your garden, here are some fascinating hummingbird facts you may not know.

■ A hummingbird's wings can turn 180 degrees up, down, forward, and back, allowing the bird to hover, fly backward, and ascend vertically, much like Michael Jordan.

■ Hummingbirds commonly beat their wings 50 to 70 times per second. But during courtship, a male's wings beat up to 200 times per second, propelling him 30 to 40 m.p.h. as he puts his best moves on a lucky female.

■ So rapid is a hummingbird's metabolism that if the bird were the size

of a man, it would need to consume 155,000 calories a day to survive. For the health-conscious among you, that amounts to about 80 gallons of yogurt a day.

■ Hummingbirds often migrate thousands of miles each year between their summer range in the Northern and Western United States and Canada and their winter homes in Mexico and Central America. Aided by uncanny memories, they return every year to the same food source. Remarks hummingbird fancier Bob Sargent of Trussville, Alabama, "We saw a bird at our house 10 days ago that we've seen for 5 successive years. Not only that, but it arrives on the same date each year."

Bob knows this for sure because he and his wife, Martha, hold a rare permit from the U.S. Fish & Wildlife Service to catch, band, and release hummingbirds in order to track their movements. The Sargents see modest numbers of hummingbirds in spring, when the birds fly north. But during the peak of the late summer and fall migration, from mid-August through early September, dozens of birds squabble over the 30 feeders distributed around their yard. Last year, Bob and Martha banded and released 550 hummingbirds. So if you're wondering why so few birds

came to your feeder, it's probably because they were all over visiting Bob and Martha.

Bob admires hummingbirds for their iron will and constitution. A good example is the ruby-throated hummingbird, the Southeast's most common species. "That bird weighs just 3 grams, half of what a marble weighs," he points out. "Yet it's able to cross the Gulf of Mexico twice each year."

A hummingbird's personality could use some refinement, admits Bob. Pugnacious and combative, the bird fiercely defends food sources against all comers, driving away much larger birds, oblivious to their size. "As pretty as hummingbirds are, they're very vicious toward other birds and their own kind," he observes.

If you're competing with your neighbors to have the most hummingbirds in your yard this year, LuAnn Craighton, Interpretive Naturalist for Callaway Gardens in Pine Mountain, Georgia, offers these tips.

First, plant brightly colored, nectar-producing flowers in your garden. You'll need flowers blooming during the migration in spring and again in late summer and early fall. Hummingbirds favor red, orange, and pink blossoms, so have plenty of these. The box (right) lists excellent hummingbird flowers.

Second, put up one or two hummingbird feeders. Choose a type you can easily clean every week to prevent a buildup of mold and bacteria. Swish hot water around in it, but don't use soap, as this can leave a film that may cause the feeder to leak. Fill the feeder with a solution of one part white sugar to four parts water. Don't add red food coloring to the water because it often contains alcohol.

Finally, leave your feeder up during the winter. Many hummingbirds that spend their summers out west enjoy winter vacations in the South. One December, Margaret Anderson and Fae Humphrey, participating in the Audubon Society's annual Christmas Bird Count in Freeport, Texas, recorded seven different species in a single day.

Undoubtedly, most of these birds had flown straight down from Bob and Martha's.　◇

**FAVORITE
HUMMINGBIRD FLOWERS**

Bee balm
Cardinal flower
Hibiscus
Impatiens
Mimosa
Pentas
Petunia
Pineapple sage
Shrimp plant
Spider flower
Tiger lily
Trumpet creeper
Trumpet honeysuckle

Restoring Nature to The Garden

(**Left**) *Dense plantings thoroughly screen this house from the street. It almost appears you're approaching a cabin in the woods.*
(**Below**) *A series of decks leads you throughout the garden and traverses soggy areas. Elizabeth's playground is on the right.*

Stephen Rusbar has a house back here. If you have a hard time spotting it, that's the whole point. A landscape architect for Natives Landscape in Covington, Louisiana, Rusbar designs gardens that re-create indigenous plant communities. His goal—self-sustaining plantings that maintain the local ecology and mask human disturbance of the original site.

When Rusbar bought the property six years ago, it was devoid of plants, save for a few tall oaks and pines. Part of the lot was low and boggy, and the soil lacked fertility. He immediately began planting large numbers of trees, shrubs, and perennials, most of them native, re-creating plant associations he'd seen in the wild. To improve the soil, he hauled in huge amounts of leaves and pine needles, spreading a layer over the soil several inches deep. Then he built a series of decks throughout the garden and over wet spots.

As the plants took hold, they quickly screened the house from the neighborhood, providing the seclusion and privacy Rusbar wanted. Each autumn, leaf litter replenishes the bank of organic matter that enriches the soil, deters weeds, and retains moisture. Rusbar encourages the garden to evolve naturally, so he seldom prunes. And because most plants are indigenous, they fend off insects and diseases by themselves, without pesticides or chemicals.

The restored habitat attracts a host of wildlife, including squirrels, frogs, butterflies, and birds. "I don't see birds nesting around houses where people have only lawn," observes Rusbar. "But I see nests in the trees and thickets around our house because it affords them the security they need. Plus, I planted food sources, such as French mulberry and arrowwood, for birds."

Native cardinal flower thrives in the garden's boggy soil. Its bright-red blooms attract hummingbirds.

Between all the beeches, bigleaf magnolias, palmettos, and giant bananas, Rusbar reserved space for a fish pond, a vegetable and herb garden, and a playground for his daughter, Elizabeth. In reality, Elizabeth considers the entire garden her playground, as she daily investigates such botanical wonders as the fragrance of banana shrub or the scarlet seeds of the wahoo.

Rusbar realizes his garden isn't for everyone. "If native plants, wildflowers, perennials, and herbs mean nothing to you, you'll probably walk right by our house and say, 'That whole yard is nothing but weeds.' That's fine with me. But I've gotten only positive comments from neighbors."

Steve Bender

The bold foliage and distinctive white blooms of flowering tobacco set it apart in the summer flower border.

The Sweet Scent of Flowering Tobacco

Summer is sweet in the South. It's not just the taste of watermelon or home-churned ice cream but the smell of gardenia and magnolia blossoms perfuming the air. Gardeners can sweeten the season even further with old-fashioned flowering tobacco (*Nicotiana sylvestris*).

The flowering tobacco offered in garden centers each spring is a carefully bred, shorter form that offers a variety of colors but lacks the intense fragrance of this more primitive species. The impact of the old-fashioned type in the garden is different too. Instead of providing color only, this flowering tobacco offers bold foliage, stately

Clusters of 3-inch-long tubular flowers are deliciously fragrant, particularly in the morning and evening.

form, and elegantly shaped white flowers. The tubular blooms are borne in pendulous clusters that eventually rise to 4 to 5 feet atop the flower stalk. Consequently, this is an ideal plant for the middle or back of the flower border. Best of all, the blossoms of flowering tobacco become even more fragrant during the evening hours, just when the air cools, the sunlight softens, and family and friends get together outdoors.

Like the shorter selections, flowering tobacco enjoys a sunny location with well-drained soil. In the Middle and Lower South, plants will probably benefit from an eastern exposure to give them a little

shelter from the afternoon sun.

In the Middle and Upper South, set transplants into the garden in spring, about the same time you set out tomatoes. In Texas, Mike Shoup grows flowering tobacco in his garden at the Antique Rose Emporium. He sets out young plants in the fall (about the same time he plants pansies), and they overwinter in the garden. Naturally these are better established and will bloom earlier than those planted in spring.

In Madison, Mississippi, Susan Haltom was pleased to have last year's plants overwinter in her garden, which is located on the southern edge of the Middle South region. "They have a vigor the second year that they just didn't have the first," she observes.

Although a single plant will produce thousands of small seeds during a single summer, only a few will survive winter to germinate in the garden the next season. However, landscape architect Ben Page in Nashville observed the first volunteer seedlings flowering in May, beginning when the plant was only 1½ feet tall.

You also can collect seeds from mature pods. Gather them in an envelope, and store in a cool, dry place during winter. Sow indoors in early spring; they germinate easily. Separate seedlings into individual pots, and protect them in a greenhouse or windowsill until the danger of frost has passed. Set plants 24 inches apart in the garden. They grow quickly once the weather gets hot and will be in bloom in several weeks.

Linda C. Askey

For mail-order sources of flowering tobacco, send a self-addressed, stamped, business-size envelope to Flowering Tobacco, *Southern Living,* P.O. Box 830119, Birmingham, Alabama 35283. ◇

FLOWERING TOBACCO AT A GLANCE

Light: Full sun to partial shade
Moisture: Moderate
Soil: Well drained
Propagation: Seeds started indoors in early spring; transplant after last spring frost
Size: 4 to 5 feet tall
Spacing: 24 inches apart

A palace and a pickup truck: When it was built by Godfrey Barnsley in the 1840s, the Italianate villa in rural northwest Georgia must have seemed as much out of place and time as this red pickup truck.

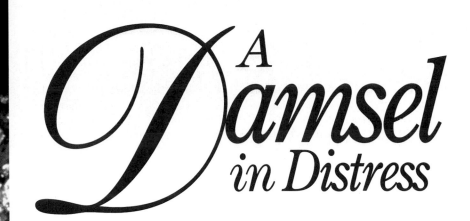

A Damsel in Distress

*Time and neglect threatened this
old estate in northwest Georgia. But
a true-to-life prince brought a happy
ending to the tale of Barnsley Gardens.*

BY MARK G. STITH / PHOTOGRAPHY VAN CHAPLIN

Late Summer, 1991

Dan Franklin, an Atlanta landscape architect, had called to gracefully badger me into going with him to see Barnsley Gardens. These ruins of an antebellum mansion and garden are about an hour's drive north of Atlanta. Dan had been engaged by the estate's new owners as a consultant in the restoration and enhancement of the extensive gardens.

Having lived in Atlanta for years, I'd never heard of it, and I listened to him talk excitedly about this place, which had been built in the 1840s by Godfrey Barnsley, a wealthy cotton merchant. Barnsley had also installed an elaborate garden around his new home (which he called Woodlands). But the family eventually fell on hard times, and the home and its gardens were badly in need of repair after the Civil War. In 1906, a tornado destroyed the mansion's roof, and Barnsley's financially strapped descendants were unable to repair it. But like a modern-day fairy tale, a prince came to the rescue. Namely, a real-life German prince, Hubertus Fugger-Babbenhausen, who bought the estate, sight unseen, in 1988.

Dan is a pretty good judge (and creator) of gardens, and this one sounded intriguing, so I agreed to go.

(In the meantime, one of the new staff members at Barnsley had contacted me, too.) So we picked a sunny, hot day and scooted north on I-75 past the outer limits of Atlanta's suburbs, got off at the Adairsville exit, and headed into the land of two-lane, rural Georgia.

Any Southerner can envision the scenery—simple houses set way off the road, a small store every few miles or so, Johnson grass in the ditches, and tail-flicking cows in the fields. Just a nice drive in the country, with no surprises. But so far, no estate either.

A few miles down the road, Dan turned left onto a dirt lane. I saw nothing but pastureland and thick woods off to the right. Frankly, I was feeling a little duped: Dan has quite a sense of humor. We drove on a little farther toward the wooded area.

Oh my! Behind the trees, set on a hillside up from the winding dirt road, appeared a beautiful, brick, ghostly shell of a mansion. A pair of arched windows atop the roofless third floor framed trees behind the Italianate structure. (Italianate? In northwest Georgia?) "Well, what do you think?" Dan asked with a wry smile. He knew I was smitten.

The dirt road continued up to the

mansion and encircled a huge, over-grown, patterned boxwood garden. At the wide steps leading into the ruins, we found a small group of people who were hard at work on the approximately 150-year-old brick structure.

I met Steve Wheaton, who had been hired as gardens manager. He led us through the tangled boxwood parterre in front of the house ("Look out for the poison ivy!" Steve warned), then out to the extensive wooded area downhill from the mansion. Narrow trails took us by old garden ponds and spillways clogged with muck. Steve spoke ambitiously of cleaning out the boxwood garden and rebuilding its central fountain, of planting hundreds of rhododendrons on a hillside across from the ruins, of cleaning out the ponds, and of reworking the trails.

And as I walked around with Steve and Dan on that hot summer day, I recall thinking that it would be years before this garden opened to the public. There was just too much to do.

*L*ate Spring, 1992

I was *so* wrong. Barnsley Gardens opened to the public in October 1991 and has entertained and delighted visitors ever since. The staff has done more than they set out to do—the addition of a replicated 1840s farmhouse, which serves as a visitors center, heightens the enjoyment of visiting an estate filled with 30 acres of lush gardens and lingering memories. The Barnsley Garden Shop, an authentic 1820 log cabin moved to the site, opened last summer and offers plants and garden accessories for sale.

The right wing of the main house, which has been almost completely restored, serves as a museum and theater displaying Civil War artifacts, period clothing, and some of the Barnsleys' original furniture. Behind the ruins is a lush perennial garden designed by Jane Bath, a Stone Mountain, Georgia, garden designer. A Confederate soldier's grave lies undisturbed among the flowers. At the

A new farmhouse-style building at Barnsley serves as a visitors center, gift shop, and cafe, as well as office quarters.

south end of the garden, a magnificent arbor, designed by Prince Fugger and detailed by Atlanta architect Roy Frangiamore, overlooks the wooded area and ponds below.

In spring, the hillsides are covered with thousands of daffodils. "We have close to 250,000 bulbs, including daffodils, iris, and others," notes Erica Glasener, garden shop manager. "We want to keep refining the garden, but we'd still like to keep some of the rustic charm," she adds.

So you probably won't ever see a roof go up over the main house or the brick stuccoed, as was the intent of Godfrey Barnsley. But you will still be treated to one of the most intriguingly beautiful historic estates you're likely to see in the area. And that is just what the original owner of the estate (whose spirit, as well as his wife's, is said to walk the grounds) would have wanted for his guests.

How to get there: Barnsley Gardens is located at 597 Barnsley Gardens Road, just off Hall Station Road between Adairsville and Kingston. From I-75, take Exit 128, go west on State 140, and follow the signs. For information call (404) 773-7480.

Barnsley Gardens schedules special events during the year, including the Daffodil Festival in March; call for specific information. ◇

A lush perennial border, designed by Jane Bath of Stone Mountain, Georgia, flourishes behind the main ruins. Delphiniums, old roses, foxglove, and coreopsis are among the plants included.

FROM A CASTLE TO THE COUNTRY: A PRINCE COMES TO GEORGIA

At first, Prince Hubertus Fugger-Babbenhausen of Augsburg wasn't enthusiastic about the idea of buying a ruin in rural Georgia.

"I had two castles in Germany to take care of," he explains. "I really didn't need another."

But the history of the home and descriptions of the rich northwest Georgia landscape lured him into the deal, sight unseen. Coming face-to-face with his new acquisition was, however, another story. Somehow the international contracts could not convey the kudzu as thick as tar, the mean snarls of weeds, and the wild trees rudely poking through once stately boxwood parterres.

But this is truly a fairy tale. And Prince Fugger, as he's called, is something of a visionary. Why not

bring back the gardens, he decided. It sounded good—except for an old Cherokee Indian curse on the land.

"I could see the headlines:

'Cursed Property Bought by German Prince,' " he grins. "We called the nearest Cherokee chief and volunteered a donation to the tribe if they'd remove the curse [reportedly fixed on the property when Barnsley built on Indian land]. They sent two medicine men down with tobacco and feathers in a briefcase.

"After their ritual, they told us the house should be harmonized now—a hawk would give us a signal. And that very afternoon, a hawk circled the property. We had achieved our harmony."

See for yourself. Walk past the delicate herbaceous borders, and along creekbeds and paths that lace the quiet land. Indeed, Godfrey Barnsley, the Cherokee Indians, and finally, a daring German Prince have achieved harmony.

September

Dahlias

CHECKLIST FOR SEPTEMBER

ANNUALS

In Florida, you may sow seeds of bachelor's-button, sweet peas, Shirley poppies, and other winter annuals in the garden later this month. Plants will grow through winter and bloom in spring in North Florida, and earlier in South Florida. Gardeners from the North who enjoyed lupines and delphiniums can grow them in Florida as winter annuals, pulling them up after they bloom. Soak the seeds overnight before planting. They will take three to four weeks to germinate. Support tall plants with a stake or wire frame to prevent them from falling over.

BULBS

Buy spring-flowering bulbs now while the selection at your garden center is best. Or order from a catalog as soon as possible to ensure receiving bulbs in plenty of time for planting. Choose the largest bulbs available for each selection. At the garden center, avoid bulbs that are soft or molded, but don't worry if the papery covering is loose. It should not affect flowering. Store bulbs in a cool basement or by themselves in the vegetable compartment of your refrigerator until you are ready to plant.

COLUMBINE

In Texas, Texas Gold Columbine (*Aquilegia chrysantha*) should be available this fall as container plants in nurseries that offer perennials. Plant them now in shady areas, such as under deciduous trees; water regularly, and apply mulch. Bright-yellow flowers with long spurs appear in May atop 2-foot-high mounds of blue-gray, evergreen foliage.

COMPOSTING

The American Horticultural Society (AHS) sponsors the National Home Compost Park, the largest demonstration of home composting methods in the country. For those not planning a visit to their River Farm headquarters, just outside Washington, D.C., they offer Compost Factsheets to explain composting methods, misconceptions, and equipment sources. To receive the factsheet, send a self-addressed, stamped, business-size envelope to Compost Sources, AHS National Home Compost Park, 7931 East Boulevard Drive, Alexandria, Virginia 22308.

FALL WEBWORMS

The unsightly webs caused by leaf-eating caterpillars are showing up in pecan, persimmon, mulberry, and other trees. Use a pole pruner to cut off branches with new webs, or spray webs with an insecticide, such as malathion or carbaryl. Include a few drops of a mild liquid detergent in the solution to help the spray penetrate the web.

FLOWERS

In Texas, sow seeds of wildflowers and spring-blooming annuals, such as snapdragons, sweet alyssum, and calendulas, now. If you're growing bluebonnets, try some of the new white or pink selections.

GARDEN MUMS

In Texas, plant mums in masses of the same color in beds or containers for a dramatic effect. After blooming, cut them back severely (down to about 6 inches high) for repeat blooms in spring. South of Waco, pinch new growth occasionally in January and February to encourage full plants and lots of flowers.

HOUSEPLANTS

If your foliage plants have spent the summer on a porch or in the garden, get them ready to come indoors. Prune plants that have grown too large for indoors. Check carefully for insects; even though you may not see a problem, small populations of pests can become large ones quickly. Consider spraying the foliage and stems with horticultural oil before bringing your plants into the house.

LAWNS

This is a good time to plant or patch fescue and bluegrass lawns. If areas are bare, loosen the compacted soil, and rake it smooth and level before sowing seeds. If you are starting over, consider planting one of the new dwarf fescues, such as Taurus, Bonsai, and Rebel, Jr. They don't grow as tall or as fast as Kentucky 31, so you won't have to mow as often. In Texas, fertilize Bermuda, St. Augustine, and other warm-season lawns a final time with a 15-5-10 or similar-analysis fertilizer. After mid-month, sow fescue or ryegrass seed. Perennial ryegrass requires less mowing and is more cold tolerant than annual ryegrass. Do not scalp the lawn before overseeding.

LETTUCE

Clear a sunny spot for a fall salad garden. Spread a 2-inch layer of compost or other rotted organic material over the bed and turn it in, loosening the soil as you work. Smooth the soil with a rake, and sow seeds of leaf lettuce directly into the garden where you want them to grow. Water gently with a fine mist. As they germinate, thin  overcrowded seedlings. In hot areas, shade the soil with an old window screen propped on bricks to speed germination.

MEXICAN BUSH SAGE

This tender perennial is showing spikes of fuzzy blooms. To preserve stems for dried arrangements, cut, strip the leaves, and hang them upside down in a dry, well-ventilated location. Then use with dried grasses and pods in a winter arrangement. You can also strip the dried flowers from the stems for potpourri. Mexi-

can bush sage is perennial in Central and South Texas; it's marginally cold hardy in North Texas. Heavy mulching can protect the plant from hard freezes.

PINE STRAW

For a few weeks you'll notice that the pine straw has begun to fall but leaves have not. This is prime time to rake clean pine straw for mulching. Set it aside, and cover with a tarp. Then let the leaves fall. After the trees are bare, put a fresh layer of pine straw on top of the leaves in your beds for a tidy appearance in winter and spring.

ROSES

Roses will flush with blooms again before it gets cold if you cut off all the hips and spent blossoms. Fertilize with a slow-release rose food, and continue spraying plants with Funginex to control black spot and powdery mildew. Also be on the lookout for mites during the upcoming dry season. You can control them with insecticidal soap. In Texas, it's not too late to prune hybrid tea and other everblooming roses back about one-

third, but do it early in the month. At about the same time, apply a 5-10-5 fertilizer for repeat blooms this fall; watch for aphids on new growth, and treat with insecticidal soap or blasts of water from your garden hose.

SPIDER MITES

These tiny, insectlike creatures can become problems on marigolds, junipers, and other susceptible plants. The mites' tiny mouthparts leave pinpoint-size spots every place they feed. Treat infested plants with insecticidal soap or Kelthane, following label directions, or wash the foliage with a strong jet of water.

TREES AND SHRUBS

In Texas, planting container-grown trees and shrubs from now through fall gives them time to become established before cold weather. Keep newly planted specimens watered and mulched to protect them from drying out or freezing.

VEGETABLES

Label the plants in your fall and winter vegetable garden when you set them out to make it easy to note which do best. Transplants usually come with labels, or you can make your own from wooden ice-cream sticks. Keeping garden notes in a simple ring binder will help you compare one year to another, and also keep you from making the same mistake twice. In Texas, sow seeds of cool-weather leafy vegetables, such as lettuce, chard, spinach, turnip greens, radishes, Tokyo Cross white turnip, and Chinese cabbage. Try direct seeding onions now for harvesting next spring; Buffalo, Sweet Winter, Texas Grano 438, and Texas 1015 are good choices.

WATERING

To conserve moisture during dry spells, mulch flowerbeds, shrubs, and the vegetable garden. A layer of organic mulch 2 to 3 inches thick also keeps down weeds. Popular organic mulches include pine straw and pine bark. Cypress mulch is very popular, but you should probably avoid it: In some places, stands of native trees are being ground up solely for mulch.

September Notes

To Do:
- Replace summer annuals with cool-weather annuals, such as pansies
- Build compost bin for autumn leaves
- Spray shrubs with fungicide after fall growth is complete
- Apply pre-emergence weed killer to lawn to control annual bluegrass
- Sow seed of cool-weather grasses
- Fertilize cool-weather lawns
- Sod warm-weather lawns

To Plant:
- Cool-weather annuals and vegetables
- Spring bulbs
- Perennials

To Purchase:
- Spring bulbs
- Annual and vegetable transplants
- Grass seed and sod
- Lawn fertilizer
- Pre-emergence weed killer

_____

_____

_____

_____

TIP OF THE MONTH

An excellent way to rid the garden of mealybugs is to place a few halves of white potatoes, preferably ones with sprouts, in the area of infested plants. The mealybugs will transfer to the potatoes. After the insects accumulate, kill them by dropping the potato pieces into a bucket filled with water and bleach. Then set out more potatoes. _Mrs. Del De Mage_
Magnolia, Mississippi

Natural Velvet

BY MARK G. STITH / PHOTOGRAPHY VAN CHAPLIN

Moss isn't something most of us encourage. Maybe if we were to see a few gardens where it is welcome, we'd see it in a different light.

The soft, green glow from Larry and Karin Guzy's moss-covered backyard could convert even the hardest heart. Yes, the Guzys were like most of us. They were conditioned to think that 1) moss is bad, 2) so you have to get rid of it, 3) even if it comes back, 4) which it probably will.

Those last two items convinced the Guzys to go with the flow, rather than fight an uphill battle. A large area of their backyard in Marietta, Georgia, was like many in established neighborhoods in the South—good-sized shade trees, lots of weeds, and some moss. But instead of trying to force the issue, they got the message. "We figured, 'Why not cooperate with what Mother Nature wanted?'" Karin recalls. "I knew the Japanese had grown beautiful moss gardens, so I figured we could do it.

"We really didn't intend for it to be so large," Karin laughs. "We just wanted it to grow around the tree roots. But then it looked so beautiful and we found there were so many different kinds, so we just let it go." Besides hand-pulling weeds in spring, the Guzys do very little maintenance on their moss garden. They will occasionally use a weak (¼ strength) solution of Roundup to control problem areas. However, ferns, hostas, and other shade-loving plants are encouraged. Watering hasn't been a problem, either. "We do have an irrigation system back there, but frankly the mosses don't need it," Karin notes.

IN PLACE OF A POND

Perhaps moss wouldn't be so maligned if people saw the pool-like oasis of green that beckons from this backyard in an old Atlanta neighborhood. The 12- x 30-foot oval patch used to be a long-neglected, leaf- and sediment-filled garden pond that the current owners discovered when they moved into the house several years ago. In fact, the whole area was totally covered with leaves.

For help in reclaiming and redesigning the backyard, the owners turned to Atlanta garden designers Jimmy and Becky Stewart. As part of their planting plan, the Stewarts suggested a moss garden where the pool

had been. The client's reaction was typical, but not negative. "I never even knew about moss gardens," she says. So the Stewarts recommended the services of Lynne Randolph and Kipp McIntyre of Mostly Moss, a moss design and consultation company. "We came in, hand tilled the area, added some gravel, and planted a 3- x 12-foot 'mother garden' where the old pond used to be," McIntyre remembers. The mother garden consisted of brownie-sized plugs of 10 different types of mosses. In addition, shredded moss was added to the area. "Even a single cell can give rise to a moss plant," he adds. As the moss took hold, established areas were swept vigorously to spread small pieces out until the entire area filled in. The owners' new "carpet" now serves as a woodsy retreat with the addition of a garden swing.

MOSSES ACROSS THE MISSISSIPPI?

Don't think that moss is just an east-of-the-Mississippi phenomenon. Dallas landscape architect Rosa Finsley is enthusiastic about using mosses whenever she can. "It's wonderful in the wintertime," Finsley says. "And it really seems to like it here." However, the heat and drought of summer can be a problem, she adds. "One thing that really helps quite a bit in the summer is to have the sprinkler system come on in the morning

for about one to two minutes." If you don't have a sprinkler system, wetting it down with a garden hose works well, too. In addition, to avoid "burning" it, Finsley uses slow-release organic fertilizers in areas where moss has been planted. She's also careful to put moss where she knows it has a chance to spread thick and lush, like it should. Shaded areas protected from strong, drying winds

are good places. "We'll even fertilize rocks, too, because moss will grow on them," she adds. However, as we all know, rolling *stones* will gather no moss.   ◇

Dappled sunlight bathes an oasis of green in this Atlanta garden. The area was once an oval garden pond that was filled in; moss was allowed to take over the spot.

Ferns and other native plants are perfect specimens to encourage in or add to a moss garden.

TIPS ON GROWING MOSS

■ To collect moss, or get it to spread, dig up brownie-sized squares and place them in a moist, well-tilled spot. Fall and spring are ideal times to collect moss.

■ Rosa Finsley makes a "moss milk shake" by taking patches of moss (especially when they are laden with spores), tossing them in a blender, and adding buttermilk. The resulting "shake" is then dabbed on stones, bare soil, or anywhere else she wants to promote moss growth.

■ To encourage mosses, Kipp McIntyre recommends an acidic liquid fertilizer, such as Miracid. Hand-pulling weeds isn't that diffi-

cult, Karin Guzy adds, because they root in the moss, not the soil.

■ Moss can't take a lot of wear and tear. And birds and squirrels love to dig up chunks of it in search of food. Some moss gardeners use plastic bird netting, like the kind you buy to keep birds out of fruit trees, to keep the critters out.

■ Mosses occur naturally throughout the South, except in the grassy plains areas of Texas and Oklahoma.

■ If you'd like a mail-order source of mosses, we know of only one: WE-DU Nurseries, Route 5, Box 724, Marion, North Carolina 28752. Their catalog is $2 and includes seven different kinds of mosses.

Dazzling Dahlias

BY MARK G. STITH / PHOTOGRAPHY VAN CHAPLIN

"Listen, y'all need to come on out here!" Richard Strong said over the phone. I detected a real sense of urgency in his voice. "I've got a lot of blooms now and will have a lot more next week!"

What Richard was so insistent about were his dahlias—a backyard

Lions International

full of them, and they were blooming to beat the band. I'm not sure what persuaded us the most to pay him a visit, but one major factor was certainly his passion for his plants. Frankly, if they were even half as good as he said they were, we'd come away with some terrific pictures.

We showed up at his house in Birmingham late one September afternoon. From the front, the house looked nice, neat, and normal—about what you'd expect in any well-kept neighborhood. Sauntering around to the backyard, we were met by Richard and his 6- to 7-foot-tall friends. Namely, cornfield-like rows of plants

Bill Holmberg

topped off with blazing, brilliant dahlia blooms, glowing like a hundred setting suns.

Richard gave us the grand tour, and we were introduced to nearly every blossom in the bunch. He had most of them in two large, raised beds—one for his 102 dahlias, the other for his wife's 80 plants. "I've been growing them since 1968," he explained. And it was easy to see he was doing something right. Here are some tips Richard shared with us that day:

■ Dahlias need rich, deeply tilled soil (about 12 inches deep) and at least half a day's sun (preferably morning) to perform well. Building raised beds

Richard Strong ties dahlia stalks to 6-foot steel bars to keep them from breaking during storms.

(about 6 inches high) with soil rich in organic matter is a good alternative to tilling up heavy clay soils. Slightly acid (pH about 6.5) soil is best.

■ Tubers are planted when the weather warms up, usually from mid-May to mid-June. At planting time, 5- to 6-foot-tall stakes should be set in each planting hole to provide protection from storms and wind. Richard uses 6-foot-long, ½-inch steel bars to provide strong support for his plants.

David George

■ Set the tubers about 3 to 4 inches deep, with the sprout at the soil surface or barely covered. Depending on the type, dahlias can be planted 2 to 3 feet apart. Fertilizing at planting time is optional—a small handful of super-phosphate, 6-12-12, or Holland Bulb Booster worked into the soil, several inches below the tuber. Reapply fertilizer monthly. Richard also recom-

My Lynda

mends spraying the foliage every 10 days with a water-soluble fertilizer (15-30-15). Stake the plants as they grow, and mulch to conserve moisture and reduce weed problems.

■ Dahlias need lots of water. If rainfall is insufficient, give them a good soaking once a week. Make sure the soil drains well, however.

■ A variety of insects and diseases can plague dahlias. Spider mites, cabbage loopers, and spotted cucumber beetles are among the more frequent pests. Mildew can be a problem in mid-August; sulfur or karathane can provide good control.

■ If you're growing dahlias specifically for cut flowers, you'll get more blooms by pinching out the top growth, much as you would mums. You'll get compact plants with more blooms. Also, pompon and miniature dahlias are better to use for mass displays in flowerbeds.

■ After the first hard frost, cut the stalks about 6 inches above the ground. Dig up the tubers carefully, using a spade or garden fork. Some growers don't clean the dirt off the tubers, storing them upside down in a basement or crawlspace. Others wash the tubers, coat them with a fungicide, and allow them to dry before storing in a cool (40 to 50 de-

Shirley Alliance

grees), dry area. Be sure to label the dahlias before storing. Mist the tubers periodically over the winter if they appear dry.

Dahlias are available in an astonishing array of colors, sizes, and forms. To get a list of mail-order sources, send a self-addressed, business-size, stamped envelope to Dahlia, *Southern Living*, P.O. Box 830119, Birmingham, Alabama 35283.

Alpine Jewel

September and early October are when dahlia growers "strut their stuff" at shows, county fairs, and exhibitions across the South. It's a good way to get an up-close look at the flowers and some expert advice from growers. The American Dahlia Society will have a free, public exhibit of dahlias at Brookwood Village mall (Shades Creek Parkway), in Birmingham, October 2-3.

Make a Succulent Wreath In an Hour

This succulent wreath has been growing in a sunny location for six months.
The glass plate underneath protects the tabletop.

Succulents are compact plants that have evolved in arid environments and taken on unusual forms. Their fleshy leaves act as tiny reservoirs of water, enabling them to survive periods of drought in their native surroundings.

By filling a wire wreath form with sphagnum moss and then inserting some of these exotic plants, you can create an unusual decoration for your tabletop.

The wreath shown here is planted with hen-and-chickens, which is a succulent with pointed leaves that grow in clusters resembling rosettes. These plants don't ever become very large but will multiply over time and eventually cover the sphagnum moss completely.

Following the steps outlined in the photographs, you can assemble this wreath in less than an hour. Place your completed succulent wreath on a waterproof plate in a warm room where it will receive full sunlight. You'll enjoy watching the plants fill out the wreath as they grow. Only water the plants when the moss has dried thoroughly, and water less frequently in winter.

MATERIALS

- Wire wreath form that separates into two halves

- Liquid plant fertilizer

- Sphagnum moss

- Roll of fishing line

- Several 4-inch containers of hen-and-chickens

- Screwdriver

Step 1: *Mix liquid fertilizer with water according to label directions; soak sphagnum moss in the fertilizer mixture, and squeeze out excess moisture. Separate wreath form into two halves; generously fill one half of form with sphagnum moss.*

Step 2: *Place the second half of the wreath form over the one that's filled with moss; then wrap fishing line around the wreath to hold halves together.*

Step 3: *Remove individual succulents from plastic containers, retaining as much of the root system as possible. Pierce the moss with a screwdriver, and insert the roots of the small plants.*

Step 4: *Continue adding plants until all of them are in place. Tuck in additional pieces of moss to cover the wire frame.*

From Simple to Simply

Before

New landscaping and major structural changes transformed this unassuming two-story house into a showplace.

Spectacular

Linda, Bob, and Beth Bible

ob and Linda Bible found a house in a nearly perfect location—Pawleys Island, South Carolina. The site joins a canal that leads to the Intracoastal Waterway, making it convenient to dock their boat just steps away from the house. Though the Bibles were taken with the beauty and privacy of the setting, the house lacked architectural character and amenities.

Realizing that the location could not easily be surpassed, the Bibles bought the house and undertook an extensive remodeling and landscaping project. Its good features became a point of departure for creating virtually a brand new structure, using the shell of the old house as a base. A new landscape plan helped

BY JULIA H. THOMASON / PHOTOGRAPHY VAN CHAPLIN

On the first floor, pediments top each of the windows.

Copper gutters, downspouts, and flashing accent the house.

Handrails were painted dark green for visual emphasis.

to integrate the house with its surroundings.

Originally the house was a simple, two-story box, two rooms deep, with doors and windows symmetrically arranged. These same characteristics are seen in 18th-century and early 19th-century Georgian houses and became the genesis of the elegant new structure. As Linda explains, "We knew we could capitalize on the basic Georgian style of the house and make it even better."

The remodeling, a collaborative effort with creative input from many sources, became a process of generally upgrading the house. Every detail of design and construction received close attention. Lindsey Bible, Bob's brother, managed the construction and also helped with the numerous design decisions.

Architect Steve Goggans of Pawleys Island designed the surround for the front door, specifying fluted pilasters that support a deep and decorative pediment. In keeping with the Georgian style, a center gable highlights the roofline; the fanlight over the front door repeats the style of the center gable. Pediments decorate the first-floor windows, and dentils add detail at the cornices. The Bibles chose construction materials of the highest quality; for example, copper flashing accents cornice returns, and heavy balusters give a substantial look to railings.

Reworking the way cars reached the house and entered the garage

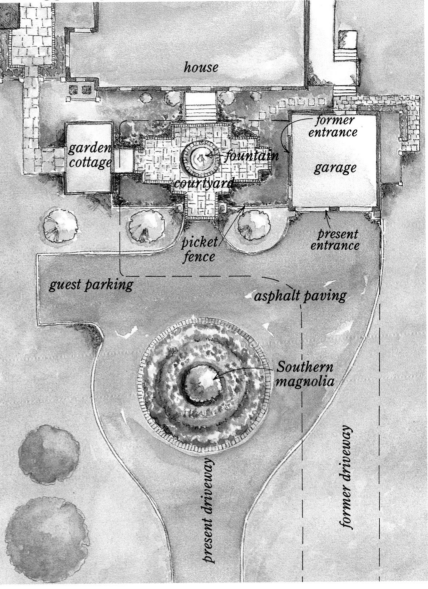

(Left) Paved in stamped concrete and edged in brick, the courtyard creates a welcoming garden space near the front door. Plantings are changed seasonally.

house

former entrance

garden cottage

fountain

garage

courtyard

picket fence

present entrance

guest parking

asphalt paving

Southern magnolia

present driveway

former driveway

became as important as architectural renovations. Both Goggans and Charleston landscape architect Robert C. Chesnut felt that bringing the drive straight in from the street would provide a more attractive approach to the house. Now, a large magnolia is the centerpiece on arrival. The tree, underplanted with annuals and perennials for seasonal color, blocks direct views of the house, lending a sense of seclusion. The placement of the magnolia tree affects views from the house as well. From the front door, the Bibles see lush greenery, not cars passing on the street.

Beginning with that reorientation, Chesnut implemented a complete plan that included a variety of land-scape renovations. To give the home a garden foreground, he developed a lush courtyard in the space between the house and new drive.

On one side of the courtyard, the garage doors were repositioned so that cars entered at right angles to the house, rather than parallel to it.

To enclose the other side of the garden, opposite the garage, Chesnut suggested building a small cottage, including storage areas and a bathroom. "They needed a storage house," he notes. "So I suggested making it a focal point out front instead of putting it in the backyard." On the exterior, narrow panels of trelliswork support thriving plantings of evergreen wisteria. The resulting U-shaped area forms a pleasant courtyard approach to the front door. The courtyard was paved in stamped concrete and is separated from the driveway by a new picket fence. With the addition of a fountain and inviting garden furniture, this area has become a convenient and enjoyable outdoor living space.

At each side of the house, new screened porches become natural extensions of rooms on the first level. The porches are L-shaped and wrap around to the back of the house. Curving steps lead to a pathway down to the boat dock and canal.

True, the setting makes the Bibles' residence distinctive and distinguished. But it's delightfully obvious that they now have a home that's as beautiful as its surroundings. ◇

October

Ornamental grasses and Autumn Joy sedum

CHECKLIST FOR OCTOBER

BANANAS

In North Florida, cut stalks back to about a foot to enjoy their foliage again next year. Cover stumps with a thick mound of pine straw until spring. Bananas take two years to fruit, so Central Florida gardeners who wish to harvest bunches can take their chances and leave plants intact.

BULBS

Throughout Florida, set out amaryllis bulbs now for blossoms next spring; plant bulb tip even with the soil surface. Plant Aztec lilies and gladioli 3 inches deep. Massing bulbs of the same color creates a more pleasing display.

CILANTRO

For a fresh supply of this flavorful herb, gardeners in the Middle, Lower, and Coastal South can sow seeds directly into the garden this month. Be careful not to cut more than half the leaves on a plant at one time during the winter. In spring, you'll probably have more than you can use.

COLEUS

Root your favorite coleus in water to enjoy indoors (and overwinter them in frost-prone areas). Just clip off 6-  to 8-inch stems, strip the lower third of leaves, and stick in a water-filled container. You'll get a healthy mass of roots in two to three weeks; then plant in pots. Place the container in a sunny window, and keep the soil evenly moist.

FALL CLEANUP

When you are cutting back and cleaning up the remains of summer gardens, leave some dead stalks in unobtrusive locations. The seeds or berries will attract birds to your winter garden.

FALL COLOR

For instant flowers in Florida, start off with transplants instead of seeds. Pansies, petunias, and dianthus are colorful October additions suitable for most of the state. Plant snapdragons in North and Central Florida. From Ocala northward, gardeners can also include foxglove. South of Lakeland, plant sweet alyssum and impatiens. In Texas, set out snapdragons, flowering kale and cabbage, alyssum, wallflowers, English daisies, California and Iceland poppies, sweet William, and calendula now. Set out seed or transplants of bluebonnets. In addition to the traditional blue, try selections such as Abbott Pink or Alba, which has white flowers.

FLOWERS

Sow seeds of poppies, larkspur, johnny-jump-up, sweet peas, forget-me-nots, and wallflowers. Scatter seeds over a well-prepared bed and rake to cover lightly. You should see seedlings this fall. They will overwinter and make vigorous plants in the spring.

HERBS

In Florida, trim back herbs, and apply a fish emulsion fertilizer. Mix 3 tablespoons to a gallon of water; apply mixture every 2 to 3 weeks for the next several months. In Texas, sow seeds or set out transplants of dill, parsley, thyme, and garlic now. Good selections of garlic for the state include Texas White and Mexican Pink; set individual cloves (with the large end down) about an inch deep and 3 to 4 inches apart.

LAWNS

Sow seed of cool-season grasses, such as fescue, in the Lower and Middle South. For best results, use one of the newer, turf-type selections, such as Rebel II. Overseed dormant warm-season grasses with annual or perennial rye for a green lawn all winter.

LEAVES

Leaves are falling, and this is a good time to start composting. It's as simple as raking them into a ring of wire fencing or a bin constructed of wood or concrete. They will compost faster if you grind them up with a bagging mower or put them through a leaf shredder. Also, add a few shovelfuls of soil to the pile as you make it.

PALMS

Florida soils are usually deficient in magnesium, causing palm and sago fronds to yellow. Scatter a generous handful of Epsom salts on the ground beneath each plant. The salts won't turn yellowed fronds green again, but will remedy the problem in new growth. Repeat the procedure next month.

PANSIES

Sprinkle a teaspoon of slow-release fertilizer, such as Osmocote, Holland Bulb Booster, or cottonseed meal, around each pansy at planting time. Two additional feedings of water-soluble 20-20-20 in December and January will help pansies growing in poor or sandy soil. Don't mulch pansies until after a hard freeze in fall. For best results, wait until November to plant pansies in South Texas and along the coast.

PERENNIALS

Divide and replant overgrown perennials, such as hostas, Shasta daisies, and daylilies now. Lift plants carefully out of the ground using a round-

pointed shovel or digging fork. You may be able to pull apart individual plants by hand; use a sharp knife or the blade of a shovel to divide thick clumps. In Florida, divide and replant overgrown perennials, such as African iris, Shasta daisies, hostas, and daylilies now.

PUMPKINS

Store your holiday pumpkins out of direct sun, and don't carve jack-o'-lanterns until a few hours before trick-or-treaters arrive. Cut pumpkins will shrivel and rot in the October heat.

RADICCHIO

Consider planting radicchio this fall; it's an attractive, leafy vegetable that adds zip to ordinary salads. Good selections to try include Guilio and Red Verona. Seeds are available from The Cook's Garden, P.O. Box 535, Londonderry, VT 05148.

SEEDS

You can save your own seeds from many garden flowers. Seeds that are easy to save include four-o'clocks, cosmos, hollyhocks, nicotiana, and black-eyed Susans. Put seeds in an envelope, label with name and date, and store in an airtight container in a dry location.

SHRUBS

This is a good time to transplant shrubs that may have overgrown their space and need to be relocated. In addition, newly purchased shrubs will benefit from being planted in fall and will establish roots before springtime. This is a great month for planting shrubs in Florida, but don't set them too deep. Form a small mound of soil on the bottom of each hole to support the shrub. To help reduce settling, water the soil while filling around the roots.

SPRING BULBS

Gardeners in the Upper South can plant all types of spring-flowering bulbs this month. In the rest of the South, delay planting until nights begin to cool. In the Coastal South, place tulips and hyacinths by themselves in your refrigerator vegetable bin for six weeks before planting. From San Antonio and Dallas south, place tulips and hyacinths by themselves in your refrigerator vegetable bin for six weeks before planting.

STRAWBERRIES

Set out strawberries in South Texas. Space plants in double rows 12 inches apart in well-prepared beds 42 inches wide. Good selections include Tioga, Douglas, and Sequoia. Plants established now will yield fruit next spring. Gardeners in the rest of the state should wait until early next year to set out plants.

SWEET POTATOES

If an early frost catches your sweet potatoes before you have a chance to dig them up, go out and clip the vines off at ground level to prevent the potatoes from spoiling. Then you'll have about a week or two to bring them in.

TREES

Fall is the best time to add trees to your landscape. Newly planted trees will establish roots before springtime. In Florida, trees native to the state may require less water and spraying. The following natives thrive throughout Florida: Southern magnolia, Southern red cedar (*Juniperus silicicola*), live oak, sabal palm, and wax myrtle.

VEGETABLES

Throughout Florida, plant radish, spinach, and Swiss chard seeds. Central and South Florida gardeners may plant carrots, brussels sprouts, and beets. In South Florida, include endive, lettuce, parsley, and celery. In Texas, plant beets, Chinese cabbage, carrots, collards, lettuce, mustard, spinach, radish, and turnips now. Sow seeds of lettuce and other salad greens at two-week intervals to ensure a steady supply.

October Notes

To Do:
- Clean plant debris from vegetable and flower gardens
- Rake and compost leaves
- Dig and store tender bulbs
- Divide perennials
- Fertilize cool-weather lawns
- Transplant trees and shrubs
- Bring tender potted plants indoors
- Overseed warm-weather lawns with annual or perennial rye

To Plant:
- In the Upper South, spring bulbs
- Trees, shrubs, perennials
- Cool-weather annuals

To Purchase:
- Spring bulbs
- Lawn fertilizer
- Compost bin for leaves
- Cool-weather annuals
- Potted mums
- Annual or perennial ryegrass seed

_____

_____

_____

_____

TIP OF THE MONTH

Before frost kills my marigolds, I cut some stems to root for winter blooms. It's easy. Just place the cuttings in a vase filled with water. In two weeks there should be a profusion of roots. Then you can pot the rooted cuttings in regular potting soil. If you remove spent flowers, your plants should bloom all winter. *Bobbie Mae Cooley Bowen, Illinois*

A Border For *All* *Seasons*

BY MARK G. STITH / PHOTOGRAPHY VAN CHAPLIN

A little land,
a little labor,
and a lot of creativity
can do wonders.
This flower garden
bears beautiful witness
all year.

Fall Border

1. goldenrod
2. sedum Autumn Joy
3. Mexican bush sage
   (*Salvia leucantha*)
4. chrysanthemum Yellowjacket
5. narrowleaf zinnia
6. lamb's-ears
7. chrysanthemum Poncho
8. chrysanthemum Debonair
9. begonia

Spring Border

1. snowball viburnum
2. Siberian iris White Swirl
3. bearded iris Blue Pacific
4. Shasta daisy Alaska
5. petunia Primetime Pink
6. pansies Majestic Giant Purple
7. chives
8. bearded iris (Ice Blue)

*F*all is often the forgotten season when it comes to gardening. Maybe it's the fact that school starts up, football season kicks off, and it's the last chance for a vacation before cold weather prevails.

The fact is, planning and planting a garden in fall can yield rewards for years to come. Take, for example, this flower border in Trussville, Alabama. Its blooms parade for three seasons, from spring through summer and into fall. The beauty of this flower border is more than stem deep, however. Here are a few lessons the creator and caretaker of this garden shared with us, along with some other tips.

Start with good soil and a sunny spot. A familiar, new-yard dilemma faced this gardener and his family when they moved into their new home four years ago: The topsoil had moved out. And the hard-packed, rock-filled red clay the bulldozers left was a Southern gardener's nightmare.

As an experienced grower, the owner knew that getting the soil "right" was the first order of business. After picking out a sunny spot about 12 feet wide and 50 feet long for the new flower border, he began amending the clay (after the fence was installed). The recipe? First, do something to help the border-to-be drain better. He put down about 3 inches of coarse builder's sand, rented a heavy-duty tiller, and worked the sand in; then he tilled it every weekend, for about three weeks, with a small tiller. To enrich the soil, he brought in several bales of Pro-Mix (a professional potting media commonly available) and tilled them in as well. The whole bed was watered down, and more sand was added and worked in. Now the real fun began—deciding on the plants and their placement.

Planning before planting. The owner really enjoys using fresh flowers in the house. As a result, most of the plants were chosen because they produce flowers suitable for cutting.

What's more, careful selection of plants that bloom at different times of the year ensure fresh flowers almost year-round. And although this garden has lots of flowering bulbs and perennials, there are woody ornamentals, such as snowball viburnum; a white-blooming flowering almond; a Nellie R. Stevens holly (used to anchor one end); and seasonal annuals and perennials.

Think small to tall. Notice in this border that the plants gradually rise in height from front to back. That's not due to trimming plants at a 45-degree angle. It's because careful attention was paid to each plant's ultimate height. Simply put, the taller plants went in the rear of the border, and the shorter ones up front.

Choose flowers for the season. All of us can conjure up colorful images of the seasons, and this gardener planned his flower garden to reflect the colors of the passing months. For example, the soft pastels of bearded iris and pure whites of other flowers are live giveaways that

Summer Border

1. tiger lilies
2. Oriental lilies
   Imperial Silver
3. coleus
4. Madagascar
   periwinkle
   Grape Cooler
5. wax begonia Gin
6. crepe myrtle
   Natchez

it's spring. Summer's garden is full of hot colors and some refreshingly cool ones. The fall garden is a study in orange, yellow, rust, and gold. Although not shown here, the winter border is interesting but quiet, too. That's when shapes and textures become dominant features.

Following the colors of the season doesn't mean you have to be predictable. For example, the hot-pink petunias in the spring border are a nice surprise, and planting marigolds in fall is a good example of using a classic summer annual in a surprisingly effective way.

Be brave with color. Bold sweeps and concentrated patches of the same plants, spaced the proper distance apart, are much more dramatic than a wimpy line of marigolds spaced several feet apart. Remember that pastels don't have the same impact-per-bloom that louder colors do, so you'll have to use more soft-colored flowers in order to get the same effect that red or yellow blooms would create.

Plant for the future. Almost all the perennials, spring bulbs, and woody ornamental plants in this garden were planted in fall. That gave them time for their roots to become established before new growth develops in spring. If you're a weekend gardener, be realistic about what you can get done during your limited time frame.

Containers in the border? Sure—look at the pleasing effect they have in the flowerbed shown here. It's a neat trick for putting color in an otherwise "dead" area, or adding a little surprise here and there. Large containers, especially, can provide a much-needed structural element in the midst of a soft-looking mass of foliage and flowers.

Annuals to the rescue. Easy-care annual flowers, such as marigolds and wax begonias, fill in the gaps between the showy perennials and provide unity. In addition, perennials used as annuals, including chrysanthemums and pansies that can be bought in season at garden centers,

really add to the show.

Use a backdrop. A wooden fence, hedge of tall evergreens, or wall can form an attractive, neutral backdrop. In this garden, a 6-foot-high wooden fence serves both functional and aesthetic purposes.

Upkeep and the real world. Holland Bulb Booster is used as a general fertilizer during the fall season. In addition, a shovelful of compost is dumped into the center of the Siberian iris and sedum each spring. Other than picking flowers and pulling a few weeds here and there, though, that's about all this gardener does—he doesn't even spray. The plants are not pampered by an irrigation system, but the hose and sprinkler will come out if rainfall is infrequent. Seasonal flowers are changed out, and the perennials are divided and shared with friends and neighbors, but upkeep is actually quite minimal. That's one of the joys of this garden: It just *looks* like someone gets out there every day to make it look that good. ◇

Splendor in the Grasses

Ornamental grasses envelop Karen Offutt and her dogs.

When Chip and Karen Offutt took stock of their garden five years ago, they weren't entirely happy. Although it boasted a beautiful setting in the rolling farmlands of northwest Baltimore County, it lacked a certain distinction. Then Karen met Jacqueline Gratz, whose Baltimore garden, featured in the July 1985 issue of *Southern Living,* showcases exotic, ornamental grasses.

Jacqueline suggested trying grasses, but Karen was uncertain, knowing little about them. And at the time, there wasn't a lot of information available. Fortunately, the country's foremost producer of ornamental grasses, Kurt Bluemel Nurseries, was located nearby in Baldwin, Maryland. So Karen paid a visit to see these plants firsthand. "That convinced me that grasses were something I wanted in my garden," she remembers.

Now, five years later, ornamental grasses sway gracefully in the breeze against a backdrop of fenced pasture and silos. As president of a local garden club, Karen gives tours of her garden and answers beginners' questions about grasses.

She feels grasses live up to their billing of being carefree plants that beautify the garden in summer, fall, and winter. They're not without faults, however. Perhaps the biggest problem is that some of them, such as switch grass (*Panicum virgatum*), Chinese pennisetum (*Pennisetum alopecuroides*), and maiden grass (*Miscanthus sinensis* Gracillimus), reseed readily. "You have to be very vigilant about getting rid of seedlings, because they take over," she warns. Moreover, seedlings often differ in appearance from their parent plant, so unless you remove them, you may

Karen enjoys the contrast between grasses and the red-flowering Autumn Joy sedum.

lose the look you originally wanted.

Grasses aren't fussy about soil, as long as the soil is well drained. Karen and Chip's original soil was a mixture of red clay and shale, so before planting they tilled in about 3 inches of cow manure to lighten and enrich it. Nowadays, about the only maintenance their grasses require is cutting the old foliage to the ground each February. They have yet to fertilize or divide them.

A garden dominated by summer- and fall-blooming grasses can look pretty blah in spring. So for early color, Karen grows lots of spring bulbs. As the grasses sprout in late spring, their elongating leaves hide the yellowing bulb foliage.

She also grows lots of perennials, such as Russian sage (*Perovskia atriplicifolia*), fern-leaf yarrow (*Achillea filipendulina*), and Autumn Joy sedum (*Sedum* x *spectabile* Autumn Joy), as companion plants. She particularly enjoys the sedum because "its nice, thick, succulent foliage contrasts with the very airy, stately looking grass."

Grasses aren't for every garden. "I'm sure you could put grasses in colonial settings, but I think they really look best with modern houses," she says. But for gardeners seeking to escape the usual azaleas and hollies bunched up against the house, ornamental grasses may be the perfect vehicle. "Grasses," she observes, "are a breath of fresh air in a vacuum of tradition."

Steve Bender

PHOTOGRAPHS: VAN CHAPLIN / GARDEN DESIGN: WOLFGANG OEHME, BALTIMORE

On a median lined with mature sugar maples, Nashville neighbors add an understory of young Yoshino cherries. (From left) Jessamine Jowers, Walter Jowers, Hannah Koonce, Suzy Newton, Steve Sirls.

Pitching In To Plant Trees

"This neighborhood is like one big extended family," states Walter Jowers, longtime resident of Nashville's historic Richland-West End section. "If one person has a good idea, it's easy to get a hundred people to support it."

Someone had a good idea at a meeting of the neighborhood association back in 1986. Instead of planting trees to beautify individual yards, why not plant trees throughout the neighborhood? Members quickly jumped on the bandwagon and embarked on an annual tree-planting program. To date, they've adorned their streets with more than 600 trees for a surprisingly modest cost.

Here's how the program works. Each September, Walter produces a special tree-planting edition of the quarterly neighborhood newsletter. This edition contains descriptions of various trees available, an order form, and advice on how to properly plant, site, and care for trees. All orders must be paid for in advance.

"Our list is a mixture of large, medium, and small trees, flowering and nonflowering," explains Walter. "Over the years, we've learned how to pick the right tree for the right site and which trees do well here and which ones die." The 1992 edition offered red maple, yellowwood, flowering dogwood, Kousa dogwood, Sargent crabapple, Yoshino cherry, red oak, and littleleaf linden.

After individual orders come in, the association's tree committee compiles them and places one large order with a Tennessee wholesale nursery. Residents benefit from wholesale prices as a result. For example, an 8-foot red maple costs only about $20. And if someone buys a tree for planting in a public space, such as a median, the association supplies a matching tree.

Trees arrive for planting in November. "We get about a dozen volunteers to unload the trees from the nursery truck," continues Walter. "We pile them onto pickup trucks and family automobiles and haul them around the neighborhood." Residents receive mulch for their trees. Volunteers even plant trees for elderly residents who can't do the planting themselves.

The association aims to plant approximately 80 trees every year to compensate for mature trees that either die or are declining. They derived this number by estimating the neighborhood's total tree planting spaces at 2,400, then divided this figure by 30, which is the average life span for an urban tree.

Walter sums up Richland-West End's fervor for trees this way: "This is an old neighborhood. Its mature, urban forest is part of what establishes a sense of place here—maybe even more than the houses. If we want to keep that atmosphere, we have to have mature, skyline trees.

"Planting trees is a good project for neighbors to do themselves," he continues. "It doesn't cost much and it's easy to do. Plus, the payoff is huge, because it'll be something your children can see."   *Steve Bender*

Letting the Breezes In

Walls and fences do a good job of closing things in—or out, depending on what side you're on. But in the sunny South, a solid wall or fence can also keep out a welcome guest—a refreshing breeze. Here are a couple of examples of how air was allowed to pass right through brick and iron (of course, with some modifications).

In Lexington, Kentucky, landscape. architect Bill Henkel had a design problem posed to him by homeowners Don and Laura Pruett. "The Pruetts wanted some privacy when they were out on their terrace," Henkel recalls. "I couldn't build on their property line, because a huge, historic red oak was right on it." So Henkel decided to set a 6-foot-high brick wall at an angle to the side property line. Because a solid wall against the terrace would have seemed a little claustrophobic, the wall was built in a "pierced" pattern.

This method of construction served several purposes. First, it let the owners see the rest of their garden, instead of a boring expanse of brick. Second, setting the wall at just the right angle screened the view of the neighbor's driveway. Third, it let more natural light into a tree-shaded area. And most importantly, the wall let air circulate, helping to cool off the shady brick terrace even more.

In Houston, landscape architects Richard Dawson and Lawrence Estes had a problem terrace to deal with. For beginners, the flagstone patio faced south. The terrace was already enclosed on two sides by the house. However, a small elm tree provided enough shelter from the afternoon sun to make it a good spot for sitting out. The terrace was right next to the driveway, so they wanted to provide a sense of enclosure and separation. But a solid wall was out of the question.

Instead, they designed an iron fence with brick columns. In doing so, Dawson and Estes created the separation of patio and driveway they thought the space needed. And the owners weren't deprived of a breeze, essential for outdoor living space.

Mark G. Stith

PHOTOGRAPH: SYLVIA MARTIN

This brick wall was built at an angle to avoid disturbing the roots of a giant red oak right on the property line. The middle area of the wall is "perforated," so breezes are allowed in.

PHOTOGRAPH: VAN CHAPLIN

A brick-columned iron fence separates the driveway (in the foreground) from a terrace on the other side. Using a solid wall would have enclosed the terrace on three sides, all but shutting it off from any air circulation.

A Drive of Distinction

Interior designer Sam Ewing wanted to make the most of every square inch of his Winter Park, Florida, lot. But because the parking area is behind his house, the narrow side yard had to serve as a driveway. City codes restricting the amount of impermeable surface area allowed on the lot posed an additional challenge.

Instead of the typical concrete driveway, Ewing used Turfblock to build his drive. An open-celled concrete paver system, Turfblock is laid directly on level soil. Ewing originally filled all the cells with sand to help hold the pavers in place.

Then garden designers Ken Hall and Rick Engle improved on the idea. They planted dwarf mondo grass (*Ophiopogon japonicus* Nana) in the sections of drive safe from tire traffic. Including this dark-green ground cover in the center strip and along the borders gives the drive a garden appearance.

Because water percolates through the mondo grass, the drive complies with city codes. Hall and Engle planted a row of crepe myrtles along the drive's edge; water draining through the driveway is available for the tree roots. Judicious pruning keeps the trunks free of lower limbs that might interfere with cars and

PHOTOGRAPHS: SYLVIA MARTIN

This strategic planting of dwarf mondo grass adds green to the drive while avoiding damage from tires.

creates a canopy of green foliage and bright summertime blossoms.

Hall and Engle left two wide strips of driveway unplanted to accommodate tires. To complement the contemporary architecture of Sam's home, they created a special treatment: Each cell of the driving surface was filled with colored concrete.

"Grandma's gravy ladle was perfect for that," says Hall. A sprinkle of small rock salt tossed on the concrete's surface before curing gave it a textured surface. Though time consuming, the concrete treatment is lasting and virtually weedproof. Another option is to forego the concrete and fill the cells with fine gravel, but this must be replenished periodically.

The Turfblock drive reflects less light than an expanse of white concrete would, so heat and glare are reduced. Attractive and durable, this driveway is an integral part of the landscape.   *Jo Kellum*

It's easy to create geometric patterns using Turfblock and ground cover.

COLORED CONCRETE

You can make small quantities of colored concrete yourself. Mix powdered concrete dye with quick-mix concrete (available in bags) to achieve the desired color contrast between Turfblock and the filled cells.

Colorful Crotons

PHOTOGRAPHS: VAN CHAPLIN

The leathery leaves of croton are notable for their colors, which are as rich and varied as those in a flower arrangement. Young leaves are green, but as the foliage matures it may become bronze, yellow, red, pink, or white. Individual croton leaves are often multicolored and may be long and narrow, curly, elliptical, or oak-leaf shaped. A variety of patterns, such as stripes and spots, occurs naturally and adds even greater interest to these plants. In their native South Pacific Islands, crotons can grow up to 10 feet tall.

For a bright display, mass small plants having various leaf shapes, sizes, and colors in a basket or planter. Choose a container that is deep enough to hide the pots. Select one croton that is slightly taller than the others, and place it at the rear of the arrangement to serve as a focal point; then surround the tall plant with smaller ones. Place the arrangement at table height, where its interesting variety is easily observable. Transplant small plants to larger containers as they grow.

You'll enjoy placing large crotons where you need an accent of color. Crotons need good light in order to maintain their vivid colors. Be sure to avoid touching the white sap of this plant; it can be irritating to the skin.

Julia H. Thomason

CROTONS AT A GLANCE

These tropical plants prefer a humid atmosphere and should not be placed in drafts.

■ **Size:** Height usually reaches 3 feet, but sometimes taller.
■ **Light:** Four to five hours of bright sunlight per day.
■ **Feeding:** Feed with standard liquid fertilizer every four weeks from March through July.
■ **Method of propagation:** Stem cuttings taken in spring.

(**Top**) *This croton adds cheerful color to a brightly lit family room.*
(**Left**) *Crotons are highly ornamental houseplants, with great variety in leaf shape, color, and pattern.*

Patrinia for Fall

Patrinia has many admirers, and they are growing in number as this sturdy, fall-flowering perennial shows up in more Southern gardens. And this is its best season, when summer gives way to fall and patrinia comes into bloom.

Although certainly not new in Korea (where it grows wild), patrinia is fairly new to gardeners here who enjoy its yellow or billowy white blooms. Introduced widely several years ago by the National Arboretum, patrinia has proved to be excellent in perennial borders throughout the South.

There are two species that bloom in the fall: *Patrinia villosa* and *P. scabiosifolia*. Both thrive in full sun

(**Left**) Patrinia villosa *bursts into a cloud of white flowers about the same time that asters bloom.* (**Above, left**) *Graceful yellow flowers are showy in the fall garden. They last a long time when cut for arrangements.*

and well-drained soil, and both come highly recommended by Durham, North Carolina, garden designer Edith Eddleman.

"The *P. villosa* is like having white foam in the garden," explains Eddleman. "It's cool and pretty. But *P. scabiosifolia* is equally as wonderful. And it can be a really good see-through plant."

Seedlings vary in height from 3 to 8 feet, so *P. scabiosifolia* can grow tall. Planted in the foreground of the flower border, it allows a veiled view of what lies behind it, adding intrigue to the garden setting.

Having grown both of these plants in the perennial border at North Carolina State University Arboretum in Raleigh, Eddleman speaks from experience: "They are both effective seeders, so most gardeners will want to cut them down before the seeds mature and the pods turn brown. However, the developing seeds are part of their charm."

The white-flowered *P. villosa* will also spread along the surface of the soil. Therefore, Eddleman recommends allowing about a 2- x 2-foot area for it to spread into a healthy clump, and then pulling off divisions from the outer edges of the plant to share with others.

Although easily grown from seeds, plants are becoming widely available. For mail-order sources send a self-addressed, stamped, business-size envelope to Patrinia, *Southern Living*, P.O. Box 830119, Birmingham, AL 35283.   *Linda C. Askey*

Patrinia scabiosifolia *makes a striking counterpoint of color when bounded by a low hedge of crimson barberry in the walled garden at Biltmore House and Garden in Asheville, North Carolina.*

> **PATRINIA AT A GLANCE**
> **Light:** Full sun, shade in Lower South
> **Soil:** Well drained
> **Propagation:** Seeds or divisions; easy to transplant
> **Difficulty:** Easy and long lived
> **Pests:** None significant
> **Season:** Late summer, early fall (earlier in Lower South)
> **Height:** *P. villosa* grows 3 to 4 feet; *P. scabiosifolia* reaches 3 to 8 feet.

Forever Fresh

BY LINDA C. ASKEY / PHOTOGRAPHY SYLVIA MARTIN

Everyone enjoys a flower arrangement and feels the pleasure that it brings—especially if the arrangement never fades. That is the case with this dried flower swag that was designed by Jenny Fitch, owner of Dovecote: A Country Garden Shop at Fearrington Village near Pittsboro, North Carolina. About 4 feet long and blanketed with dried materials, the arrangement captures the essence of autumn in the dried leaves, pods, and flowers of the preceeding season.

The swag shown can be constructed on any length of 1 x 4 lumber and displayed horizontally on a sideboard, as a centerpiece, or over a mantel or door. It also can be hung vertically on a wall or door, or as one of a pair on either side of a mantel. Jenny also suggests using a semicircular form cut from plywood to make an arch over a door or mantel.

Regardless of shape or length, the assembly is the same. Cut blocks of florist foam in half lengthwise with a knife; then shave off the squared edges. Wrap the chicken wire firmly over the foam, pressing it to the board. Staple the wire to the back of the board. Trim any stray pieces of wire with wire cutters. Cover the back with felt. Sheets of sphagnum moss can be attached with a hot-glue gun to the bottom and sides of the board form. This will protect furniture from scratches and will help conceal the mechanics behind the arrangement.

Jenny begins her swag with magnolia leaves that have been preserved in a 50% solution of glycerin and water. After a couple of weeks, they become like leather, brown and flexible. Each leaf is attached to a florist pick and stuck into the dry foam.

Their dark color makes the magnolia leaves a perfect frame for the lighter and more colorful materials that will fill the center of the swag.

Once a base of magnolia leaves is in place, Jenny fills the swag, layering different plants and textures. As you can see from the list of Jenny's recommended materials (below), there are more kinds of dried plants than could be used in a single swag. So select your favorites from what you have, and add more of your own.

Jenny dries her materials by hanging them from the rafters of her workroom. This is an ongoing process through the growing season. When flowers, leaves, or pods are right for gathering, they are brought indoors. Then when enough variety and quantity is on hand, she makes her swags.

Rather than spacing individual pods or flowers evenly throughout the swag, Jenny uses bunches. For example, she positions a handful of poppy pods near a single stem of hydrangea. Because the poppies are clustered, they have the texture of hard, round objects, similar to a lotus pod. In contrast, the hydrangea is soft and fluffy, but echoes the dry, parchment color of the pods. ◇

TOOLS AND SUPPLIES
1 x 4 pine board of desired length
knife
florist foam
chicken wire
staple gun
wire cutters
felt
sphagnum moss
hot-glue gun
glycerin
florist picks

PLANT MATERIALS

lotus pods
cinnamon sticks
pinecones
strawflowers
iris pods
deodar cedar cones
pomegranates
poppy pods
dock seedheads
bittersweet
roadside grasses
cockscomb
hydrangeas (all types)
teasel
gomphrena
Coronation Gold yarrow

The base of the swag is a piece of 1 x 4 pine cut to the desired length and covered with florist foam, chicken wire, and sphagnum moss.

okra pods
dried herbs
coneflowers
Autumn Joy sedum
rabbit tobacco
artichokes
birds' nests

Treated with glycerin:
magnolia
boxwood
goldenrod

Purchased:
pepper berries
safflowers
cinnamon sticks
statice

(Above) *A swag of dried leaves, flowers, and pods captures a part of summer to be enjoyed year-round.* **(Left)** *Jenny Fitch makes such arrangements as this dried swag for Dovecote, her garden shop at Fearrington Village near Pittsboro, North Carolina.*

November

Paperwhites and Yuletide sasanquas

CHECKLIST FOR NOVEMBER

AMARYLLIS

If you buy a loose bulb, select a container that is about an inch wider than the bulb (usually an 8-inch pot). Set the bulb in the pot with about an inch exposed above the potting soil. Water thoroughly; then place the pot in a bright window. Rotate the container every couple of days to keep the stalk from leaning toward the light.

ANEMONES

It's time to plant Greek anemones (*Anemone blanda*). Their tiny, 2-inch-wide flowers are borne on 4- to 6-inch stems. Set the tubers about 3 inches deep in an area with good drainage and some shelter from afternoon sun. For best effect, plant in masses of 25 or more. In Florida, pre-cool the tubers for 8 weeks; then plant.

ANNUALS

Gardeners in the Middle and Lower South still have time to set out cool-season annuals, such as pansies, snapdragons, English daisies, and such for bloom in winter and early spring. And also don't forget to plant seeds of sweet peas, forget-me-nots, poppies, and larkspur.

AVOCADOS

Yellow leaves may indicate whiteflies. Shake the foliage to see if a cloud of the insects takes flight. Treat infestations with insecticidal soap. You can make your own by mixing 2½ tablespoons of mild dishwashing detergent with the same amount of vegetable cooking oil in 1 gallon of water. It's a good idea to test first on a small branch.

CAMELLIA SCALE

Mottled green leaves on camellias, euonymus, tea olive, and citrus are good indicators of scale insects. To be sure, check the undersides of leaves for white, crusty deposits. Spray according to label directions with a systemic insecticide, such as Orthene or Cygon, or you can apply a dormant oil spray to the underside of the foliage.

CHILDREN'S TREES

A good garden project for a child is to plant an oak tree. Acorns are plentiful right now, and many will have begun to sprout already. Help your child plant 2 or 3 fresh acorns about an inch deep and several inches apart. That way you will get at least one (pull out the extras). Mark the spot with a stake, and label it with the child's name and date.

COLD PROTECTION

In Florida, prepare for sudden cold snaps by building a PVC freeze frame to protect your tropical specimen plants. Glue pipe to form a simple frame slightly larger than the plant. Heed freeze warnings, place the frame over the plant, and drape with an old bedspread.

CREPE MYRTLES

Sooty mold, a black film that is a by-product of aphid infestations earlier in the season, is commonly found on crepe myrtle foliage. Though unsightly, it will not harm the tree. The easiest solution is to leave it alone, as crepe myrtles will soon defoliate anyway. Then in spring, start a spray program to control aphids.

FRUIT TREES

Prevent damage from hungry rodents by keeping all grass and mulch away from the trunk. An 18-inch-tall collar of chicken wire or commercial tree wrap will deter rabbits and other above-ground munchers. Move any container-grown citrus indoors or to a protected area before freezes hit your area. Water them every week or so to keep the roots from drying out. Also mulch fig trees with 12 inches of hay or other mulch to protect them from freezing weather. Don't water during the dormant season.

GARDEN COLOR

Winter residents returning to South Florida at Thanksgiving can still start flowerbeds. Set out transplants of impatiens, red salvia, begonias, geraniums, and dusty miller.

HOUSEPLANTS

Yellowed and falling leaves are part of the readjustment tropical plants go through when they are moved from the sunny, humid outdoors to the dry, heated indoors. Plants should stabilize in a few weeks, with sufficient light and moisture. If problems seem to continue, check leaves for spider mites or scale. Spray as needed with insecticidal soap or horticultural oil.

LAWNMOWER

After you've given your warm-season lawn its last cut, drain remaining gasoline from the tank. If you don't drain the gas, pour a gas conditioner into the tank to keep the gas from going bad (available at repair shops and dealers). Disconnect the spark plug wire, and store the mower in a protected place.

LAWNS

Apply a second application of nitrogen fertilizer, such as 16-4-8, to cool-season lawns (including fescue and bluegrass) before Thanksgiving. Apply as recommended on the label, and water well to wash fertilizer granules off the grass and down to the soil. In Florida, continue to mow St. Augustine and Bahia lawns at the usual 3-inch height. Though a slower growth rate means less frequent mowings, remember that no more than one-third of the grass blade's height should be removed during mowing. Apply a broadleafed weed-killer, such as Ortho Weed-B-Gon, to control clover, henbit, chickweed, and dandelions in warm-season turf. Check the label carefully before spraying; don't apply to newly seeded lawns. Be sure to clean your sprayer thoroughly after applying herbicide.

MULCH

Now is a good time to add new mulch to planting beds to replace organic mulch that has washed away or disintegrated. A layer of mulch 2 to 4 inches thick will help conserve moisture throughout the dry season.

OAKLEAF HYDRANGEA

Plant this attractive native shrub now. Best known for its huge panicles of white flowers in summer, the deeply serrated leaves turn a luscious reddish burgundy in fall. Winter

finds the plant's slender stems covered with peeling bark. Choose a spot in your landscape with good soil in partial shade.

OVERSEEDING

In North Florida, overseed lawns with annual ryegrass at the end of the month. Spread seeds at a rate of 5 to 15 pounds per 1,000 square feet, depending on how thick you want the ryegrass. Use a drop or whirlybird seeder, and rake the surface lightly to shake the seeds down to soil level. Don't overwater; excessive runoff could wash away seeds before they sprout.

PECANS

In Texas, consider planting pecans for a beautiful shade tree that offers the bonus of delicious nuts. Cheyenne, Desirable, Choctaw, and Kiowa are good selections of pecan trees for East and Central Texas. Wichita, Western, Kiowa, and Cheyenne grow well in West Texas.

PERENNIALS

Fall is the best time to plant perennials such as coneflowers, Shasta daisies, daylilies, and goldenrod. Divide overcrowded plants or those you want to propagate. Begin by cutting back excess foliage; then lift the entire clump with your digging fork. Shake away the soil, and gently pry pieces of the crown apart. If it's stubborn, use a sharp spade to slice through the crown, dividing it into several pieces. Set them back into the garden at approximately the same depth they were growing originally. Tuck them in with enriched soil, and water well. In Texas, cut back asters, chrysanthemums, and other fall-blooming perennials after they flower. Clip mums down to about 4 inches or the first set of leaves; clip asters down to about 8 inches.

PRUNING

Azaleas have already set their buds for next spring, so avoid pruning until after flowering. Poinsettia bracts have also already formed, so wait until the leaves fade before cutting back outside plants. After danger of frost has passed, trim poinsettia stems to a height of 12 to 18 inches.

ROOT CROPS

Throughout Florida, sow carrot and radish seeds this month. Plant in alternating rows, because the fast germinating radishes will serve as markers for slow-to-appear carrots.

VEGETABLES

Gardeners in Central and South Texas still have time to plant carrots, radishes, mustard, spinach, and turnips. In South Texas, you can set out transplants of broccoli, Brussels sprouts, cabbage, and cauliflower now. In North Texas, plant spinach, radishes, Bibb lettuce, and other cold-tolerant greens in cold frames or other protected areas.

WATER GARDENS

Remove yellowed foliage from hardy water lilies so they don't decay at the bottom of your pool. Also clean the pool of tree leaves that may have fallen in.

November Notes

To Do:
- Continue garden clean-up
- Rake and compost leaves
- If necessary, lime lawn and planting beds
- Dig and store tender bulbs
- Clean and store garden tools and lawnmower
- Collect and store seeds from summer annuals
- In Coastal South, purchase and refrigerate spring bulbs at least eight weeks

To Plant:
- Trees and shrubs
- Spring bulbs

To Purchase:
- Spring bulbs
- Trees and shrubs
- Lime
- Soil test kit

_____
_____
_____
_____
_____
_____
_____
_____

TIP OF THE MONTH

Stop weeds that sprout from stray birdseed by cooking the seed to prevent germination. Spread a thin layer of seed on a cookie sheet that has raised sides. Bake for 8 minutes at 300°. This sterilizes the seed, but doesn't affect nutritional value.   *Mrs. Frank Reynolds Florence, South Carolina*

BEAUFORT'S SNOW

Lowcountry holidays—balmy days with gardens surprisingly full of flowers—are sweetened with the fragrance of paperwhites.

BY LINDA C. ASKEY / PHOTOGRAPHY VAN CHAPLIN

Long before florists used pots of paperwhite narcissus in holiday decorations, gardeners in Beaufort, South Carolina, were planting the bulbs outdoors. Lifelong resident Milton Parker remembers, "We used to see them blooming beneath the palmetto trees on Boundary Street as we came into town. When we were children, we would sneak out and pick some for the Thanksgiving table."

Although most of those bulbs have gone the way of roadside maintenance, paperwhites are not entirely gone or forgotten. Once they grew so thick they were known as "Beaufort snow," but they continue in local celebrations and in old gardens, thinner now for competition from tree roots and shade. These paperwhites, passed from one generation of gardeners to the next, are still available between friends, as well as readers of the state market bulletins.

The traditional Christmas centerpiece at the Parker household is still made from paperwhites, red cedar greenery, and nandina berries. These paperwhites, planted in symmetrical beds outside, represent a new generation of bulbs bred for bigger and showier blooms.

Selections such as Israel, Jerusalem, and Bethlehem were developed in Israel where the bulbs naturalize, much as they do in the Carolina Lowcountry and across the Lower and Coastal South. Gardeners in this country may also find these selections sold under their Israeli names—Omri, Sheleg, and Nony.

Frances Parker remembers her grandparents planting bulbs shallowly, so the tip showed. In the sandy, coastal soil this was necessary because they tended to sink deeper as the years went by. To slow their sinking and to nourish the bulbs, they used to put an oyster shell beneath each one.

Although she still plants her bulbs at a shallow depth, Frances skips the oyster shell. "I just don't have time," she sighs. But she does use Holland Bulb Booster fertilizer beneath each paperwhite she plants, and she fertilizes established beds with a hose-end applicator filled with water-soluble fertilizer.

However, gardeners faced with colder climes and heavier soil should follow the recommendations of Dr. August De Hertogh of North Carolina State University. He recommends that gardeners in the Lower and Coastal South plant their paperwhites so that the base of the bulb is about 5 inches deep.

For a good landscape effect, plant lots of bulbs, spacing them so that you wind up with 10 to 15 bulbs per square foot. And don't stop with only a handful. Plant enough so that you'll have some to cut for arrangements indoors *and* plenty to perfume the garden.

Because paperwhites do not need a cold period before blooming, they start to grow as soon as they are planted and flower in November and

December. And they are one of the few bulbs that gardeners along the coast can count on to bloom year after year.

However, gardeners in the Middle and Upper South who plant paperwhites in the fall run the risk of the flowers getting frozen. Bulbs take five to six weeks to bloom, so even if they manage to flower before frost, the show will not last six weeks to three months as it does in the Lower and Coastal South.

Gardeners in Texas need to keep their zone in mind when planting paperwhites. Although the foliage and buds can withstand light freezes, open flowers are susceptible. In areas where the soil freezes, the bulbs will be killed.

Gardeners in the Middle South can cheat a bit by choosing more of a sheltered location, such as a south-facing slope, and hoping for a mild winter. In Birmingham, Galilee paperwhites have grown well outdoors for the past five years, and last year bloomed throughout December and January.

In the Upper South, the best bet is to grow them in containers, even outdoors. That way they can prosper in the bright light and cool temperatures of the garden, and then they can be whisked indoors at the threat of cold weather.

The paperwhites most commonly sold at garden centers are the white selection called Ziva, an improved one that is intensely fragrant, large-flowered, and dependable. Two other white selections include Galilee (Gallilea, Galil), a good, hardy one for use outdoors, and Jerusalem (Sheleg), a tall, large-flowered favorite.

For color variation, look to the two-toned selections that sport a brighter yellow cup. They are Israel (Omri), Nazereth (Yael), and Bethlehem (Nony). The old-fashioned ones are the bright-yellow Grand Soleil d'Or and the doubled yellow-and-white Constantinople.

The cream-and-yellow flowers of the paperwhite selection called Bethlehem bask on a sunny Beaufort porch with pots of alyssum and Johnny-jump-ups.

Build a Shade Frame

Gardeners are notorious for pushing the limits of the growing season. They can't wait to put out store-bought spring vegetable and flower transplants, even if the calendar says more frosts are due. And they can't wait to put their homegrown seedlings out in the garden, even if the plants aren't quite ready for the cold, cruel world.

That's why something like this simple wooden shade frame can be handy to have around. Not only can it protect cool-weather plants from frosts (and snow, if you have such in your area), but it can also shade them when the weather warms up. The net result is a longer growing season for lettuce, cabbage, kale, and other cool-weather vegetables. What's more, you can set seedlings you've grown indoors directly out in your garden, and then set the shade frame over the young plants. There's no need for a cold frame or other means to acclimate (or harden off) tender seedlings.

To build a shade frame like this, you'll first need to construct the supporting framework, made of ripped, pressure-treated 2 x 4s. Each frame "half" measures 2 feet wide and 4 feet long, although you could make them longer. Use a rabbet joint, or a butt joint and angled metal braces to join the corners. For more support, you may want to add another piece, cut slightly shorter than the end pieces, to the middle of the frame.

After you've made the frames, join them with two ordinary cupboard hinges so they can fold flat for easy storage. Now you're ready to attach the lath strips (usually available in lumber shops in 1- to 1½-inch widths) with construction staples or brads. To prevent splitting the lath strips, pre-drill the holes before nailing them onto the frame. Space the strips

about an inch apart, which reduces the amount of sunlight reaching the plants by 50%. If severe cold spells or heavy snows are forecast in your area, mulch heavily inside the frames with straw, grass, or hay for additional protection.

The frames can also serve as drying racks for large vegetables, such as loofah gourds, or can be used for rinsing off root crops, such as potatoes or carrots.

A folding wooden shade frame can extend the cool-weather garden by as much as three weeks. Lath strips help protect tender plants from extremes of temperature and sunlight.

Plants for Low Light

BY JULIA H. THOMASON

PHOTOGRAPHY VAN CHAPLIN

"Low light" never means "no light," but a surprising number of plants have a tolerance for being away from a window. This is a boon to anyone who enjoys houseplants but has less than ideal light for growing them. If you have a spot away from a window where you'd enjoy seeing a plant—on a coffee table or in the corner of an entry hall—try one of the four plants suggested here. As long as these plants receive indirect light from one or two windows in the room, you will be pleased with their good looks as well as their durability.

You can arrange several of them together on the floor or on a large tabletop, adding interest with a piece of sculpture or garden ornament. Smaller plants may be displayed individually on a desk or bookshelf.

As you care for plants in low-light situations, remember that they need less frequent watering and less fertilizer than plants living in a brighter environment. In an air-conditioned room, corn plant and sansevieria are best, and only need watering once every two weeks.

SPOTLIGHT ON LOW LIGHT

Native to the Philippines, Chinese evergreen (*Aglaonema* sp.) has handsome 6- to 9-inch-long leaves, which are dark green and marked in a range of variegations. The popular Silver Queen Chinese evergreen bears distinct silver-gray markings and grows 1 to 2 feet tall. Let the soil dry slightly between waterings. During their active growing season (March to September), fertilize every two months using a water-soluble fertilizer, such as 20-20-20, diluted according to label directions.

Often called snake plant or mother-in-law's tongue, *Sansevieria trifasciata* is a very dependable plant that offers some unusual foliage effects. The upright, linear pattern of growth makes it one of the most sculptural of house plants. Position a sansevieria against a simple background to make the most of its unique appearance. When watering, give it a thorough soaking followed by an extended drying-out period. Water only when the top ½ inch of soil feels dry. A half-strength application of liquid fertilizer with every watering will help keep it at its best.

Corn plant (*Dracaena fragrans* Massangeana) can grow to be a tall plant—6 to 7 feet, or more. It has 18- to 32-inch leaves that radiate gracefully from a woody stalk. The leaves are green with a gold band marking the center. Dracaena Janet Craig has long, narrow, dark-green leaves that are ribbed. Its airy yet compact form makes it ideal for placement on the floor by a chair or table. Corn plant needs good drainage; do not overwater. Feed monthly with half-strength liquid fertilizer.

Golden pothos (*Epipremnum aureum*) resembles philodendron, but its heart-shaped leaves may be variegated yellow, white, or silver. Often called devil's ivy, this vine may be trained to climb or cascade over the side of a container. Golden pothos is excellent for filling out the base of tall plants that have similar lighting requirements, such as corn plants. Water golden pothos when the top 2 inches of soil is dry; then water thoroughly. Feed golden pothos monthly with a water-soluble plant fertilizer, at half the strength recommended on the label.   ◇

This hand-carved sculpture of a deer rests among baskets of golden pothos (left) and Chinese evergreen that flank the tall sansevieria.

Double potting ensures adequate drainage for this dracaena Janet Craig. The handsome porcelain jardiniere surrounds a clay pot placed in a waterproof saucer.

Small containers of golden pothos fill out the antique copper pail that holds this corn plant. An antique stand elevates the arrangement located near an old cypress column.

Carefully spaced columns, built of brick and then stuccoed, support the treated-pine pergola. Wisteria softens and shades the structure.

Arbor at the Entrance

Jackson, Mississippi, architect Ken Tate likes columns. In fact he likes just about any type of classical architectural element. Not just for the detail itself, but also for what he can do with it. "That's what is so wonderful about classicism," he says. "You can manipulate it."

For the Hattiesburg home of Cathy and Richard Conn, Tate used a classical device, the pergola, in a not-so-classical way. The pergola—an Italian term for arbor—is used at the front of this French-Colonial style house to define the entrance and to serve as a 10- x 40-foot transition between the outside and the home's interior.

In a more formal situation, a pergola would have seemed out of context. "I never would have used the pergola on a house that didn't have a wooded site," Tate explains. "It wouldn't look right."

The pergola is a simple structure . . . joists, beams, and columns. But careful attention to detail in both design and construction give this exterior space the richness of an interior room. The six columns are of the Tus-

can order, the simplest of the classical orders. Although readymade wood columns are available, the architect chose to have these made from brick and stuccoed over. The cost is comparable, and brick columns don't rot, an important consideration with Tuscan columns since they do not have

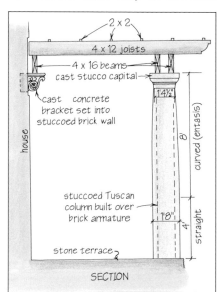

the plinth base that some other orders use to protect the column from water at the ground line.

This column gradually tapers toward the top with a slight convex curve, called entasis. The ancient Greeks developed this concept to make columns appear straight.

The columns are carefully located so the spaces between them line up with the front entrance and two pairs of adjoining French doors. At the center span, this necessitated using two pairs of columns. Doubled heavy timber beams span across the top of the columns. At the house, another beam is supported on cast-stone brackets projecting out from the front wall (see sketch). These brackets were cast locally from a mold made from a carved wood original. Then the brackets were set into the brick wall of the house, which was then stuccoed over.

Joists, cut from 4 x 12s, span from the house out to the columns. The ends are finished with a decorative cut. Above the joists, 2 x 2s of treated pine form a trellis for wisteria.
Louis Joyner

PHOTOGRAPHS: SYLVIA MARTIN

(Above) *The new side garden performs definite functions: Taller trees in the background help screen out the side wall of the neighbor's house; a dense planting of monkey grass forms a soft contrast to the architecture.* **(Right)** *Previously, the view from the porch of this house in San Antonio left a lot to be desired.*

Putting It All Aside

What do you do when your property doesn't have a front yard? Or a backyard? Or for that matter, not much of a side yard, either? You either get creative or get someone who *is* to help you get the most from what little land you do have. That's what faced the owner of an attractive San Antonio residence.

That wasn't the only unpleasant thing she faced. To create a more appealing entrance for the new house, which was tucked into a narrow lot, the front door was located on the side. While that solved one problem, it created another, recalls landscape architect John S. Troy, who was called in to help.

"The view from the 'front porch' was just the side wall of the neighbor's house and garden wall," says Troy. "There was nothing to look at." His skillful design makes the long, narrow strip of land perform many functions.

First, fitting several trees, such as red oak, live oak, redbud, and mountain laurel into the garden helps screen the large expanse of wall that the front door faces. Then, dense plantings of ground covers, flowering shrubs, and perennials provide year-round interest. "The owner really wanted the look of a forest of plants—a bit overgrown but not claustrophobic," Troy adds. The gentle splashing of a small waterfall and pool help mask noise from the street or neighbors.

The sound of water trickling into a small pond tucked among the lush greenery helps screen out noise.

Because the front door is hidden from the street, the garden also works as an invitation for visitors to explore beyond the wrought iron gate at the entrance. "You see the garden first, not the front door," says Troy.

Other details also help the garden succeed as a quiet retreat. Instead of designing a concrete sidewalk to the gate at the rear, Troy used large native stones from West Texas for a natural-looking pathway that matches the casual mood of the garden. Another stone pathway meanders out to a low, stacked-stone wall that arches out from the wall of the neighbor's house. "The paths aren't connected, so you get the feeling of different spaces," Troy adds. Night lighting extends the enjoyment of the garden to evening hours.

The result of the design is a garden that looks larger than it is and does a better job of creating a sense of seclusion than some larger gardens. Considering the homebuilding trend of fitting more house on less land, it's a magic trick that may need to be performed more often.

Mark G. Stith

This wooden planter is an easy weekend project. It's designed to hold an inexpensive plastic planter,
making it a snap to change out seasonal plantings.

A Pretty,
Practical Planter

Sometimes, you just bump into a neat idea. That's what happened in the case of this attractive wooden planter. Senior Garden Photographer Van Chaplin and I were visiting a garden in Athens, Georgia, when Van spotted a nice wooden planter near the back door. "You know, that would make a great little project," he said. And an idea was born.

To make the planter even more versatile, we thought it would be a good idea to design our version so you could drop in (and dress up) one of those inexpensive plastic planters you can buy at large discount stores, hardware centers, or most anywhere that sells garden equipment. With our

design, you can easily change out seasonal flowers, herbs, or even small vegetables for year-round appeal. Buy your plastic planter first; that way you can check to be sure our measurements will fit the plastic planter you've purchased.

Van, who is as skilled with woodworking tools as he is with a camera, drew up a quick sketch and set to the task in his basement. A few saw cuts and hammer taps later, out came one fine-looking wooden planter.

Stock lumber was used for convenience. First, make the box out of 1 x 6s; then build the trim and base around it (Van suggests using waterproof glue at all joints). Use 6-penny

finishing nails to join the box. Predrill the nail holes to avoid splitting the wood. The base is made of 1 x 4s routed at the top for a more finished look; you can trace around a coffee can to lay out the cuts on the sides and ends of the base. The same router bit (Roman ogee) was used for the base and trim pieces; the top trimwork sits slightly above the box, flush with the lip of the plastic planter. Attach the trim with 4-penny finishing nails. The box is bottomless, to avoid the potential problem of standing water and also to save weight, but is braced to add strength and support for the plastic planter.

To get the particular look of the

The planter's clean lines and good looks make a perfect accent for anywhere you need a spot of color.

planter shown in the photograph, the wood was primed and then painted with several coats of exterior latex. The total cost for the project, not including plants, was about $30.

Mark G. Stith

The lip of the plastic planter should sit on the top edge of the box; trim fits flush or slightly above the lip.

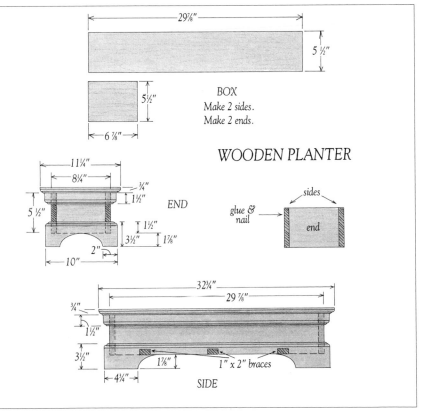

29⅞"

5½"

6⅞"

5½"

BOX
Make 2 sides.
Make 2 ends.

WOODEN PLANTER

11¼"

8¼"

¾"

1½"

5½"

END

1½"

3½"

1⅞"

2"

10"

glue &
nail

sides

end

32¾"

29⅞"

¾"

1½"

3½"

1⅞"

4¾"

1" x 2" braces

SIDE

December

Moss topiaries

CHECKLIST FOR DECEMBER

AMARYLLIS

Plant gift bulbs outdoors after holiday blossoms fade. Set bulbs in 8-inch-deep holes. Although amaryllis won't bloom again this year, expect blossoms each spring starting next year. In North Florida, keep amaryllis in pots until cold weather has passed to avoid killing foliage.

ANNUALS

In Florida, it's never too late to add color to your landscape. Gardeners throughout the state can plant pansies, petunias, and snapdragons in full sun. Dianthus and verbena will also do well in Central and South Florida. In Texas, it's time to give established pansies, larkspur, sweet peas, and other winter-hardy annuals a dose of 20-20-20 liquid fertilizer. Do not fertilize if freezes are forecast. Keep a 2- to 3-inch layer of mulch around each plant to protect it from cold weather.

ASHES

Save ashes from the fireplace, and add them to your compost. However, be certain all embers are extinguished. Leave the ashes in a bucket several days before dumping them into your bin.

BERRIES

Clip sprigs of holly to tuck into bowls of fruit, gift ribbons, evergreen wreaths, and napkin rings. To keep them looking fresh, spray foliage with acrylic floor wax.

BIRDS

Add color and activity to your garden this winter by feeding birds. If you don't have a feeder, put one on your wish list for the holidays. And don't forget to ask Santa to bring some birdseed, too.

BRIGHT FOLIAGE

Include variegated croton leaves in your holiday arrangements. Hang leaves upside down in your home or garage a week before you need them so leaves will dry.

BROCCOLI

In Florida, promote a second crop by leaving broccoli plants in the ground after harvesting heads. Fertilize with 6-6-6 granular fertilizer, at a rate of ½ cup per 10 feet of row. Side shoots often produce as much as the original harvest.

BULBS

Plant spring-flowering bulbs as soon as possible in the Upper South. Gardeners in the Middle and Lower South can set out bulbs until the end of the year. Gardeners from Dallas southward should wait until the end of the month to plant pre-chilled bulbs, such as tulips and Dutch hyacinths. Plant them in masses to obtain the best effect; choose a sunny area with good drainage.

CAMELLIAS

In Florida, select camellias now while they're in bloom throughout the north and central parts of the state so you can get the color you want. Cool-weather planting lets them get established before next summer's heat stress.

CATALOGS

As the garden catalogs arrive this month, organize them according to what they offer. Group them as "seeds," "perennial plants," "trees and shrubs," or "herbs." While thumbing through them, highlight entries that you find appealing. When you have the time to fill out orders, be sure to comparison shop, looking for packet or pot size, price, shipping cost, and any guarantee.

CITRUS

In Florida, remove unripened fruit if this is your citrus tree's first crop. First fruit is usually low in sugar and not as tasty as subsequent crops. Removing new fruit also encourages tree growth.

COASTAL PLANTING

Look for salt-tolerant plants if you live along the coast and want to add to your landscape. Natal plum (*Carissa*), dwarf yaupon holly, oleander, and coontie (*Zamia floridana*) are good salt-tolerant choices to plant for seaside landscapes.

FLOWER ARRANGING

Crystal and glass vases can't sparkle when they are streaked with dried scum lines. Unfortunately, the narrow necks of many vases make them difficult to clean. Jan Midgley from Rockville, Maryland, passed along an idea from her mother: Fill the vase with water, and drop in effervescent denture tablets.

GERANIUMS

In frost-prone areas of Florida, store geranium roots for replanting next spring. Knock soil from roots, and trim foliage. Store in a cool, dry room through the winter. Cut dormant roots into 4- to 6-inch pieces next spring, and plant. Water regularly and new shoots should appear in a few weeks.

GIFT PLANTS

Poke a few holes in the decorative foil or wrapping of gift plants, such as poinsettias, kalanchoes, azaleas, and

Christmas cactus. Such wraps prevent the pot from draining adequately after watering. Besides, placing the plant and its plastic pot inside a basket or cachepot may look even better in your home.

LAWN CARE

Continue mowing once a month in Central and South Florida, but raise the cutting height. Allow St. Augustine lawns to grow to a height of 3 to 4 inches, but keep Bermuda about 2 inches high. Mow overseeded ryegrass lawns in North Florida when the grass gets about 2 inches high. Cool-season grasses, such as fescue and ryegrass, need about an inch of water per week to continue looking their best, especially in winter. Even dormant Bermuda, St. Augustine, and Zoysia lawns need occasional watering if rainfall is insufficient (below 1 to 2 inches per month).

LEAVES

To reduce the size of your leaf pile and hasten composting, grind your leaves in a leaf shredder or gather them up with a bagging lawnmower. When you put them in your composter or leaf pile, include a shovelful of soil every few inches to add the bacteria necessary for decomposition.

POINSETTIA

For longer lasting displays, buy plants with the central, yellow flowers not fully open. Once home, place the plant near a sunny window but away from forced air vents. If the pots are wrapped in foil, poke a few holes in the bottom to allow excess water to drain away; use a saucer to catch the overflow.

PRIMROSES

For a fresh alternative to pansies, try planting primroses in their place. Look for pots of the Pacific Giants series or other selections. Although they tend to be more expensive than pansies, they are also somewhat more shade tolerant.

TOOLS

When putting away your tools for winter, wash or scrape off soil. Remove rust with a file or steel wool. Then wipe with an oily rag, or spray with cooking spray to protect the steel surfaces from dampness and rust damage.

TREES

If all the trees in your neighborhood are mature, enjoy them, but remember that they cannot last forever. Consider where you would like to have additional trees, and plant them this winter. Then if you should lose one of the giants, there will be a replacement already growing.

VEGETABLES

Remove fall garden debris. Mulch beds of carrots, beets, salsify, and parsnips for digging as you need them this winter. And while the season past is fresh in your mind, note selections that performed well and those that did not. You'll need these notes when you get ready to plan your garden for next year. In South Texas, seed broccoli, cabbage, and lettuce indoors or in cold frames; transplant to the garden when seedlings are 4 to 6 inches tall. It's too early to set out purchased transplants directly in the garden. Cut asparagus to the ground, and mulch after frost.

WATERING

Winter is Florida's dry season, so remember to check your landscape frequently for signs of drought. Frequent supplemental watering may be necessary, especially in areas with sandy soil. Always water in the morning to discourage fungal growth.

WINTER STORAGE

Because water expands when it freezes, it can damage hoses, water timers, and sprinklers. Drain these, and put them away if not in use. If damp, terra-cotta pots and ornaments can crack or crumble as a result of a freeze. Remove plants and soil from terra-cotta pots; then store them upside down in a dry location.

December Notes

To Do:
- Buy Christmas tree early for best selection
- Gather greens for holiday decorations
- Rake and compost leaves
- Mulch trees, shrubs, and perennials after the first hard freeze
- Water evergreens thoroughly
- In Coastal South, continue to refrigerate spring bulbs

To Plant:
- In Middle, Lower, and Coastal South, trees and shrubs
- In Lower South, spring bulbs

To Purchase:
- Live and cut Christmas trees
- Christmas tree lights and stand
- Poinsettias, kalanchoes, Christmas cactus, and other seasonal flowers
- Tools and garden equipment to give as presents

_____

_____

_____

_____

TIP OF THE MONTH

We used to have our bluebird house nailed to a post. Each time we lifted up its roof, we found a blacksnake inside. So we took the house off the post and hung it at post height between two trees, using heavy wire. We wired a brick to the house's bottom to anchor it and keep it steady. Bluebirds soon began nesting in it. And we had no more trouble with snakes.
Mrs. Toby Kozak
Henderson, North Carolina

GARDENING
PLANTS AND DESIGN

An Unexpected
Twist

Mix fruit and blooming plants to give a fresh look to the season.

BY MARK G. STITH AND MARY McWILLIAMS
PHOTOGRAPHY CHERYL DALTON

You'll love the ease of these great new decorating ideas for the holidays. All you need are a few containers of flowering bulbs (purchase them in bloom, or pot them per our tips) or a few camellia blossoms clipped from the garden. If you dress them up in a unique basket or bowl and accent them with fresh fruit and a few "Saint Nick-knacks," you've got some special, seasonal arrangements.

The crisp fragrance of citrus along with sweetly distinct paperwhites will add a special bouquet to the season. Put an 8-inch pot in a wooden bowl, and surround it with lemons.

Camellias grace the season with their stunning ruffled faces. The peppermint variety combines with the ruby-red blossom in this arrangement. Fruit makes a wonderful container for flowering plants with coarse stems. Insert the stem directly into the orange.

A simple wicker basket provides the perfect container for this majestic red amaryllis. Spanish moss, vines with red berries, and bright-red apples complement the still life.

If that happens, you may need to stake the flower stalks with bamboo (especially top-heavy flowers, such as amaryllis). However, you don't need to keep the flowers in bright light once they have fully opened.

A cool room temperature (60 to 70 degrees) also helps prolong the blooms. "It's fine to place the arrangement on the mantel for a special occasion, but the flowers will last a lot longer if you move them to a cool windowsill afterward," says Sally Ferguson, director of the Netherlands Flower Bulb Information Center. "Just make sure the petals don't touch the window if it's freezing outside."

The heated air inside many homes can often be quite dry, which is bad news for indoor plants. Be sure to check the container every day or so for dryness. Add water as needed, but don't allow the bulbs to sit in water or they will rot.

Paperwhite narcissus and **amaryllis** can be purchased either pre-potted or as loose bulbs. It's not too late to pot them yourself—"You can get paperwhites to bloom in three weeks," declares Angelyn. Amaryllis can take from four to eight weeks. You might consider buying some already in bloom to enjoy now, and pot some to bloom later. Because the blooms last about two weeks before fading, it's a good idea to plant a few bulbs now for an extended show.

Both types of bulbs are often sold in kits that include a container and potting media. If you buy a loose amaryllis bulb, choose a container that is only a few inches wider than the bulb—a shallow, 8-inch pot for a large bulb is typical. For containers without drainage holes, fill the bottom inch of the container with pebbles or fine gravel. Fill in potting soil around the bottom half of the bulb, leaving the top half exposed. Place the container in a sunny, south-facing window. Water thoroughly, but allow the soil to dry out slightly between waterings. If the light comes from a single window, turn the pot slightly every few days to keep the stalk from tilting toward the light.

One way to prepare paperwhites for indoor blooms is to place about an inch of fine gravel or pebbles in a wide-rimmed saucer. Nestle the paperwhites down so about a third of the bulb shows above the gravel. "It's okay to let the bulbs touch," says Ferguson. "The more bulbs you can fit in the container, the better the display." Fill the saucer about half full with water; then gently tip the saucer to drain off any excess water. Keep the container in a cool location and away from strong light for about two weeks or until roots form (a gentle tug on the bulb will let you know when roots are well developed). Then move them to a sunny window until blooms appear. Once they are in flower, move them away from direct sun. Again, cool temperatures mean longer lasting flowers. And don't let the bulbs dry out or the flowers will quickly wither—and won't recover. "Amaryllis and paperwhites develop lots of roots, so they can dry out quickly," Petrovsky adds.

For **camellias,** take a container filled with water outside with you; clip the stems about 6 to 8 inches long; then plunge them immediately in water. You can store the blooms in the refrigerator for several hours before using them. Make a fresh, angled cut before inserting the stem into the citrus. ◇

Because the flowers are the star attractions of these festive displays, it's important to keep the blooms looking good for as long as possible. "You can count on the tulip flowers for about a week to 10 days," advises Angelyn Lewis, who created several of these arrangements to decorate her home in Madison, Georgia. "The amaryllis and paperwhites can last two weeks." Here's how to keep the flowers from flopping, as well as how to pot your own bulbs.

Hardy bulbs, such as tulips and hyacinths, must be pre-chilled for as long as three months before they will bloom properly. Although it's a little late for you to do that, others have been thinking ahead. Garden centers, florists, and grocery stores that sell fresh flowers often have pre-chilled bulbs potted and ready to go. Unless you've waited until the last minute and need flowers in full bloom for that special occasion tonight, it's better to buy containers with flowers that are in bud—the blooms will last longer when they open.

"Potted bulbs need bright light," says Vincent C. Petrovsky, floral designer and manager of Gardenstyle in Palm Beach. "They can take the winter sun; otherwise, the stems will get leggy," he adds.

New Walk Says Welcome

Some homes just seem to radiate Southern hospitality. It starts before you even get to the door. For example, this wide front walk in Orlando extends an invitation that starts at streetside. Interlocking pavers made of precast concrete form a colorful and textured path; matching pavers on the new porch steps complete the welcome.

Michel and Barbara Petiot recall their family's experience with this do-it-yourself project. "There was a broken concrete slab to start with," Michel remembers, "and the old porch steps were uneven. There were only three steps, and they were too high."

Kelly McMahon, Barbara's son, removed the existing steps and replaced them with four concrete steps. When calculating the riser heights (the vertical part of the steps), Kelly allowed room to add pavers.

When Michel and Kelly took out the old concrete walk, they discovered the ground beneath was sufficiently compacted to serve as a base for the new paver walkway. After leveling the soil, they dampened it to help set the pavers firmly in place.

Pressure-treated 2 x 4s were used along each edge of the walk to help align the pavers and hold them tightly. Bordering the walk is a single row of pavers laid end to end in a running bond pattern. This also helps contain the walk with minimal shifting. Between the borders, the pavers were laid in a basket-weave pattern. After allowing several months for the pavers to settle, the Petiots removed the 2 x 4s and let their St. Augustine lawn grow right up to the walk. If using a sand bed, leave the boards in place, or substitute metal edging.

Using a basket-weave pattern for the new walk works especially well with brick-shaped pavers because it creates rows of squares. The charming, finished walk leads you from the picket gate at street level up the steps to the front door. *Jo Kellum*

Four colors of pavers were mixed in this entry walk: Charcoal gray, tan, and gray-and-tan mixed pavers predominate, while a smattering of mixed red-and-charcoal pavers were included as accents.

Topping off the steps with matching pavers ties the walk to the porch. The basket-weave pattern is continued from the walkway.

PHOTOGRAPHS: SYLVIA MARTIN

2R + T = 27

You can use this formula to dimension your steps. The combined heights of two risers (2R) plus the width of one tread (T) should equal 27. When determining riser heights, consider the effect of adding pavers. These brick-shaped pavers are 2⅜ inches thick. A mortar bed adds about another ½ inch of height to each step.

Unforgettable Ladew

BY JULIA H. THOMASON

PHOTOGRAPHY VAN CHAPLIN

From Ladew Topiary Gardens in Monkton, Maryland, we bring you ideas for quick, yet elegant, decorations to make a part of your own Christmas tradition.

Sixty-four years ago, Harvey Ladew laid out extensive gardens, sculpted majestic topiaries, and redesigned and renewed his old Maryland farmhouse. Today, his magnificent home and elaborate topiary gardens are open to the public.

Listed on the National Register of Historic Places, the house and grounds are beautiful in all seasons. But at Christmas, Ladew Topiary Gardens is an especially warm, welcoming, and festive place. For several days in December, it opens for an annual "Christmas in an English Country House" celebration.

Under the guidance of executive director Lena Caron, volunteers adorn first-floor rooms with fresh greenery and handmade decorations. It's traditional at Ladew that all decorations be made from boxwood and other kinds of natural greenery.

Lena and the volunteers have generously shared their ideas for natural holiday decorations. These designs are so easy to duplicate, you'll be delighted with your own splendid results.

(Left and inset)
The tree in the Oval Library glows with leaves and dried plant materials given a shimmering coat of gold spray paint. Colorful ribbons cascade to the floor.

Boxwood topiaries flanking a portrait in the Elizabethan Room were made by filling chicken wire cones with dried maple leaves; then boxwood cuttings and decorations were added.

GOLDEN ORNAMENTS FOR THE TREE

Gather several dozen dried leaves, seed-pods, and clusters of berries from the garden. Look for a variety of shapes and sizes. Place a few items at a time into a tall cardboard box, and apply gold spray paint. Place miniature white lights on your tree; then add the gold ornaments, positioning some of them deep within the branches. Tie a dozen long, silky ribbons to the top of the tree, and let them curve over the branches and down to the floor.

BOXWOOD TOPIARIES

You'll need chicken wire and dried leaves. Cut a 15- x 15- x 15-inch triangle of chicken wire (vary the size of the triangle for a larger or smaller topiary). Overlap one side of the tri-angle onto another, forming a cone; bend the exposed ends of wire to the inside, to make the cone hold its shape. Cut away about an inch of chicken wire at the top of the cone. At the bottom, trim away excess wire (or bend it inside), so that the cone will stand straight. Pack the

cone with dried leaves. Insert 4- to 6-inch-long cuttings of boxwood into the form at an angle, covering it completely. Set into a planter or clay pot, and decorate with bows or ornaments.

HOLIDAY CANDLEHOLDERS

Tape over the hole in a small clay pot. Spray the pot gold. Cut an 18-inch-long piece of gold ribbon, braid, or wire. Wrap it around the pot, and insert a votive candle.

MOSS TOPIARIES

Select a 2- to 4-inch-high clay pot, and seal the hole with masking tape. Mix plaster of Paris according to manufacturer's instructions. Cut a stick that's twice the height of the pot. Pour about 2 inches of plaster into the pot. (Adding more plaster than this may cause the pot to crack.) Use tape to keep the stick vertical until the plaster hardens. Select a plastic foam ball that is the same diameter as the pot. Use white glue to attach green sheet moss to the ball. Punch a hole in the ball, place glue on the end of

(Left and Inset) *Handmade topiaries and candleholders rest among Harvey Ladew's crystal inkwells and other desktop accessories.*

the stick, and insert it in the hole. Glue sheet moss to the plaster. Trim the topiary.

You can easily add color to the moss when it begins to turn brown. In a spray bottle, mix two parts yellow food coloring with one part green; add water, and spray the mixture onto the moss. Mist lightly for best effect.

Note: When foliage is first cut at Ladew, it is sprayed with an antidesiccant to help it retain moisture and stay green longer. This is a step you can easily do at home, using an antidesiccant spray such as "Wilt Pruf," purchased from a nursery or garden center. When using an antidesiccant, follow product instructions.

For more information contact Ladew Topiary Gardens, 3535 Jarrettsville Pike, Monkton, MD 21111; (410) 557-9466. The house and gardens are open for public tours April through October. Admission is $5 for adults and $1 for children. "Christmas in an English Country House" takes place 11 a.m. to 4 p.m. December 10 through 12. ◇

(Left) *Moss topiaries are easy to make and to individualize with ornaments and ribbon. They are elegant yet playful additions to many settings.*

PHOTOGRAPHS: TINA EVANS

(**Above**) *Strawberry bush is a loose, gangly plant easily distinguished by its green stems and showy seedpods* (**above, right**).

Wahoo — It's Strawberry Bush

Did you say you have a shaded, natural area that you're looking to embellish? You could plant azaleas or hollies and be like everyone else on the block. Or you could give way to your maverick side and try something truly different. The plant under consideration isn't some exotic rarity brought back by explorers from Tibet. No, it's a shrub native to our own Southern woods that goes by the name of strawberry bush.

At least that's one of its names. Another is hearts-a-busting, which sticklers for good grammar correct to hearts-a-bursting, and those given to romantic flings of fancy call it hearts-bursting-with-love. Believe it or not, all these names can be logically

explained. They describe the plant's remarkable seedpods, which ripen in early fall to resemble strawberries. With the onset of fall, the pods split open, revealing bright, orange-red seeds that hang like drops of blood from the pod's purple insides.

Lanky and multitrunked, strawberry bush (*Euonymus americana*) grows 6 to 8 feet tall. It suckers to form small colonies but doesn't spread aggressively. Stems and trunks stay bright green all year, a valuable feature for the winter garden. In spring, look closely to spot the small, yellow-green flowers that rest atop the leaves.

The ornate seedpods that follow these flowers aren't the shrub's only

STRAWBERRY BUSH AT A GLANCE
Size: 6 to 8 feet tall
Light: Sun or shade
Soil: Moist, fertile, lots of organic matter
Pests: None serious
Propagation: By seeds or cuttings
Range: Throughout the South

fall attraction. Lance-shaped leaves that change from nondescript green to soft, creamy-yellow tinged with pink merit attention as well.

Take a cue from nature when deciding where to plant strawberry bush. In nature, it frequents shady stream banks and open woodlands. So try it as an understory shrub in a naturalized area where plants aren't neat and trim. Don't plant this shrub in formal settings where its loose form looks unkempt.

Although strawberry bush prefers light shade, it tolerates full sun as long as it's supplied with moist soil containing copious organic matter. Unlike other kinds of euonymus, it's seldom beset by scale. Propagation is easy. You can either dig up suckers or root cuttings.

Incidentally, Native Americans had their own word for strawberry bush. They called it "wahoo," a name that's easily explained. If you were a plantsman who'd just discovered this singular shrub, you'd probably yell "wahoo," too.   *Steve Bender*

For a list of mail-order sources of strawberry bush, send a self-addressed, stamped, business-size envelope to Strawberry Bush, *Southern Living,* P.O. Box 830119, Birmingham, AL 35283.   ◇

Twining evergreen stems of potato vine blanket an old garden wall in the Carolina Lowcountry.

Brazilian nightshade makes a spectacular show by producing lilac flowers and red berries at the same time.

Twine a New Vine

Potato vine blooms year-round in clusters of white flowers.

No group of plants adds maturity and romance to a garden like vines. Two of the newest twining arrivals in Southern gardens are relatives of tomatoes, eggplants, and potatoes—and one look at the flowers will reveal their family resemblance. However, the similarity ends there, for these vines distinguish themselves by their ornamental habit and unceasing bloom.

The hardier of the two is *Solanum jasminoides,* sometimes known as potato vine, although no potatoes are produced, and for that matter, no jasmine-like fragrance. However, its vigorous growth, clean foliage, and delicate sprays of white flowers are making it a newfound favorite with many gardeners.

Trials at the North Carolina State University Arboretum in Raleigh have shown it to be much more cold-hardy than reference books indicate. It has grown there for 10 years. Although not always evergreen, it has proved root-hardy.

In the Lower and Coastal South and during mild winters in the Middle South, potato vine is evergreen. In a tough winter, the plant will drop its leaves. If the freeze is severe, the vine will die to the ground and grow back from its roots. In the Upper South, gardeners should consider it a worthwhile annual, taking cuttings in autumn, wintering young plants in a window or in a greenhouse, and then replanting in spring.

You can expect about 10 feet of growth the first season, although the longer your season, the longer your vines will grow. But don't worry; they can be cut back anytime they stray too far. For best performance, plant in full sun to partial shade in well-drained soil that has been amended with organic matter.

The other vine is *Solanum seaforthianum,* commonly called Brazilian nightshade. Gardeners love its sprays of lilac-blue flowers. An added bonus is that they continue to bloom at the same time that panicles of glossy-red berries ripen.

Unfortunately, it is even less cold tolerant than the potato vine, so plant it in a sheltered location if your region is not frost free. In Beaufort, South Carolina, Frances Parker reports that her Brazilian nightshade has lost its leaves during light frosts and died to the ground when the thermometer dips to 20 degrees. But the vine continues to sprout again, twining over and through her hedge of sweet bay.

Because the vines grow so fast, Frances trains them onto topiary forms. Then they can be moved to shelter during cold weather.

Unlike their edible relatives, these vines are poisonous, except to birds. They love to nest in the tangled stems and feast on the red berries.

Linda C. Askey

For sources of these plants, send a self-addressed, stamped, business-size envelope to Solanum Vines, *Southern Living,* P.O. Box 830119, Birmingham, AL 35283.

LETTERS TO OUR GARDEN EDITORS

African violets: I bought an African violet this year, and it bloomed for months, then stopped. It hasn't bloomed since. Will it ever bloom again? *Jean Feigly*
Herndon, Virginia
Relax. It's quite common for African violets to rest between periods of bloom. Just make sure yours receives plenty of bright light, but no hot sun. Feed it once a month with water-soluble African violet fertilizer. Your plant should resume blooming before too long.

Amaryllis: I have a beautiful amaryllis bulb and want to know if I can plant it outside in the ground. Also, when should I cut off the leaves? *Ara Foshee*
Judsonia, Arkansas
Your amaryllis is probably an indoor type because this is the most common. It won't survive freezing temperatures, so bring it indoors for the winter. Keep in the same pot even if you take it outdoors for the summer, because an amaryllis blooms best when potbound. Don't cut off the leaves until they turn yellow and start to wither. You can help induce dormancy by gradually reducing water in late summer and fall.

Bermuda Grass: Each spring, brown spots appear in my 5-year-old Bermuda lawn just as the grass begins to grow. They disappear by July. Could you suggest the cause and a cure? *Grace George*
Ada, Oklahoma
The cause is spring dead spot, a mysterious disease that usually doesn't affect Bermuda until the grass is at least 3 years old. The spots reappear in the same places each year, but gradually spread. The fungus that causes them is most active when the soil is cool and moist. To control, spray benomyl on the spots in spring according to label directions. And avoid applying heavy doses of nitrogen fertilizer in late summer and fall.

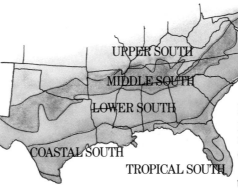

Blackened beans: What's causing black puncture marks all over my string beans? I've been told that a pumpkin bug or stink bug is doing it, so I've sprayed with Diazinon and carbaryl. *Mrs. Thomas Spencer*
Talladega, Alabama
We suspect the marks are caused by a beetle with a long snout called a cowpea curculio. Female curculios puncture the skin of bean pods and lay eggs inside. To control the insects, spray or dust with rotenone just as the pods are forming, before the curculios appear. Reapply as new beans form. Be sure to follow label directions carefully, and try to keep the spray or dust off the flowers, lest you kill the bees that pollinate the plants.

Bougainvillea: I have a beautiful bougainvillea growing outside in a large hanging basket. The limbs are as much as 3 feet long and hang down on all sides of the basket. How should I care for this plant to get through the winter? Also, should I prune it severely to make it more manageable inside? *Mrs. Leonard H. Aiken*
North Augusta, South Carolina
Bring your bougainvillea inside before the onset of freezing weather. Give it your sunniest window. Cut the plant back to a manageable size. Throughout the winter, keep the soil just barely moist, and don't fertilize. When the plant begins actively growing in February or so, increase watering, and give it a little water-

soluble houseplant fertilizer every two weeks. Don't shift it to a bigger hanging basket—bougainvillea actually blooms better when it is potbound.

Butterfly bush: Please explain the proper care for butterfly bush. I am mostly concerned about whether to cut it back, by how much, and when. Also, will it survive in our winter temperatures? *Nancy Grob*
Austin, Texas
An old-fashioned shrub prized for flowers that attract butterflies, butterfly bush (*Buddleia* sp.) is hardy throughout the South. It does best in full sun and moist, fertile, well-drained soil. Because it blooms on new growth, cut it back rather hard in winter. This encourages new, vigorous growth in spring.

Camellia: My camellias always have lots of flowerbuds, but very few of them open. They either drop off or get burned by cold weather. Can you help me with this problem?
Doug Horne
Moultrie, Georgia
To reduce the chances of bud drop, mulch camellias thoroughly in early winter to mitigate extremes of soil moisture and temperature. In addition, these shrubs do better in a sheltered location. Don't put them up against a wall of the house, as the extra heat may cause the buds to open prematurely and subsequently freeze.

Camellia pruning: The camellias growing near our breakfast room are quite big. Can we cut them back?
Mrs. I. A. Campbell
Charlotte, North Carolina
Don't prune your camellias in the fall, unless their size really bothers you. If you do, you'll cut off all of the flowerbuds for next year. Instead, wait to prune until after the plants bloom. Cut them back as much as you want—new foliage will sprout

from the trunks. However, it usually takes a number of years for severely pruned camellias to regain an attractive form.

Chinese hibiscus: My Chinese hibiscus plants are big and green but produce very few flowers. What do you advise? *Rose Matus*
Lighthouse Point, Florida
The key to getting a Chinese hibiscus (*Hibiscus rosa-sinensis*) to bloom is plenty of summer sunlight. They are "long-day" plants, meaning that they bloom best when provided with at least 12 hours of sun per day. Fertilize every two weeks throughout the summer with a water-soluble, bloom-booster fertilizer. Make sure the soil is evenly moist and well drained. In fall and winter, blooms will decrease as the plant enters a resting phase. So stop fertilizing and reduce watering this fall. Winter is a good time to do any necessary pruning.

Clay: I'm having a heck of a time breaking up the clay soil in my vegetable garden. No matter how much I till and mulch, the soil clumps up and sticks together. Please recommend a solution to this vexing problem. *Mike Brackett*
LaGrange, Georgia
Making good soil out of red clay is harder than keeping your teenage daughter off the telephone. It takes a lot of hard work—basically, tilling in huge amounts of organic matter, such as pine straw, shredded bark, ground-up leaves, compost, manure, and peat moss. Over a period of time, this material coats the clay particles and keeps them from lumping together. Organic matter also attracts earthworms, which help to loosen the soil. If all this sounds like too much work, you might consider building raised beds and filling them with good soil.

Corn plant: My corn plant has yellow spots and brown tips on its leaves. It gets morning sun, and I keep the soil inside the plastic container fairly moist. I'd appreciate your advice. *James L. Turnbull*
Johnson City, Tennessee
It sounds like the problem is too much water. Corn plant (*Dracaenafragrans massangeana*) is one of those invaluable houseplants that

thrives on neglect. When growing indoors in partial sun, it likes the soil to go dry between waterings. One watering every two weeks is usually about right. When you do water, do it thoroughly, so that the excess runs out of the drainage holes.

Dogwoods: Can you give me some information about new dogwood selections that are resistant to the anthracnose disease?

Karen Lovell
Huntsville, Alabama

EDITORS' NOTEBOOK
"Somebody went nuts with the spray paint." The first time you spy the gaudy, metallic-purple berries of a beautyberry, that's the logical conclusion. Nothing else in the garden flaunts this color. Of the several species available, our native beautyberry (*Callicarpa americana*) is the most common. A lanky, unkempt shrub, about 6 feet high and wide, it points branches and leaves in all directions, looking like the hair of some hapless soul who's just had a radio dropped in his bathwater. A better candidate for home gardens is purple beautyberry (*C. dichotoma*), from Japan. This graceful, arching shrub grows about half as large. Don't wait until its leaves drop to harvest berry-laden branches for decorations, because an early freeze might turn the fruits brown. Instead, cut branches as soon as the fruits ripen in fall. The leaves will wither almost immediately, but the berries last a long time indoors. For mail-order sources, send a self-addressed, stamped, business-size envelope to Purple Beautyberry, P.O. Box 830119, Birmingham, AL 35283. *Steve Bender*

A research program at Rutgers University recently released several new hybrids of our native flowering dogwood (*Cornus florida*) and its Japanese cousin, kousa dogwood (*C. kousa*). They're named Aurora (white), Constellation (white), and Stellar Pink. They resist anthracnose, a disease that many feared would spell doom for our native dogwoods. However, scientists now think it isn't that serious. The disease doesn't survive hot weather, so only dogwoods growing at high elevations appear endangered.

Elm: Our beautiful, 36-year-old elm lost all of its foliage in August. A few years earlier, a limb or two appeared unhealthy and we removed them. What could cause it to die so suddenly? *Nell Holloway*
Shreveport, Louisiana
Sometimes trees die as a delayed reaction to serious drought or damage suffered one or two years before. But from your description, it appears your tree may have been diseased. Two common insect pests of most elms are Dutch elm disease and phloem necrosis. The first is spread by elm bark beetles and the second by leaf hoppers. The symptoms look very similar. Most notable is the yellowing, wilting, and dying of foliage in the uppermost part of the tree. The disease then progresses downward. Once either disease appears, it's almost always fatal. American elm (*Ulmus americana*) is especially susceptible. Fortunately, Chinese elm (*U. parviflora*) is a reasonable substitute for the native elm. It resists disease, grows fast, makes a fine shade tree, and is widely available.

Fail-safe flowers: My property has either swampy sand during the rainy season or desert drought during the rest of the year. What annuals will bloom continuously under these conditions? *Bridget Tolomeo*
La Belle, Florida
Few plants thrive in both wet and dry soil. We suggest you build raised beds, so that the soil drains adequately during rainy weather. Then use plants that prefer good drainage and tolerate drought. Such fail-safe flowers include narrow leaf zinnia (*Zinnia augustifolia*), globe amaranth (*Gomphrena glo-*

bosa), spider flower (*Cleome hasslerana*), rose verbena (*Verbena canadensis*), melampodium, blue daze (*Evolvulus nuttallianus*), wax begonia, and lantana.

Fiddle-leaf fig: Some of the leaves of my fiddle-leaf fig have brown, rusty patches of no particular shape on them. There is also a slight yellowing. Can you tell me the cause and cure? *Wanda G. Taylor*
Gautier, Mississippi
It sounds as if your fiddle-leaf fig (*Ficus lyrata*) is under attack from a disease called anthracnose. Fortunately, this isn't a serious problem, and you don't need a chemical spray. Just pick off and destroy infected leaves. When you mist or water the plant, make sure that water doesn't sit on the leaves for a long time, as this promotes disease.

Firethorn: Can you diagnose the problem with a firethorn that's espaliered against my chimney? Last spring, the plant developed numerous dead, brown areas among healthy foliage. *Gale Davis*
Virginia Beach, Virginia
It sounds like your firethorn (also called pyracantha) fell victim to a disease called fireblight, which turns leaves, berries, and twigs dark brown or black. To control fireblight, prune all affected branches and twigs back to healthy wood. Remove blackened berries, too. After each cut, disinfect your pruners by dipping them in a solution of 1 cup of bleach to a gallon of water. Throw the diseased material away. In spring, spray your plant while it's blooming with streptomycin or copper sulfate according to label directions. Follow up by spraying again two weeks later. If you'd rather not prune or spray, consider replacing your firethorn with a fireblight-resistant selection, such as Mohave or Navaho.

Holly berries: We have a lot of native hollies on our property, but they never have any berries. Why?
Nancy Fuhrman
Southside, Alabama
American hollies (*Ilex opaca*) have separate sexes, and you need both to get berries. So you probably have mostly males or mostly females. The only way to tell the difference be-

tween fruiting and non-fruitingplants is to closely examine the small flowers in spring. If the flowers contain a fat, green pistil in the center, the plant is female. If they contain a ring of yellow stamens, the plant is male. Only the female plants form berries.

Holly tree: Something ails my holly tree. It's absolutely laden with berries, but every leaf has ugly splotches. What do you suggest?
Anna Woodward
Suffolk, Virginia

EDITORS' NOTEBOOK
Here in the South, common wisdom says to plant pansies in the fall. This way, the plants will develop vigorous root systems during winter, and you'll get many more blooms in spring. In most years, this is exactly what happens. But every once in a while, fickle weather upsets the proverbial applecart. Following a stretch of relatively mild days, a Canadian cold front roars into town and quickly turns contented flowers into limp, green mush. Here are two suggestions to keep your pansies from suffering this dire fate. First, well-fed plants fend off cold better than lean ones. So feed your plants in fall with water-soluble, general-purpose fertilizer right after planting them. Then sprinkle a teaspoon of slow-release fertilizer around each plant. Second, pay attention to weather reports. The day before a serious cold front hits, cover your plants with several inches of pine straw, fallen leaves, or hay. Leave this insulating blanket in place for several days until the weather moderates. When you remove it, you'll find your plants pert and green, ready to bloom again. *Steve Bender*

Your holly is under attack from holly leaf miner, an insect whose larvae bore into the leaves. This pest is especially prevalent in the Upper and Middle South. The best way to combat it is to spray your plant with Cygon, an insecticide, in mid-May. Be sure to follow label directions.

Hostas: My hostas were beautiful last year, but this spring the leaves have gotten holey. What causes this, and what should I do about it?
Ella Barnes
Alexandria, Virginia
The holes are probably the handiwork of slugs. To control these pests, sprinkle some slug pellets around your plants. Be sure to follow label directions carefully. Don't spread the pellets where they're likely to get into fish ponds or be eaten by birds. If you prefer to use something less toxic, try spreading wood ashes, ground lime, or diatomaceous earth around your plants. Slugs don't like crawling across ashes or lime. And diatomaceous earth pierces their skin, causing them to dry out and die.

Hummingbirds: Your "Winged Wizards" article advised us to leave our hummingbird feeders up for the winter. Shouldn't you remove feeders in areas where temperatures fall below freezing to encourage hummers to go south? Otherwise, they may stay where the nectar is and freeze to death. *Susan Young*
Madison, Alabama
The advice to leave your feeder up for the winter came from experts in the Lower and Coastal South, where many hummingbirds do overwinter. However, leaving your feeders up in the Upper and Middle South would be futile, so we regret misleading readers about that. In any case, don't worry about killing hummingbirds with kindness. They can easily survive a few days of freezing temperatures. Moreover, leaving your feeders up for the winter will not keep the birds from migrating to their normal wintering grounds.

Hydrangeas: We have four beautiful hydrangeas, about 5 years old, in full bloom. Can I transplant these and, if so, when?
Mrs. John Carpenter
Comanche, Texas

Don't move your hydrangeas during the heat of summer, or you'll probably kill them. Wait until after they drop their leaves in fall. Try and get as big a root ball as you can, and plant them at the same depth as they had been growing previously. When new growth begins the next spring, prune off any dead wood above the uppermost green buds.

Impatiens: I loved the impatiens I had this year and want the same ones next year. Do you have any suggestions about how to keep them from dying this winter?

Troy Purvis
Brandon, Mississippi

In the Lower South, where you are, impatiens growing in a very protected spot will sometimes overwinter, if you cover them in fall with leaves or pine straw. But the chances are less than 50-50. You'd do better to overwinter the plants indoors. One way is to pot up your plants this fall, cut them back, then bring them inside to a sunny room. Or you can root cuttings in potting soil or water and grow them indoors this winter.

Ivy: We have English ivy growing up the trunks of tall pines and hardwoods. It has almost reached the tops. Will this harm the trees?

Wayne Smith
Columbia, South Carolina

While English ivy (*Hedera helix*) sometimes smothers small trees, it seldom harms mature trees. So unless you object to its appearance on the trunks, leave it alone.

Jackson Vine: I'm looking for an evergreen vine that won't harm mortar to grow on a wall. In North Alabama, people love to grow something they call "Jackson vine." Will it grow here? If not, can you suggest some other good substitutes?

Mary J. Hicks
Nashville, Tennessee

Jackson vine (*Smilax smallii*) should grow for you, although it may be injured during severe winters. It climbs by tendrils but won't dig into and damage mortar the way English ivy or Boston ivy will. This native vine also features glossy, evergreen foliage, which people enjoy using in holiday decorations. And unlike other forms of smilax, it's spineless. Suitable substitutes include Car-

olina jessamine (*Gelsemium sempervirens*), Confederate jasmine (*Trachelospermum jasminoides*), and trumpet honeysuckle (*Lonicera sempervirens*.)

Jasmine: I've enjoyed the fragrance of night-blooming jasmine in Florida and along the North Carolina coast. Are there any jasmines that will withstand the winters of Winston-Salem?

Page Lowry
Winston-Salem, North Carolina

EDITORS' NOTEBOOK

Long stretches of hot, steamy weather tell me it's getting near blackberry-picking time. If you've never partaken of homemade blackberry cobbler topped with vanilla ice cream, life has not been kind to you.

Because blackberries don't ship well, you hardly ever find them sold fresh in supermarkets. So if you want them, you have two choices. One, dress in long pants, long-sleeved shirt, and boots, and head to a wild blackberry patch.

Your second option is to plant domesticated blackberries this fall. You'll need a sunny site with moist, well-drained soil and plenty of organic matter. Avoid spots where tomatoes, potatoes, peppers, or eggplants grew recently, as the soil there may contain verticillium, a serious wilt disease.

Your county Extension agent can suggest a selection for your area. Don't automatically gravitate toward thorn-free types. Thorny blackberries tend to be tastier—a little suffering always makes the reward seem sweeter.

Steve Bender

Most of the fragrant jasmines are semitropical and tropical, and so aren't reliably hardy outside of the Coastal and Tropical South (in Winston-Salem). Of course, you can grow jasmines indoors. Just make sure you give them plenty of bright sun.

Kiwi: I would like to grow tropical kiwi here in west central Florida, but have seen a statement to the effect that they will not fruit in this state. Is that true and, if so, what's the explanation?

James H. Pannell
Dunnellon, Florida

According to Judith Caldwell, who is a small-fruit expert at Clemson University, kiwi is not a tropical fruit, as it requires some degree of winter chilling to flower and set fruit. The most popular selection, Hayward, needs between 900 and 1,200 hours of temperatures below 45 degrees to produce a decent crop. It's doubtful that your area of Florida receives this much cold. You may get some fruit during cold winters, but other years you might not.

Lady Banks rose: I have a Lady Banks rose growing on the east side of my house. In the four years it's been planted, it has had only one small cluster of blooms. Does it have to be very old before it blooms? What am I doing wrong?

Marilyn Ryan
Cocoa, Florida

Lady Banks rose is a fast grower and often flowers when quite young. So there must be another problem. Perhaps your rose isn't getting enough sun. The best flowering occurs in full sun. You may also be pruning it at the wrong time. Prune your plant in late spring, immediately after it finishes blooming. If you prune it in summer or fall, you'll cut off the flowerbuds for next year.

Lupines: While vacationing in Bar Harbor, Maine, I fell in love with its beautiful native flower, the lupine. I brought back seeds and wonder whether they will tolerate our hot summers and sandy soil?

Joy H. Burris
Florence, South Carolina

Although wild lupine (*Lupinus perennis*) is said to grow from Maine to Florida, we doubt that seeds collected in Maine will thrive in South

Carolina. This is because native populations adapt to the local climate over time. Thus, a South Carolina population might fall victim to Maine's severe winters, while a Maine population might wither during South Carolina's blistering summers. But if you wish to try, sow seeds as soon after they ripen as possible into moist soil, and barely cover. Transplant seedlings into permanent locations, as established plants resent disturbance. The site should receive shade during the hot part of the day. Water freely during summer droughts. If, despite all this, your plants fail to overwinter, treat them as cool-weather annuals and sow new seed each fall.

Marigold: I used to be able to grow beautiful marigolds. But for the past three years, my plants grow nicely, and then wilt and die almost overnight. I'm sure the problem is my dirt. Can you advise me about what to do?   *Joe K. Cathcart*
Winnsboro, South Carolina
It sounds like your marigolds are being attacked by a disease called stem wilt, which does indeed live in the soil. The only way to eradicate it is to fumigate the soil before planting with a product called Vapam. Be sure to follow label directions carefully. If you'd rather not fumigate, try planting your marigolds in a different spot.

Mulch: Does fresh cedar sawdust mixed with fresh horse manure make a good mulch for a vegetable garden?   *Chris Garrett*
Greensboro, North Carolina
We don't recommend mulching your garden with fresh sawdust and manure. As it breaks down, the sawdust would likely deplete soil nitrogen. And the manure might burn your plants. We suggest you put both into a compost bin and let them decompose over the summer. Then till them into the soil this fall. For a good mulch, use pine straw or shredded bark.

Peace lily: The leaves of my peace lily turn brown and yellow on the tips. The plant sits near a window. Is there anything I can do to prevent this?   *Annie McCollister*
Russellville, Alabama
Peace lily (*Spathiphyllum* sp.) may

develop brown or yellow tips on its leaves for several reasons. First, you may have let the soil dry out briefly. Peace lily prefers consistently moist, well-drained soil. Second, the indoor air may be too dry. To correct this, place the plant on a gravel-lined saucer filled with water or in close company with other houseplants. Third, a cold windowpane could freeze leaf tips that touch it. Finally, chlorinated water could be the culprit. To evaporate chlorine, let the

EDITORS' NOTEBOOK

Depending on your background and temperament, the critter on this tree could be a blessing, a curse, or tomorrow night's dinner. I've never experienced the third alternative and, Lord willing, never will. But I do know about the first two. My wife simply adores squirrels, an affectation I attribute to her being a nongardener. I, however, recoil from such bitter memories as watching these rodents strip my fig trees of figs, pick the only pear from my pear tree, chew all the flowerbuds off of my Exbury azalea, dig up my newly planted annuals and leave them dying atop the ground—not to mention brutish raids on my bird feeder. Short of violence, the best solution is that of my mother. She traps the fiends, then releases them in the woods. Since she's had her trap, Mom reports she's taken away well over 400 squirrels. If you would like a mail-order source for traps, send a self-addressed, stamped, business-size envelope to Squirrel Trap Editor, *Southern Living*, P.O. Box 830119, Birmingham, Alabama 35283.
Steve Bender

water stand overnight before using.

Roots: We have two beautiful, 50-foot dawn redwoods. I tried planting azaleas under them, but the surface roots of the trees sucked up all the water and destroyed them. Is there any way to keep these roots from surfacing? If not, what can I plant under the trees?   *M. N. Jones*
Osceola, Arkansas
A handsome, deciduous conifer, dawn redwood (*Metasequoia glyptostroboides*) naturally develops surface roots as it ages. Unfortunately, we don't know of any way to prevent this. Our advice is simply to spread a layer of mulch under the trees and leave it at that or plant a shade-tolerant ground cover that doesn't need deep, moist soil. Liriope, mondo grass, or English ivy would probably work.

St. Augustine: We're worried about losing our St. Augustine lawn to a winter freeze. I've been advised to winterize my lawn by adding sulfur to my last fertilizer application this year. Will this help to protect against cold damage? What do you think about covering the lawn with hay or with a thermal cover made for greenhouses?   *Mrs. Neil Rohan*
Aledo, Texas
We've never heard of anyone protecting their lawn under hay or a thermal cover, so we can't help you there. As for adding sulfur, sulfur doesn't increase winter hardiness by itself. However, by lowering the pH of alkaline Texas soil to a level the grass prefers (about 6.5), it may make the grass healthier and stronger. To determine if your lawn needs extra sulfur, have a soil test done. One element that has been shown to increase winter hardiness is potassium. Consider applying a winterizing 8-8-25 fertilizer (the last number represents potassium) in the fall. A final thought—improved Bermuda grass grows well in Texas and is hardier than St. Augustine. If your lawn is sunny, you might consider it as an alternative to St. Augustine.

Scales: A brown scale gets on the fronds of my Boston fern. Eventually the fronds fall off. What should I spray on the fronds?
Mary Sue Collins
Laurel, Mississippi

If the brown scales are only on the undersides of certain fronds, they may not be scales at all, but spore cases instead. Spore-bearing fronds naturally wither as the spores mature. However, if the brown bumps appear irregularly spaced on both upper and lower surfaces or on the stems of the fern, scales are the likely problem. Spray according to label directions with refined horticultural oil, being sure to wet both surfaces. You may have to spray more than one time if the infestation appears serious.

Screening: I'm interested in large screening plants for my backyard. I live in northwest Tennessee, only 5 miles from the Kentucky line. I've been told that this is too far north for wax myrtle. Can you recommend a good substitute?
David W. Parks
Union City, Tennessee
You might try wax myrtle's hardier and slower growing cousin, bayberry (*Myrica pensylvanica*). This large shrub grows about 10 feet tall and is semi-evergreen. Other substitutes that are fully evergreen are Eastern white pine, Canadian hemlock, and Leyland cypress.

Tree-lined drive: We would love to have a tree-lined driveway but don't have 150 to 200 years to wait for mighty oaks to give us the effect we'd like. Do you know any fast-growing trees that would produce a "tunnel effect" similar to that of Rosedown Plantation in Louisiana?
Mrs. C. Smith
Memphis, Tennessee
We're afraid that no tree grows fast enough to produce an effect like that of the live oak allée of Rosedown Plantation in a single lifetime. But this doesn't mean you can't have a very attractive tree-lined drive in 15 to 20 years. Good, fast growing shade trees for your area include willow oak, red oak, red maple, tulip poplar, and Japanese zelkova. Resist the temptation to start with balled-and-burlapped trees taller than 10 feet. These trees often have much of their roots cut off and grow slowly for four to five years after transplanting. Instead, look for trees 7 to 10 feet tall grown in large baskets or pots. They'll cost a lot less and grow a lot faster.

Vegetable garden: We're putting in a vegetable garden and have been asked which way the rows will run. Does it matter?
Cheryl Rappold
Covington, Louisiana
Not really. Just make sure that tall vegetables don't shade out shorter ones. For example, if you're growing corn and okra and your rows go east-west, plant these two on the garden's north end. Because the sun will shine from the south for most of the day, the corn and okra will get plenty of light but won't shade plants

EDITORS' NOTEBOOK
Maybe old dogs can't learn new tricks, but old garden editors can. During a visit last summer to the Dallas Arboretum, I saw sweeps of caladiums growing in full, blazing sun. Has the staff taken leave of their senses? I asked myself. Are they making caladium stir-fry? Wrong on both counts. Bob Brackman, the Arboretum's director of horticulture, explained that they're using a different type of caladium than the familiar, fancy-leaved ones. The new type is shorter with smaller, lance-shaped leaves. Given the right conditions, it grows perfectly well in full sun and also lasts four to six weeks longer in fall than fancy-leaved types. Bob advises planting the new caladiums about 4 inches apart so that the leaves will shade and cool the soil. Keep the soil moist, but don't water in midday, as this will burn the leaves. Water instead before 9 a.m. For a list of mail-order sources, send a self-addressed, stamped, business-size envelope to New Caladiums, P.O. Box 830119, Birmingham, Alabama 35283. *Steve Bender*

behind them. If the rows go north-south, plant tall vegetables on the east end. That way, shorter plants will get strong midday and afternoon sun. Of course, if all of your vegetables are about the same height, the arrangement is of little consequence.

Vines: Please advise me of a good vine to cover my new pergola and shade my garden swing. What about clematis?
Robert Smith
Columbia, South Carolina
Clematis probably wouldn't do the trick, as it doesn't grow thickly enough to provide much shade. Better choices include Carolina jessamine, Cherokee rose, Lady Banks rose, and trumpet creeper.

Wild azaleas: We recently purchased a wooded lot with many wild azaleas growing on it. These plants have no leaves on the bottom and no shape. They only bloom on the very top branches. Could you please advise me as to when and how to prune them? I would like them to be full and bushy.
Brenda McGee
Vienna, Georgia
Native or "wild" azaleas are large, deciduous shrubs that naturally become tall, open plants with relatively little foliage at the bottom. Pruning them back immediately after they flower will reduce their height without removing flowerbuds for next year. However, native azaleas will never be as dense and compact as evergreen types. We suggest you leave your shrubs alone and enjoy them in their woodland setting. If their legginess bothers you, plant ferns, wildflowers, or other low-growing, shade-tolerant plants at their feet. Or add some evergreen azaleas to your garden.

Wild roses: Last year, I planted seven hybrid tea roses. This year, they looked like wild roses, growing in all directions with small, single flowers. What happened?
E. Martin
Irvine, Kentucky
Hybrid tea roses are often grafted onto rootstocks of *Rosa multiflora*, which is a noxious weed. It appears that the tops of your roses died and the rootstock took over. To get good roses again, you'll have to replace your plants.

Index

Structures 24
  arbor 182
  pergola 83
  shade frame 179
Sulphur butterflies 35
Summer roses 95
Swag, dried flower 170
Sweet potatoes 159
Swimming pools 82

T
Texas mountain laurel 49
Tilling 25
Tobacco, flowering
  (*Nicotiana sylvestris*) 137
Tomatoes 61, 115
  planting 25
Tools 189
Transplants 77
Tree borers 133
Trees 189
  citrus 60
  dogwoods 201

elms 201
fast-growing 205
fig 48
fruit 24, 174
holly 202
planting 145, 159, 165
pruning 34
redwood 204
Tropical fruit 25
Trumpet honeysuckle
  (*Lonicera sempervirens*) 91

V
Vegetables 189
  gourmet 16
  growing 10, 18, 114
  harvesting 94
  planting 25, 35, 49, 61,
    115, 145, 159, 175, 205
  root crops 175
Vines 205
  Brazilian nightshade
  (*Solanum seaforthianum*) 199

Ivy (*Hedera helix*) 203
Jackson vine
  (*Smilax smallii*) 203
  potato (*Solanum jasminoides*)
    199
  training 77
Voles 115

W
Walkway 193
Walls 42, 53, 66, 166
Water gardens 175
Watering 145, 189
Webworms 144
Weeds 25, 115
  in birdseed 175
White-flowering plants 86
Winter storage 189
Wreath, succulent 150

Z
Zinnias 115
Zoysia 26